Losing Afghanistan

Losing Afghanistan

An Obituary for the Intervention

Noah Coburn

Stanford University Press
Stanford, California

Stanford University Press
Stanford, California

Printed on acid-free, archival-quality paper

Printed and bound in Great Britain by
Marston Book Services Ltd, Oxfordshire

Library of Congress Cataloging-in-Publication Data

Coburn, Noah, author.
  Losing Afghanistan : an obituary for the intervention / Noah Coburn.
    pages cm
  Includes bibliographical references and index.
  ISBN 978-0-8047-9663-7 (cloth : alk. paper) —
  ISBN 978-0-8047-9777-1 (pbk. : alk. paper)
1. Afghan War, 2001– —Political aspects. 2. Nation-building—Afghanistan. 3. Economic assistance—Afghanistan. 4. Afghanistan—Politics and government—2001– I. Title.
  DS371.412.C63 2016
  958.104'7—dc23

2015020748

ISBN 978-0-8047-9780-1 (electronic)

Typeset by Thompson Type in 10/14 Minion

*To Sediq Seddiqi, Farid Ahmad Bayat,
Mohammad Munir Salamzai, and
Mohammad Hassan Wafaey, with thanks
for long conversations, sharp insights,
warm hospitality, and the hope they
give me for the future of Afghanistan.*

Contents

Images

Abbreviations

ALP	Afghan Local Police
ANA	Afghan National Army
ANP	Afghan National Police
ANSF	Afghan National Security Forces
AO	Area of Operation
AWP	Alliance Wind Power
BUDS	Basic Underwater Demolition/SEAL school
CERP	Commander Emergency Response Program
COIN	Counterinsurgency
COP	Combat Outpost
DAFA	Délégation Archéologique Française en Afghanistan
DDR	Disarmament, Demobilization, Reintegration
DFID	Department for International Development (UK)
FOB	Forward Operating Base
GIRoA	Government of the Islamic Republic of Afghanistan
HTS	Human Terrain System
IA	Insightful Approaches group of companies
IAM	International Assistance Mission
IED	Improvised Explosive Device

ISAF   International Security Assistance Force

KLE   Key Leader Engagement

NDS   National Directorate of Security

NGO   Nongovernmental Organization

PRT   Provincial Reconstruction Team

RESAP   Renewable Energy Sources in Afghanistan Project

RFP   Request for Proposal

ROE   Rules of Engagement

SEALs   Sea, Air, Land teams

SIGAR   Special Inspector General for Afghanistan Reconstruction

UNAMA   United Nations Assistance Mission to Afghanistan

USAID   United States Agency for International Development

VSO   Village Stabilization Operation

Losing Afghanistan

1 Surveying the Intervention from Above

The mountains surround Bagram like the walls of a castle.
Café owner near Bagram

Above

If one had been looking down from above the Shomali Plain just north of Kabul during the late 2000s, the most noticeable thing would first have been the way the plain seems to pour out from the Hindu Kush Mountains, a shocking fan of green amid the gray hills. From the streams and larger waterways that eventually merge to form the Kabul River, countless irrigation channels split off. Powered by gravity, these channels hug the sides of hills, naturally highlighting the area's more gentle topography, in contrast with the surrounding sharp mountains. In the spring and summer, neat green fields and orchards spread out alongside these water sources; where water is abundant, grapes, figs, and other fruits are grown and, in drier, less fertile areas, wheat. Mud walls divide the fields, turning the landscape seen from above into puzzle pieces. Narrow, zigzagging boundary lines tell the stories of land feuds and generations of inheritance as the land has been divided and redivided among sons and grandsons.

Settlements in the plain have a similar logic to them. Most spread out from hilltops above the fields, slight rises where the land is less easily cultivated. As in much of Afghanistan, large walled compounds with a central courtyard are favored. Over time, as a family grows, often extensions are added as sons marry, and many of the settlements seem to sprawl out like thick bushes, linked by narrow pathways that also mark property boundaries.[1] Except for the occasional small town, usually just a slightly larger cluster of houses, this pattern of fields and settlements repeats itself across the plain for over fifty miles.

Floating above here, the viewer's eye is drawn to the southern part of this fertile plain, where an odd slash runs southwest to northeast, breaking up the rhythm of fields and houses. As one looks closer, two distinct dark lines become visible—two roads to nowhere.

The slashes are two asphalt runways, 3,500 meters long, straighter and wider than any of the roads in the area. Although these are striking in and of themselves, the topography around the runways raises even more questions. The organically spreading compounds, whose mud walls sometimes blur into the fields next door, are replaced by dozens of neat rectangles, laid out in a well-organized grid pattern that appears almost stamped on the landscape like a strange crop circle. The greens and soft browns are exchanged for grays and blacks.

The area is Bagram Airfield, one of the key centers for international military operations in Afghanistan. The airfield contains several connected bases and houses military personnel from the various countries making up the North Atlantic Treaty Organization's (NATO's) International Security Assistance Force (ISAF). As with much of ISAF's presence in the late 2000s, however, most of the soldiers are American. This airfield was at one point the busiest American Department of Defense airport in the world with an average of 1,200 people moving through its terminal daily.[2]

The smaller rectangles, primarily to the west of the runway, are living quarters for the troops, packed tightly together; the larger ones are hangars, administrative buildings, a hospital, a prison, and other facilities. Closer to the runway there is a group of larger rectangles and other odd shapes at regular intervals. These are large cargo planes, smaller helicopters, and other aircraft, including strange hybrids like Ospreys, which take off like helicopters but fly like planes and look almost insectile. They are parked near the runway with blast walls between them to ensure that if one is hit with a stray rocket the explosion will not set off a chain reaction. These concerns about protecting aircraft are not overcautious; in 2012 a small group of lightly armed insurgents destroyed six Harrier jets causing more than US$200 million in damage at Camp Bastion, a similar base in the southwest of the country.[3]

As odd as these vehicles are, for the observer from above, most remarkable are perhaps the edges of this area. In nice crisp lines, the neat outer walls of the base, occasionally punctuated by a guard tower, outline the perimeter and then stop; almost immediately on the other side the fields and flowing compounds typical of the Shomali begin again. In some cases, the

Figure 1.1. Guard tower. Photo by Gregory Thielker.

fields come right up to the walls of the base. To the southwest of the base there is a much larger cluster of buildings and a traffic circle: the central bazaar for the town of Bagram. To the more rural east of the base wall are the faint traces of compounds that have been razed by the international troops, concerned that insurgents might use them to launch attacks. From above, it is as if an alien city has been simply dropped into the otherwise green, fertile plain.

In some ways the view from the ground was even more disorienting at the height of the intervention. As one walked through the town of Bagram there were few vantage points in the area, the military having secured any spot from which insurgents could fire rockets into the base. This was a trick learned from the mistakes of the British in the first Anglo–Afghan war in 1842; they faced constant sniping from compounds near their cantonment, which similarly abutted local communities. The lack of vantage points meant that I and the others in the bazaar were always forced to look upward at the base walls, never sure of what was happening within. High walls with the occasional guard tower loomed over the bazaar, and yet people seemed to have become accustomed to the international military presence. There was an occasional sonic boom as a jet took off, but this did not halt conversations.

On a typical day, traffic in the bazaar would come to a brief pause when a patrol came through. Chatting with a local store owner, four patrol vehicles, or MRAPs as they are usually called (because they are Mine-Resistant Ambush Protected), and an armored vehicle that appeared to be a cross between a Humvee, a pickup truck, and a giant tow truck came rolling through. The MRAPs were close to twenty feet tall and looked like khaki dinosaurs, with long hornlike guns sticking out of the turrets on top. Atop the first, a young man in dark wraparound sunglasses swept his gun across the crowd, which had paused to let them through. The other vehicles had guns but no men; instead the guns were attached to video cameras. The guns swiveled eerily as the camera peered out unblinkingly at the pedestrians.

Despite the presence of the latest military technology, the history of occupation here runs deep. Just north of the base, the road descends toward the river, drawing close to the ancient field where Alexander the Great camped. Here, in the first half of the twentieth century, French archaeologists excavated a treasure trove of gold and Silk Road wealth, ranging from Chinese porcelain to Roman statues. Many of these artifacts toured Paris, New York, and other Western capitals as a part of the *National Geographic*–sponsored *Bactrian Gold* exhibition. As we drive down this track, a nineteenth-century citadel built adjacent to the site suddenly towers above. It has been transformed to a small, impenetrable, but oddly quiet, military base. This is one of several satellite bases that surround the main airfield at Bagram. HESCO barriers and sandbags stand twenty feet high on top of the ancient walls at this smaller outpost. Rolls of razor wire are wrapped lackadaisically around the slopes below. Just inside the tangle of wire, on the slope of the hill leading up to the smaller base, a charred building sits, long abandoned, with DAFA, the name of the French Archeological Alliance, spray painted on its side.

The base stands over the river and another smaller, quiet bazaar that has been built up alongside it. From the small cluster of shops, it is impossible for the Afghans walking through the market to tell whether there are Afghan or America soldiers within—or no one at all.

Tilting at Windmills in Kabul

Not all the building associated with the international intervention in Afghanistan was so menacing and disruptive of the local landscape. In 2009, Alliance

Figure 1.2. AWP Workshop, Kabul. Photo by William Locke.

Wind Power (AWP) sat under a broad corrugated roof on a small side street in western Kabul. Filled with tools and half-finished projects, it looked like many of the other workshops in the area and not unlike one that you might find in a small town in America. This neighborhood, one of the more planned areas of Kabul, was shaded by trees and cleaner than the haphazard settlements that had grown up on the hills around it. The crush of Kabul traffic, however, was still ubiquitous, and snarls could spring up unexpectedly when young nomads moved their flocks through town.

Set up in part by William Locke, who owned a 23 percent stake, AWP was remarkable for several reasons.[4] In a country where power was unreliable and often produced by smoky diesel generators, AWP and its dream of providing wind energy offered the promise of clean, sustainable, and, most important to local communities, cheap and easily accessed power. Owned primarily by a group of young, dynamic Afghans, who for the most part came of age after the most brutal fighting in Afghanistan, working with Will's support and relying initially on international grants, the business also offered a model for wider economic growth in Afghanistan and a way for independent Afghan businesses, with a helping shove from the international community, to stimulate real internal growth.

AWP was in many ways the perfect development project for the later 2000s in Afghanistan: It was Afghan led, with international assistance on technical aspects and in funding start-up costs but still privately owned. It produced a product, energy, that was in economic demand, that Afghans were willing to pay for, and that would seriously improve quality of life. More reliable electricity allowed students to study at night and families to watch news on the television and to connect with a wider world after charging their cell phones. For the security oriented, energy in more rural areas would give communities light at night and hopefully increase the ability of local Afghans to call security forces when threatened by insurgents. AWP had something to offer every aspect of the intervention: hearts and minds won for those counterinsurgency practitioners, business growth and investment for neoliberal development experts, increased access to educational opportunities for human rights advocates.

Will also seemed to have started the company at an opportune moment: Between 2002 and 2008 the U.S. government spent an average of $25.1 billion per year in Afghanistan. In 2010–2011 that average jumped to $106.2 billion.[5] AWP was founded in 2008, after Barack Obama had made winning this "just war" a centerpiece of his campaign strategy and as the resulting international funds really began flowing into the country. Yet, although an ideal project, like so many others, AWP's story is unique and, despite being set up with some of the "best practices" from the development world, the company struggled.

Too Good to Succeed?

Will started the company with Amir, a young Hazara student with an entrepreneurial spirit. While looking for someone to help them make fiberglass blades, they met Farouq and Abdul, both Tajiks who had experience welding. All of them became partners in the project. Symbolic of the growth of business in the 2000s, this group represented two of the major ethnic groups that had caused severe damage to the neighborhood they were now working in during the Civil War of the 1990s. But this was a new era, and such young men were looking forward, not back.

Originally the group wanted to name the company Afghan Modern Power, which would have given it the apt acronym of AMP, because it was always important in Kabul's nongovernmental organization (NGO) scene to have a catchy acronym as a name. For unclear reasons, however, the official at the government licensing office told them their name was unacceptable, a typically vague answer from the Afghan bureaucracy. Needing to come up with a new name on the spot, they ended up with Alliance Wind Power, or AWP, which was slightly less catchy but close enough, Will supposed.

For the outside viewer, the AWP had a distinctly Afghan–international hybrid feel. Its workshop looked like many of the others found crammed onto the rough streets outside the center of Kabul, and, as with almost everything in Kabul, a thin layer of dust covered the equipment and half-finished projects. At the same time, AWP maintained an international feel that most other Afghan businesses did not have.

The company, for example, had a website entirely in English, with action photos of their various projects. On the "Contact" page of the website they gave the typical if somewhat cryptic address of "Across from Architects Union of Afghanistan, Darulaman Road." Such an address seems strange only to those who are not familiar with the way in which Kabul's building boom, combined with the chronic refusal to label streets or assign house numbers, made people consider addresses such as "Behind the Old British Embassy"—one of my first addresses in Kabul—completely appropriate.

Similarly, navigating Afghanistan's ethnic and linguistic diversity was a challenge for the few businesses that were truly trying to cater to both an international and a domestic audience in the 2000s. As a result, the website contact lists told English speakers to contact Will (and included both his email address and cell phone), Dari speakers to contact Farouq with his details, and Pashto speakers to contact Amir. Along with the contact list, next to a group photo of the AWP crew, a caption helpfully pointed out that Will was on the far right, Abdul was second from the right, and Amir was on the far left. In the photo, the crew stands outside their workshop, looking sternly at the camera. To understand, however, how Will ended up in this picture working with this ethnically diverse wind company on a dirt street in one of the most booming parts of Kabul, one must step back several decades.

Although for many American twenty-somethings the thought of relocating in the mid-2000s to Afghanistan may have seemed daunting as security deteriorated, Will's move to Afghanistan in 2006, he says, "did not feel abnormal in the slightest." His parents had worked there in the 1960s and 1970s, living in Jalalabad; one of his older brothers was born in Kabul. Will's family left the country before the chaos that spread across the country in the 1980s and the 1990s began but stayed in close contact with many of their friends from the country, and Will grew up eating kebab and hearing stories about the country.

In 2004 the senior Lockes returned to Afghanistan with many other foreigners during what was essentially the first wave of relief workers returning to the country, many of whom had worked in the country before or among Afghan refugees in Pakistan. Will's father, a doctor, began working at a prominent Kabul hospital. They moved to a quieter area west of the center, away from the embassies and government buildings, which was popular among many of the longer-term expats. Shortly afterward, Will's older brother, wife, and young daughters joined the family in Kabul. Will, in the meantime, was in college in Pennsylvania, where he majored in engineering and minored in philosophy. After graduation, he spent some time working for an NGO in Dhaka and then went traveling in Australia.

Lacking much of a plan, Will decided to visit his parents, as many twenty-six-year-olds do when at a loss for what their next step in life should be. And so, Will "moved back home" to Kabul.

Luckily for him, however, this was also a time of growth in development spending, particularly on construction projects. Government and NGO programs were all growing, and qualified workers were in short supply. Many relief workers seemed to have degrees in international affairs or management, but few had studied engineering. Will discovered that his technical background was in high demand, and he was much more employable than he would have been back in America. As a result, he quickly found a volunteer position with International Assistance Mission, or IAM.

In 2006 when Will arrived, IAM was in and of itself unique. Founded in 1966, it is the longest continuously serving NGO in the country. An "international Christian organisation serving the people of Afghanistan through capacity building in the sectors of Health and Economic Development," IAM was notable for its commitment to staying in Afghanistan during both the Civil War and the Taliban period.[6] By 2006, IAM's international staff was going through a period of expansion and was a mixture of newer arrivals, like Will, and those who had decades of experience in the area. Except for having completely evacuated for a couple of months just after the September 11, 2001, attacks, IAM as an organization had a longevity and continuity that most other groups in the country lacked.

IAM's position, however, also reflected some of the cultural tensions that came with the growing international presence. In a country where conversion from Islam to another religion was punishable by death, faith-based organizations, even those that did not proselytize, needed to maintain a low profile. As "people of the book," Christian groups had been able to work in the country relatively undisturbed in previous decades. This, however, had been shifting. In other Islamic countries, such apostate laws may have been on the books but were rarely implemented. In Afghanistan, since the passing of the new Afghan Constitution, there had been several cases where individuals had been sentenced to death for conversion or other perceived religious violations.

In one case, a man from the north of the country was arrested during a custody case after converting to Roman Catholicism sixteen years before. Only after significant international pressure was the man released and allowed to seek asylum in Italy, despite an outcry from Afghan religious leaders and the inconvenient fact for many of his supporters in the international community that his detention was likely legal under Afghan law at that time. In fact, the Afghan Constitution mentions both adherence to the country's conservative brand of Islamic jurisprudence and respect for the UN Declaration of Human Rights.[7] Much of the time these systems quietly coexisted. The contradictions and tensions at the points where culture, development, and the law meet grew, however, as the intervention went on.[8] Although the man was released, he was still forced to leave the country, essentially exiled from his family and community. The case generated a good deal of hostility toward the international community in the Afghan press, and many suggested that this was just another case of the West imposing its values and laws on Afghanistan.

Such cases made navigating relationships difficult, but Will also benefited from IAM's sensitive awareness of cultural issues. Due in part to its long-term commitment to the place, international volunteers at IAM were required to learn either Pashto or Dari, something that few other NGOs or international organizations were prioritizing during the busy years of expansion of the international presence. Finding internationals who spoke Pashto was particularly problematic because there were few Pashto language programs in Europe or America. Dari is a close cousin of Farsi, and it was much easier to find language programs that taught Farsi in the West; to get a head start on language learning, I had enrolled in one of these courses in Boston, just around the corner from my apartment, before first traveling to Afghanistan in 2005. As a result, most international organizations relied heavily on translators. In contrast with this approach, IAM offered six months of intensive language training for those who were planning on working long term in the country.

Because Will was not initially sure he was going to stay in Afghanistan much more than six months, he chose the more relaxed route of three classes a week, which, as he put it, got him "up to speed with things like buying in the bazaar or using a taxi, plus greetings." In addition to facilitating communication, however, it also gave Will a certain amount of cultural capital, the ability to forge friendships and earn the trust of the Afghans with whom he worked. This gave him a significant advantage over most internationals in the country, particularly those diplomats and officials working brief rotations in various Western embassies.

After Will had spent three months in Kabul, improving his language skills and working on a technology project for IAM, several of his colleagues approached him about working on IAM's Renewable Energy Sources in Afghanistan Project, or RESAP. RESAP provided electricity to rural Afghan communities using renewable energy sources, emphasizing technology that was especially appropriate for Afghanistan.[9] Particularly in the 1990s, RESAP became rather well known for running a series of micro-hydroelectric power projects in small villages in the mountains north of Kabul, above Bagram Airfield.

By 2006, based on its earlier success, RESAP was considering other forms of renewable energy beyond their hydroelectric projects. Solar energy, popular with other development projects, was difficult because solar panels, largely made in China, were expensive and difficult to repair, and rechargeable batteries were costly.[10] So they began exploring options, including wind energy. This was appealing to IAM because, although RESAP had had good success with micro-hydro plants in various villages in the foothills of the mountains, for areas farther away from such reliable and quickly moving water sources, there were challenges. One of the areas that appealed to Will almost immediately was the Shomali Plain around the international airbase at Bagram. This area is flatter than the foothills that surround it. The rivers here are large but slow moving, so hydroelectric generators make less sense. The area also receives a fair amount of consistent wind that made it well situated for generating power on a village-level scale. Smaller wind turbines could even potentially be connected to water pumps, greatly expanding the amount of cultivable land beyond the narrow confines of the areas that gravity-driven irrigation channels reached. The amount of farmable land is a concerning issue in the Shomali, which has seen a drastic population increase in recent years as refugees returned from abroad. With this potential in mind, IAM gave Will and his associates funding to initially set up AWP under IAM's management, with the idea that it would soon become an independent company.

Owned jointly by an American and Afghans of various ethnicities and working to generate clean, renewable energy on a small scale in a strategic area that had received a good amount of international aid just as Obama was announcing a significant increase in troops and spending of all types to Afghanistan, AWP seemed well positioned to succeed. Despite this, six years later, AWP closed up shop, having completed a few small projects but falling far short of its real potential. Later, as I discussed with Will how he might have done things slightly differently, he focused on details like the size of the blades they manufactured and the types of batteries they purchased. Even in his reflections he was constantly tinkering with how the turbines could have been better constructed. Stepping back, however, these changes seem minor and unlikely to have had much impact. Instead, even as Will second-guessed some of these small decisions, I increasingly got the feeling that AWP, much like the intervention itself, was doomed from the start.

In many ways Will's story was unique. His family had deep ties with the place; instead of using armored SUVs or even a Corolla with an Afghan driver, Will was known for traipsing around Kabul on his 150 cc Chinese dirt bike, which you could hear coming from a couple of blocks away; he seemed more committed to the place than many of the international workers who seemed to be just passing through. But in many ways the story of every Afghan and every member of the international community in Afghanistan during the fateful years around the surge was unique, making it difficult to tell a single collective story of the intervention. As I tried to make sense of the intervention myself and spoke with both Afghans and internationals about it, I was struck by how, looking back, the people I spoke with all seemed to have the urge to tinker with how they could have changed the projects they were a part of, and several themes began to emerge regarding the struggles individuals faced during the years of the surge.

This book will look at Will's experience in Afghanistan, along with the experiences of three other very different individuals. None of them ever met each other, but as I traced their journeys through the intervention I could see that they intersected and overlapped numerous times, particularly in the places that were hubs of the international presence, like Bagram Airfield. These individuals come from very different places and have very different experiences of what the intervention was. Ronald Neumann, as the American ambassador

to Afghanistan, worked on policy issues that seemed far above Will's considerations about the cost of fiberglass and wood. But Neumann also had deep
family ties to the place, his father having served as American ambassador to
Afghanistan in the late 1960s and early 1970s, and as a young man Ron had
visited him there. For others, the intervention was a war, a direct result of
the attacks of September 11, and Navy SEAL Captain Owen Berger was often
frustrated by the complex layers of development, state building, and counterinsurgency that marked the intervention. For some, like Omar Rassoul, an
Afghan businessman working with the international community, this meant
serious opportunities to earn money and help his family. Despite these differences, however, there are patterns and lessons that can be drawn out of how
Will, Ron, Owen, and Omar lived through the intervention. These lessons will
help us begin to look at what exactly the intervention was and what repercussions it had on the Afghans and internationals that were a part of it.

When we study wars and other conflicts, focusing too much simply on the
battlefields and even the political negotiations ignores the ways in which conflicts are actually having an impact on those involved and shaping the ways
people make decisions and perceive the world around them. With Afghanistan's political future still far from certain, this book attempts to begin the
processing of writing a more nuanced history of the intervention in Afghanistan, a history that looks at how individual lives were shaped socially and economically by the vast resources that flooded the country.

In the end, the ultimate failure of Alliance Wind Power had little to do
with Will, the design of his projects, or the effort that he and his colleagues put
into the company. Particularly as money and troops surged into the country
in 2009, the constraints put on Will as he applied for funding and attempted
to navigate the new political economy that the international presence created
pulled him increasingly into a system that restrained his ability to make the
decisions he needed to make. His situation grew only more challenging with
increased competition from those larger international contractors who prioritized short-term profits and Afghan government officials and merchants who
became increasingly talented at diverting international development funds.
All of this constricted the real creative potential of AWP, eventually dooming
his project.

And so AWP was added to rusting tanks and other archeological shards of
empires that are scattered around Bagram Airfield.

2 Intervening

FOR THE LAST CENTURY, the standard approach of anthropology students nearing the end of their graduate studies has been to pack up their notebooks and travel to some distant land to study a new, "exotic" people, to record their lifestyles and culture. This is, in fact, to some extent, what I originally went to Afghanistan to do in 2005. During my graduate research, I spent twenty months researching a local community of potters, who were well known in the country but who had never been the focus of a long-term study. These potters lived in a small town called Istalif, about an hour north of Kabul, in an area that was relatively stable during my time there. I spent my time studying their workshops, surveying in the bazaar, interviewing in guesthouses, and chatting about the production of pottery, its sale in the market, and how that shaped everything from whom they married to how they felt about the national government.[1]

For the most part, the young men spoke to each other mostly about daily concerns: how they were going to set up a new business, an orchard they were considering buying, or whether they would be attending the wedding of a distant relative in Kabul that weekend. These daily decisions ultimately shaped how families and clans formed alliances, which in turn shaped much of the town politics. As an anthropologist who was mostly interested in politics on a local level, I spent most of my time trying to determine which families were arranging marriages between their children and which were feuding over land. I eventually became convinced that the ways in which these families cooperated was the real reason the area remained so free of violence during the time that I was there, whereas so much of the country was becoming increasingly mired in insurgency and more general instability.

Sitting in the bazaar, the shopkeepers and I watched local convoys of French troops pass by and NGOs breeze through town, funding short-term projects. Rarely did either of these groups linger or stop to discuss projects with the potters or other members of the community. The town was in an area that was fairly progovernment, so there was little reason for the international military to take notice of the potters or their neighbors. Although NGOs did run a series of local development projects, they were for the most part small and did not drastically influence local politics. Instead, both young men and local leaders treated NGO funds as just another resource to take advantage of and attempt to exploit. During my time there, life in the town was shaped somewhat by the macro-economic and political shifts generated by the international presence, but, on a day-to-day level, few townspeople interacted directly with the people who made up the intervention. Particularly as the decade wore on, however, and more and more troops and money entered the country, the international presence came to mean more and more, even in my quiet town. This also shaped my own thinking, and I began to ask myself, what was this international intervention, and how could I, as an anthropologist, make sense of it?

Life in a Time of Intervention

Even while I was researching in this small bazaar, the international presence was, of course, always there. Sitting on a hilltop in town we could watch the planes take off and land at Bagram in the distance, and young men would occasionally speculate about what was happening at the base across the plain. Stories had come back into town about young men who had made their fortunes working on the base or, more often, doing contracting work for those working on the base; these tales only added to the local lore about Bagram. These stories intertwined with tales about other men who had made their fortunes in Dubai or in Europe, and it was almost as if the base was in one of these far-off countries or, at least conceptually, a gateway to them.

One man told the story of a distant cousin who had become wealthy selling carpets on the base. They talked about how the soldiers knew nothing about the quality of carpets and would buy almost any souvenirs they could find. The men had heard that any merchant with a special badge could get onto the base, and these badges took on an almost talisman-like quality in the

Figure 2.1. UN vehicle. Photo by the author.

stories, a golden ticket to the rich market inside. Like a talisman, however, no one seemed to know how to acquire one of these miraculous badges or how they worked. Beyond this, the details about the base were hazy rumors. What was going on behind those walls?, the young men wanted to know.

When I returned to the country a year later in 2009 my role changed. Now working for a series of research organizations and think tanks, I began studying the internationally sponsored elections in the country and evaluating several projects that were meant to help ordinary Afghans gain greater access to justice. Instead of speaking with potters and farmers, I spent more time with the Afghan officials, diplomats, policy makers, and journalists who worked in these areas. Instead of sitting in the bazaar, talking about the harvest or about a new business scheme that some young man had in mind, I was now spending my time in the offices of Afghan government officials and ministerial meeting rooms and inside embassy walls. Here we debated the effectiveness of programs, how policy should change, and the political future of the country. At the same time, however, I also began to wonder, what were all these programs doing, and how were they shaping the lives of the potters whom I had worked with? Even as I continued to visit my friends in Istalif on the weekends, that world now seemed rather far away.

The connection between the potters and these programs seemed tenuous. Although I was hired first in 2009 to work on a project to support the Ministry of Justice based on my experience conducting research in the field, the irony was that there had been almost no justice officials in Istalif at all. The only official figure other than the local police was a lone prosecutor who had to bring his cases to the city when he had them. Mostly, however, he complained about how little he had to do in the town and was rarely there, preferring to spend his time at his home in Kabul. Researching the justice system, it was almost as if I were hired to look at how life should be from the international perspective, rather than how it actually was.

Still, it seemed to me that improving access to justice was an important thing and, with land feuds a common point of contention among the potters, those in Istalif I spoke with about it agreed that this was a good project to be working on. So if money was going to be spent on projects to improve it, I decided it was better that they be well informed. As a result of my previous experience in the country, I felt that I had something to contribute, though I soon discovered that it was not always what other members of the international intervention wanted to hear. While the international community often talked about giving Afghans this or that, whether it was public health, education, or democracy, they rarely asked how Afghans felt about these things or whether they wanted them at all. So, as I conducted research on justice and the approaching elections, I tried to look at both what the international community was attempting to deliver (in this case, justice and democracy) and also whether Afghans really thought they needed these things at all.

Sometimes the answers surprised those working in the international community. For example, millions of dollars were spent in the early years of the intervention on the judicial system, building courthouses and training prosecutors. Few in the international community bothered to ask whether communities actually wanted local courts and whether prosecutors would be useful. In fact, most of those in local communities whom I interviewed were happy with courts in distant provincial capitals where they could bring serious criminal cases, but they wanted to be left in peace to resolve things like land disputes on their own. When they did resolve these land disputes, oftentimes they wanted to be able to register the decisions in local civil courts; yet, in the rush to fund prosecutors who would take on high-profile narcotics or terrorism cases, little money was left to support the underfunded and under-staffed civil courts where residents could bring these more low-level cases.[2] Thus, I ended up visiting brand-new courts that were almost entirely empty and unused, while also visiting local civil affairs offices that were crammed full of people but receiving almost no international support.

While my initial time in Afghanistan was spent researching a relatively small town, I found that on my return I moved in a different world. I found my-self at meetings at the Ministry of Justice (working on an internationally sup-ported policy on using local structures to increase access to justice), at various NGOs and think tanks (collaborating on research projects), at the American embassy and the U.S. Agency for International Development (USAID) (brief-ing the international donors paying for the projects), and occasionally on mil-itary bases (looking at how ISAF was working with local justice issues or sim-ply to check in when traveling in one of the less-secure provinces). With the economy in Kabul growing and NGOs scooping up much of the housing near government offices and the embassies, it made sense for many young interna-tionals like myself to share large houses or compounds. With many on short-term rotations and demand for rooms so high, internationals moved in and out of rooms in shared compounds regularly. As a result, over the next couple of years, I lived with journalists, relief workers, engineers, lawyers, and artists who were American, Canadian, British, Swiss, Kenyan, Sri Lankan, Afghan-American, Afghan-German, Australian-Indian, Pakistani-Swede, and seem-ingly every other combination imaginable. The more I moved in this world that was distinct from Afghan communities, though often engaging with Afghans in strange ways, the more I struggled to understand what we, this odd collection of internationals, were doing in Afghanistan. As Afghans in-teracted with the growing body of internationals, how did they understand the international community, and what did this do to shape the way the inter-vention changed over the course of the decade?

As the initial relative stability of the early 2000s was replaced by a grow-ing insurgency, as development projects struggled to show serious returns, and as the governance efforts failed to bring about the services and stability that most Afghans wanted, internationals and Afghans alike debated where the international intervention seemed to have gone astray. Unsurprisingly, military officials always seemed to suggest that the solution was military, dip-lomats supported a more aggressive diplomatic approach, and development types called for more funding for their projects. Everyone tended to suggest that if only his or her own project received more funding, media attention, and diplomatic support, all would be well. Surely, these divides must be part of the issue. The anthropologist in me increasingly focused on the fact that this eclectic group of people who made up the international intervention, despite their differences, seemed to have developed a unique and insular society, and I wondered to what extent this society, and the structures and practices it created, had actually shaped the outcome of the intervention.

Could we claim that this odd group of diverse people who made up the international community had its own distinct culture? They certainly spoke a unique language (for example, the insistent use of acronyms), they had distinctive dwelling structures (razor wire everywhere), a peculiar style of dress (fashionable but conservative, billowy skirts for many of the female NGO workers, the casual expat headscarf for some, military fatigues for others), and unique economic structures (where was all this money paying for these various people coming from, and, more important perhaps, where was it going?). At the same time, however, they were not always easy to study. One of the tricky things for the anthropologist trying to understand the international community was that there was no central square, no bazaar, no mosque, where everyone went to gather, and yet the international community was still clearly a *thing*. Moreover, it was a thing that was rarely analyzed as a whole.

As people have come to think of the intervention as unsuccessful in Afghanistan, analysis has been done on the resiliency of the insurgents, the opium economy, continued grievances among local communities and the corruption of President Hamid Karzai's government. A few pieces have turned the focus back on aspects of the international presence, whether to examine military challenges or some of the political hurdles that those delivering aid and state-building funds faced. Those assessments that did look at the American role, such as the detailed investigations launched by the Special Investigator General for Afghanistan Reconstruction (SIGAR), tended to look on a project-by-project basis to try to find where money was wasted, producing detailed and sensational reports that were difficult to decipher for anyone not trained in auditing.

But what if, instead of looking at these individual aspects, we try to focus on how these pieces came together, and not just the intervention today but its predecessors who were there before the Taliban and even before the Soviet invasion? In particular, writing an entire history of the intervention risks drifting too high up into the clouds to notice what the individuals were doing below, but what if we focused on certain individuals and lives during the intervention? What if, instead of looking just at a policy level, we attempted to look at how economics and politics interacted with the strange culture of the international community? What would we notice? How did this odd social and political group shape the way the intervention unfolded and the ways that both Afghans and internationals came to see the intervention? What can the stories of Will, Ron, Owen, and Omar tell us when we listen to them together?

Cups of Tea and MREs (Meals Ready to Eat)

One of the reasons analyzing the international community is not easy to do is the fact that the international community was composed of so many different pieces. Discussing this idea of the international community's culture in Afghanistan, Owen Berger was quick to point out that there was not just one culture but a group with many subcultures. A Navy SEAL captain who had served in both Afghanistan and Iraq on multiple tours, Owen told stories that were often accounts of his frustration not just with his counterparts in the Afghan National Army but with the slow, plodding movements of the conventional American military. SEALs and other Special Forces guys, he argued, "had their own culture." This was not merely the fact that they wore specific uniforms, oftentimes with no insignia, or were allowed to grow facial hair, unlike other members of the military. Instead it had to do with their training and the way that they approached the problems they were faced with in Afghanistan, which were different from those of the more conventional forces.

SEALs, Owen argued, were mission oriented. They were trained to secure a beachhead or take out a target. Each of these was "a kinetic event." It was left to the conventional army to build bases and hold ground. SEALs were also a community; these members of the Special Forces all knew each other and took pride in their collective identity. When the movie *Lone Survivor* was released, depicting the travails of a SEAL reconnaissance team on a mission gone astray, SEALs back home discussed how accurate the personalities of their fallen comrades were portrayed. In contrast with this, when *No Easy Day*, the ex-SEAL account of the killing of Osama bin Laden, was released, most in the community joined together in disparaging the attempt to make money off the mission, as well as potentially leaking classified documents.

The SEALs were united in part by the fact that they had all gone through the same training together, referred to as BUDS (Basic Underwater

Demolition/SEAL school), and they identified each other by the class in which they had graduated. When they were not deployed, almost all lived in Norfolk or San Diego, where they went to each other's weddings and knew each other's kids. This created an almost family-like atmosphere that contrasted with the stiff hierarchy of the conventional soldiers Owen was often interacting with in Afghanistan. These pieces of the international military coexisted but did not always fit together comfortably. Of course, such divides were relative and seem minor compared with the split between civilian and military. In our conversations Owen would often drop phrases like "you guys think . . ." to refer to all civilians in Afghanistan, whether they were journalists, diplomats, or anthropologists. On a day-to-day basis, however, in a world that had only limited contact with civilians, it was clear that the divides between branches of the military were what made Owen's job most frustrating.

Stepping back, how would one analyze these cultural differences between branches of the military and civilians and make sense of all these various parts of the international community? On the surface, the easiest divisions to identify were those among soldiers, diplomats, journalists, and NGO workers (and to a lesser extent, researchers and academics like myself). But even these simple categories were somewhat deceiving. During the surge there were diplomats assigned to NATO headquarters and soldiers who worked as liaisons at the embassies. Journalists left and returned as policy specialists, and NGO workers set up shop as consultants. Karl Eikenberry, an American general, served as the commander of the NATO forces in Afghanistan, only to return later as the American ambassador. Peter Jouvenal, a well-known cameraman during the war with the Soviets, returned and set up a popular expat bar in Kabul called the Gandamak Lodge.

How would we classify these figures or, for example, Will's associates at IAM? They were for the most part fulfilling the role of relief workers, but many were clearly motivated on some level by their religious beliefs. Was this then similar to the divide between soldiers who were expected to be there out of a sense of duty and patriotism, and mercenaries who were there for the paycheck? And what did this say about the numerous soldiers who came as part of the military and had returned as security contractors, earning enormous paychecks from large international security firms that protected everything from NATO's supply lines to small NGO guesthouses? As each group tended to maintain its moral superiority and disparage others privately, these groups all bumped into each other and ultimately intertwined uncomfortably.

Of course categorizing by profession is only one approach. Another way of organizing the international community would be to focus on country of origin, which was unevenly mixed. Although on the military side the Americans, followed by the British, Germans, Canadians, and Australians, clearly dominated NATO's forces in the country, countries like Malaysia, Hungary, and Macedonia also supplied troops. In fact, in terms of troops per population of the home country, Tonga was actually the leading contributor for much of the intervention with one soldier for every 2,000 citizens, while the United States was second with closer to one for every 5,000.[3]

Within this conglomeration of military forces, there were certain reputations and hierarchies. The Australians, for example, were particularly engaged in counterinsurgency practice and had a large presence at the Counterinsurgency Academy on the outskirts of Kabul. Different regulations and reputations also shaped these groups. The Germans had strict rules of engagement and could fire only when they had been fired on. As a result, they were looked down on by the military from other nations, who criticized them for primarily remaining on their base and limiting their patrols "outside the wire." At the same time, however, the Germans, with a more lax policy about alcohol, had a highly regarded bar at their base in the north, so despite the criticism, soldiers from other groups were happy to go visit when they had missions based out of the German base.

But the military was not divided simply by different nations sending troops to join the NATO forces. Within the U.S. military, as Owen suggested, there were tribes and subtribes. This was most apparent as President Obama ramped up the Marine presence in southern Afghanistan. Helmand in particular became known as Marineistan, due to the demand by Marine leadership that Marines be stationed in contiguous areas where they could be supplied by their own Marine helicopters and convoys.[4] Such restrictions limited the integration of the different American military branches. At this point, some military officials joked uneasily that there were not forty-two member countries in ISAF but actually forty-three because the Marines acted like their own member country in the coalition.

Difference in command and structure was reinforced by difference in culture and approaches to war. In the U.S. Marine Corps, "every Marine is a rifleman." Smaller than other branches of the U.S. military, with a history of rapid force response, Marines liked to say that they had come to Afghanistan to "hunt the bad guys." In contrast with this, the Army, with its more lumbering bureaucracy where soldiers were more often specialists, was on occasion criticized and other times praised for its more long-term view to its missions. If what was wanted was a large base constructed with complex logistics, it was probably a better idea to call them. Even the Coast Guard played a role, with a small contingent brought in at Bagram especially as troop levels first increased and then again as they decreased. As specialists who had more experience with the logistics and art of packing containers than other branches of the U.S. military, they were used to help organize the packing and shipping of equipment in and out of the country.[5]

These variations in culture could easily rankle more hierarchal officials. This was true with the subtle differences in ranking of officers. Owen's status as a captain in the Navy was the equivalent of an army colonel. Despite this being fairly common knowledge in all branches of the American military, other officers would on occasion pretend to get confused or to forget how the system worked to undercut the SEALs who were seen as entering and taking attention away from other troops. These rivalries ranged from good-natured joking to serious confrontations over territory or what was referred to as "battle space." Within a unit's battle space the commanding officer was sovereign with all the soldiers in that area invested in maintaining that sovereignty and calling for outside support only when absolutely necessary.

The sudden increase in demand for military personnel also meant that some units were assigned missions that did not always fit comfortably with their training. On Owen's first tour in Afghanistan, his team was assigned to support an Afghan National Army (ANA) unit. This type of work was particularly challenging for the Special Forces soldiers who had been taught primarily to fulfill short-term, clearly defined missions. Suddenly thrust into an advisory role, Owen was not expected to perform tasks as much as support others who were doing the missions. This meant organizing the training of ANA commandos, mentoring their officers, and spending time with them all less officially.

Owen described how at first he went about all this in a businesslike manner, fulfilling the requirements as his orders dictated. After a while, however, it was clear that relations between him and his counterpart, an ANA officer he was meant to be supporting and mentoring, were cool at best. Owen's translator finally stopped him and told him, "Listen, you need to sit and drink tea with him." Owen laughed in recollection of the notion; why would you want to drink tea with a guy when everything could be discussed in a five-minute meeting? Owen preferred the Meals Ready to Eat or MRE approach of the military, where all the subsistence you needed was enclosed in a series of pouches that could be torn into and eaten in a matter of minutes. Of course, what Owen came to realize, and his translator was pointing out, was that Owen's mission was really about relationship building, not "kinetic events." And, in Afghanistan, relationship building is all about drinking tea and visiting. Visiting demonstrated to both the colonel and, perhaps even more important, to the men serving under the Afghan colonel that Owen was taking the training seriously and that they were actually partners in all this. Taking time to establish a rapport, however, was something that Owen pointed out had not been a part of his training. But, if tea drinking was going to lead to a successful mission, then Owen, falling back on his SEAL mentality, would do whatever it took.

Even more difficult, perhaps, were the cultural differences between the nascent ANA and Owen's brand of professional militarism. Owen complained about Afghan soldiers going home on leave. Once on leave the soldiers were difficult to track, some returning weeks late, others not returning at all, making it difficult to determine exactly how many soldiers were available for missions. Variables that Owen had no control over, like these, made his systematic approach and lengthy preparations seem useless. Additionally, drug use was high, literacy was low, and, although there were occasionally strong officers, the recruiting and maintaining of Afghan soldiers was clearly a challenge in a different way than it was in the American military. Yet Owen and others who were paired with ANA units felt pressure to make sure the two were performing effectively together.

Policy makers in Washington and officers higher up were calling for an "Afghanization" of the war. The international public wanted to see that progress was being made, and they did not want to see Americans dying in what was increasingly considered an Afghan war. One of the best ways to demonstrate this was by having the ANA take the lead on missions and the Afghan National Police (ANP) to focus on maintaining local security. This meant a series of cooperative missions as well as a reaching out between international forces and local security groups. Around Bagram this took the form of NATO donating furniture and security barriers to the local police headquarters, along with plenty of time for photo ops for both the local police commander and the soldiers from the airbase, which were then posted by American military media outlets.[6]

Of course, when it came to completing more military missions, the ANA struggled, particularly early on, often relying on the support of the international troops they were partnering with. Looking back at his mission, Owen had developed some sympathy for the young ANA soldiers; he saw their half-hearted attempts to engage the Taliban as logical—they would, of course, have to be living with these people once the international community left. Furthermore, if things went sideways, they could always call in international reinforcements, who were much better equipped. Who wouldn't sit back and give way to the SEALs?

But what bothered Owen more was the lack of cooperation on the international side of things. This was a frustrating world, not just of bureaucracy, but of multiple bureaucracies, where getting anything done required paperwork in different languages that went to different headquarters. These bureaucratic divides within the international effort were only exacerbated by the difference in lifestyle and culture of different groups. Outside the military and the predictable nationalism of the embassies, NGO workers, journalists, and others tended to clump together around certain professions, though even here nationalities seemed to clump together around clichés: South Africans were military minded and always appeared to make up a large percentage of the security contractors; Scandinavians worked for human rights groups; and cultural NGOs had a relatively high number of French expats, who particularly enjoyed working with contemporary Afghan artists.

The international military was not the only group with territorial concerns; even within the NGO world, there were discussions about where certain groups should and should not be working, oftentimes on a more conceptual level. In the case of contractors, there was a clear advantage to not sharing information and attempting to monopolize certain types of contracts whether they were road construction or assistance to the justice sector. There was often a rush to secure the advice of certain experts when calls for proposals by USAID were released. So when a new justice initiative was announced, my colleague at the United States Institute of Peace and I suddenly found ourselves getting a stream of phone calls from grant writers looking to set up meetings so that they could claim certain sectors of justice support as their own. Experts were scooped up on short-term projects to demonstrate that the contractors were using those with the most knowledge of the situation. Even nonprofits worked to secure their own niches. In many cases this was simple division of labor with one women's rights group focusing on women's shelters and another working on employment opportunities, but in other instances there were territorial divides. The Aga Khan Foundation, for example, was known primarily for working with Ismaili communities in the north of the country, while the Norwegian Refugee Council focused much of their efforts in the west. Moving into another organization's territory without proper consultation was seen as impolite at best and, in more extreme circumstances, predatory.

These divisions helped create rather different social worlds in which members of various groups circulated. Peter Jouvenal's Gandamak Lodge was an inn and bar frequented by old-school journalists in a building that was the former home of one of Osama bin Laden's wives. After growing in popularity as a watering hole, it moved to a new location near the Iranian embassy, its stone basement a place where aspiring spies tended to congregate. In contrast with this, NGO workers filled a series of international-oriented restaurants and guesthouses around town, including the Lebanese Taverna, which was destroyed by an insurgent attack in 2014. The UN guesthouse was a place for international diplomats to go for a swim on a Friday afternoon before it was shut down and was replaced, in part, by the German Club, which had some of the only tennis courts in town.

These groups occasionally mingled with diplomats, but protocol and force of habit meant that most of those working in embassies tended to move between meetings and various embassy parties. Diplomats such as Ronald Neumann, who was the American ambassador to Afghanistan from 2005 to 2007, had clearly defined social circles of diplomats and high-ranking Afghan and international officials. Within the walls of the American embassy compound, Neumann was known to take the occasional break by playing volleyball with the embassy's Marine guards, though this type of social mobility was rare among high-level diplomats. Restrictions on whom one was interacting with put certain constraints on whom someone like Neumann was able to speak with and how he gathered his information. Many of his stories of his time in Afghanistan are of trying to get out of the U.S. embassy compound to visit the provinces, hoping to get a sense of what was actually happening.

Expats like Will, who moved between different groups, were more difficult to classify. Will, working for an organization that was driven by Christian values, interacted a good deal with the missionary community, who primarily lived in residential neighborhoods far from the embassies in the west of Kabul. At the same time, however, Will's more liberal social views meant that he also enjoyed drinking at the international bars with the younger journalists and NGO workers. His engineer's eye and interest in taking apart motors gave him a vocabulary that allowed him to talk more easily to military folks than some other NGO workers could. Ultimately, this flexibility helped him a great deal. Once the surge in international funding came in 2009 and the American embassy started looking at investing in the development of renewable energy, as one of the few with real on-the-ground experience with wind energy in Afghanistan, Will was increasingly pulled into a circle that involved officials from donor agencies like USAID and, like sharks smelling blood in the water, the large-scale contracting crowd who generally went after such contracts. This combination would have serious repercussions for Will and his partners at Alliance Wind Power and their work in the Shomali Plain around Bagram Airfield.

Sites of Interaction

As had become clear to me while sitting in a sleepy bazaar, watching potters work in their workshops and sell their wares, it was possible for the intervention in Afghanistan to be both everywhere and nowhere. At times, you would hear stories of journalists or travelers reaching mountain villages that thought the Taliban were still in power; at other moments, with international troops traipsing across local fields, the intervention was impossible to miss. Across Afghanistan the impact of the intervention was uneven. Instead, most felt only a few of the effects of the international presence, often indirectly, through changes in the economy. This could be good and bad, and new roads often meant improved access to health care but could also mean more insurgent groups moving through the area or the growing spread of narcotics. Other changes in things like governance meant that there were more government offices across the country, but the fact that the Afghan government populated these offices with many former jihadi commanders meant that these outposts were filled with corrupt officials who had been there in less formalized positions for the past decades.[7] At the same time, however, a handful of meaningful sites of interaction between Afghan communities and the international presence became key to discussing and understanding the intervention more broadly across the country. These sites became symbols of the intervention but also flashpoints where the power, violence, and inequality of the conflict were most real and visible.

Figure 2.2. Outside Bagram. Photo by the author.

I first became interested in the area around Bagram Airbase having passed through several times while studying Istalif, which was just above the Shomali Plain about an hour to the west.[8] Technically an airfield, with an ISAF airbase there composed of troops and bases from a variety of NATO countries, as well as a larger American presence, the base was the key military installation north of Kabul. It was also home to the headquarters for RC East (the Regional Commander Center for the east of the country). In the rather odd geography of the intervention, this meant that Bagram oversaw NATO operations in the east of the country, particularly operations in provinces like Nangarhar, Kunar, and Nuristan, areas that were culturally and politically much different from Bagram, despite the fact that Bagram itself was located at close to the center of the country.

As I traveled through the district and the growing town around the base, two of the things that were remarkable were the bustle of trucks and merchant activities in the market compared to the quiet bazaar I had been studying and the rather hostile attitudes of the people I interacted with around the base toward the international presence more generally. In Istalif, while I had faced some challenges during my research, one of the things I had been most surprised about was how willing people were to speak with me about all manner of things. Most in the town felt ambivalent about the international presence; generally, they were grateful that the Taliban had been expelled and that certain NGOs were working in the area but also frustrated by the lack of more effective aid and sustained growth. As time wore on, they became increasingly frustrated by the reckless spending of the intervention but were benefiting from it to such an extent that they did little more than grumble. Most of the hostility toward the international presence that I encountered came from groups who felt they had been excluded from the development aid that international organizations had brought to the area. For the most part, however, people in Istalif were more than happy to speak to a curious foreigner asking questions about their town. They took me on rambling walks up the valley and told me stories about where different militias had camped during the Civil War. Part of their willingness to engage with me was probably just that, in a quiet bazaar, an odd American asking questions about genealogies and pottery making was an intriguing distraction. A larger part, however, was that the Istalifis in town were fiercely proud of their history, and the idea that I was writing a book about it appealed to many of them. Theirs was a long history and one that they knew had not been told much abroad. As residents of a town that had seen tourists visit during the 1960s and 1970s when it was a popular hillside escape from Kabul, when I first arrived in 2005, many were hopeful the town's reputation could grow again as the country became peaceful.

In contrast with this, the people around Bagram were more suspicious of me as an international, but they were also clearly more suspicious of each other. They had had much more experience both with international journalists passing through and with internationals from the base arranging consultations and meetings aimed at creating a group consensus about development projects or security initiatives. The community, however, had become increasingly convinced that these were largely just rubber stamps for those inside the base, who could say that they had done some sort of community consultation. As a result, whenever I chatted with people, they wanted to know what my "real" intentions were. Most were still happy to talk about their experiences of the last decades of the conflict and particularly about the nearby base. Others were less so. On one of my first visits to a more rural area a little to the north of the base an older man chatted with me and my driver, answering some of our questions before concluding almost jovially, "If you come back here, we will probably kill you." We left rather soon after that.

On a certain level this was peculiar because the area seemed to have benefited economically a good deal from the international presence. It had certainly gained more in terms of international funds than Istalif had. Around the base NATO forces and their contractors worked to employ young men as translators and laborers, generating income for many families. The international military had also set up programs aimed to co-opt local community leaders by delivering small-scale development projects. The shops had a much greater variety of goods and merchandise, and there was evidence around the bazaar of new buildings and near-constant construction.

Yet, in the town of Istalif, which had seen far fewer internationally sponsored programs bringing aid to the area, although people increasingly grumbled about the waste of the foreign troops, few were openly hostile to them. This struck me as an odd contradiction; in the places where the international community was spending the most to "win hearts and minds," Afghans were the most opposed to the international presence. Somehow where the most effort was being exerted, it seemed that hearts were being lost.

The influx of funds into the area dominated public life and politics in the Shomali Plain around the airfield. Most conversations seemed to loop back to the uneven economic growth in one way or another. As I began to explore some of the contradictions in the area further, one Afghan analyst in Kabul suggested to me, in the past ten years "no part of Afghanistan has changed more than the road through the Shomali," and this seemed to be true. Despite Bagram's relatively small size historically, there were dozens of new and half-completed shops in the bazaar near the entrance to the base. These shiny glass facades contrasted sharply with the mud shops in the further reaches of the bazaar, which had yet to be renovated. Even here, however, shopkeepers were talking about expansion.

Shops had also sprung up at a shocking rate along the road that linked Bagram to Kabul. On the drive north from Kabul, the city used to end abruptly as one climbed onto the plain, but as traffic swelled it became increasingly difficult to determine where the city ended and the rural areas around the base began. Instead, there sprang up a near-constant string of shops along the road to Kabul with growing rows of houses behind them. The towns along the road, key sites from Afghan history like Qara Bagh, Kalakan, and Mir Bacha Kot, were increasingly difficult to distinguish from one another as they sprawled outward. It was almost as if there was a bread-crumb trail of development and business growth tethering Bagram to Kabul, thirty miles to the south.

The bazaar adjacent to the base also had a rather international feel to it considering the fact it was a historically rural area. In the second-story teahouses across from the main entrance to the base, Pakistani and Indian merchants discussed business with Afghans who seemed to hail from almost every corner of the country. Bollywood films on satellite stations played on television screens above them. Imports arriving from China and the Persian Gulf were mixed in with local produce in the bazaar, and the variety of goods in the market was generally found only in major cities in Afghanistan.

The vast amounts of money coming into the area created odd scenes. On the highway south of town was the delivery entrance to the base. Here rows and rows of trucks waited patiently in a concrete holding area, lined up to be inspected before delivering their goods onto the base. Atop one building nearby were dozens of discarded treadmills, covered in the gray dust. It was difficult to tell whether they were going to be used for spare parts or whether some local businessmen had gotten ahold of them, not known what to do with them in a country where few people jog, and left them there to rust.

Although the economic makeup of the area had shifted, some things had not changed in the community, such as the importance of land. Owning land continued to be a key measure of wealth and status, and people had a complicated relationship with the land around the base. In one sense, locals pointed out, the mountains provide water for the area, and the irrigation channels that descend from them flowed for much of the year as the winter snows slowly melted from the high mountain passes. At the same time, however, trouble came out of the mountains as well. The mountains to the south and the east were used by the mujahideen, the various anti-Soviet militias, to attack the Soviet soldiers occupying the base in the 1980s. Later during the Civil War in the 1990s, Hizb-e Islami used the mountains to attack Jamiat-e Islami, the principle group that formed a part of what became known as the Northern Alliance, which controlled most of the floor of the plain. When the Taliban finally took Kabul in 1997, some of the most devastating fighting took place on the plain as the Taliban pushed northward and Jamiat pulled back. A deminer who had worked in the area complained to me about the haphazard way that both Jamiat and the Taliban had left mines scattered around the base. The

Soviets, he said, at least tended to leave them in predictable patterns that were easier to map. Along with the occasional mine explosion, the long runway and huge hangars remained inviting targets, and the Taliban regularly lobbed poorly aimed missiles at the base.[9]

The increased international presence on the base and the growing demand for space for new businesses also distorted the value of the land. In this fertile area, producing numerous high-value crops, disputes over land were already complicated on both a family level, as sons argued over inheritance, and on a tribal level, as groups migrated to the plain from other parts of the country.[10] Through the late 2000s, however, the base continued to expand, putting pressure on land prices as well.[11] Concerns about attacks from adjacent compounds led ISAF to attempt to rent much of the land surrounding the base. Similarly, in Kabul, the U.S. embassy became increasingly surrounded by an eerie street of unoccupied houses that had been emptied out for security reasons. In the Bagram area, families and communities debated about whether to rent their land to businesses or the military or to maintain a more conservative approach by continuing to farm. Renting the land could earn them significant economic funds but potentially incur retributive attacks by insurgents or simply disgruntled neighbors.

Stories about the base and the potential for earning money by leasing land further complicated these debates. One man described to me how ISAF representatives came to his family to arrange the rental of some land, presumably because there were security concerns about its proximity to the base. They agreed to a contract but had failed over the past year to pay any rent whatsoever, the man said. It was unclear to the man why this had occurred, but speaking with other men from the area, they had decided as a community not to allow anyone in the area to lease any additional land to the military.

Perhaps because of the variety of tensions, in conversations around Bagram what many speakers dwelled on was the clear sense that things could have been different. As one of the parts of the country that suffered the most under the Taliban, the area was quick to embrace the international presence initially. After I asked the principal at the local high school to describe the Taliban era in the area, he responded that the Taliban "in just four years took the area back forty years . . . they shut down our schools, they put our intellectuals, religious leaders, and farmers in prison; they cut our trees and burned our homes. But as soon as the international forces came to Bagram, things began to normalize."

In 2001 international troops were generally welcomed to the area as Taliban fighters vanished, fleeing to the south and the east, rarely looking back. In the early 2000s, the damage done by dragged-out fighting between the Northern Alliance and the advancing Taliban in the 1990s was slowly being repaired. A decade later, however, the promise of peace and prosperity had largely not been fulfilled. Money had entered the area, but it was increasingly in the hands of a small elite, and, although incidents involving the Taliban remained fairly rare, unarmed men seldom dared travel the area alone at night. Kidnapping continued to be common, as were more general shakedowns. Household incomes had grown, and more children were in school, but in comparison to the amount of money that was spent during the international intervention it had become obvious to people on both sides of the wall of the base that individuals were continuing to suffer as opportunities were wasted.

For many the base now symbolized their ambiguous relationship with the international intervention. As the school teacher continued:

> In general, we don't have much connection with the base . . . they contact our leaders only when they need to employ translators or laborers. Sometimes they talk in the media as if they are completely in contact with the communities outside the base. But this is a lie, and I have never witnessed them coming out to ask about our problems. The district of Bagram and the base are like two different regions separated by thick concrete walls that never permit citizens to pass from one side to the other. We are not allowed to enter the base, and they are not allowed to enter our villages without permission from the district governor.

An Ethnography of the Intervention

As I tried to wrap my mind around some of these tensions and ambiguities, it became increasingly clear to me that many of the analyses of the conflict in Afghanistan and of the intervention were inadequate. Even the strongest, most vivid accounts seem to be missing some key aspects, and few could explain to me some of the contradictions I found in the communities around Bagram. Why was development money not leading to more development? Why was a military presence making things more dangerous? How do we reconcile both the good and the bad aspects of the intervention without falling into a political debate that blinds us from the lessons that we could be learning?

To study these issues some have looked at the ways in which policy decisions were made, such as Bob Woodward's *Obama's Wars* and Rajiv Chandrasekaran's *Little America*. Other memoirs, in particular, have critiqued diplomatic approaches, such as pieces like *The Other War* by former American Ambassador Ronald Neumann and *The Long Way Back* by Canadian diplomat Chris Alexander. Military accounts range from histories of entire campaigns, such as Doug Stanton's *Horse Soldiers*, to memoirs by generals, like Stan McCrystal's *My Share of the Task*. Some of these are more thrilling narratives of missions gone wrong, like Marcus Luttrell's *Lone Survivor*, whereas others, like Carter Malkasian's *War Comes to Garmser*, were more thoughtful critiques of the application of counterinsurgency strategy. More analytical pieces have assessed the role of warlords toward the beginning of the conflict (Antonio Giustozzi's *Empires of Mud*) and how those roles have evolved (Dipali Mukhopadhyay's *Warlords, Strongman Governors, and the State in Afghanistan*). Astri Suhrke's *When More Is Less* provided a sharp critique of using development in stabilization operations while Scott Smith's *Afghanistan's Troubled Transition* did the same for elections.

All of these pieces, however, focus on only one aspect of the intervention. Rereading my own notes from interviews and conversations around Bagram, those whom I interviewed focused first on local politics, but eventually these conversations moved into concerns about the local economy, the role of former warlords, and the evolving social landscape. Trying to analyze these notes, the approaches of most of the writing on the intervention felt too narrow to really understand all of the aspects of what was happening in the area. The intervention was not simply a military mission that had been sidetracked, a failure of diplomacy, or an issue with how development projects were being implemented; it was all of these things uncomfortably intertwined. Was there a way to bring these pieces together? Was there a way to better understand the lived experience of the intervention? My own training as an anthropologist pushed me to take a more holistic approach to these questions. Instead of sectioning off various pieces, could they be kept together within one framework? The Afghans I was speaking with certainly were not separating the military from the developmental from the diplomatic when they looked at the international presence. As I thought about trying to avoid these divides in my own writings and articles, I began to wonder, was it possible to write an ethnography of the intervention?

Ethnography generally attempts to take a holistic approach, looking at a group of people from a variety of angles, examining what they do, how they interact, and what they believe to try to move us away from our own cultural tendencies toward a more nuanced view of how different cultures work. Usually, after an extended period of fieldwork, the anthropologist would then record these observations in a carefully organized book-length analysis. Particularly in the first half of the twentieth century, the typical ethnography was rather formulaic. It gave a brief introduction and went through chapters such as history, population, ecology, social structures, kinship, economics, politics, and, often last, religion. Others include chapters on residence patterns and mythology.

This approach was rightly criticized for its overly static and bounded portrayal of culture. It also attempted to understand other cultures in strictly Western terms (that is, by assuming that a culture had a "mythology" that was worthy of a chapter, this oftentimes created something that might not have even been there in the first place).[12] In many ways, anthropology and the academic world in general have moved past this approach, favoring thematic studies that focus on one aspect of a culture. Even before the rise of postmodernism, anthropologists had grown weary of the idea that one could simply sum up all the pieces of a society and categorize them in one monograph, not to mention the fact that almost every group had had, by this point, some graduate student live with them and write such an ethnography.

The strength of the ethnographic approach, however, remains in the ways in which anthropology weaves together political, economic, and social concerns in a manner that demonstrates the complicated tapestry of human life. As the case of Bagram demonstrates, culture and politics are not narrowly bounded the way that some early anthropologists may have assumed. Instead, ethnographies need to be flexible, to move among sites, times, and people to demonstrate how culture shapes the lives that people live.[13] In this case, such an approach allows us to take a broader, more nuanced view of what the intervention was and how it affected people.

How did the merchants like Omar living around the base, Will who worked near the base, Owen who fought alongside the troops on the base, and Ambassador Neumann who led the American presence in Afghanistan understand the intervention? Accounts that fail to mention the way that military aspects of the intervention related to political aspects, which related to economic aspects, social aspects, religious aspects, and so on, are missing the broader context of what has happened in Afghanistan. Accounts that try to emphasize the international politics of the intervention ignore the way in which the intervention is a lived experience that is, in many ways, the sum of a series of individual decisions that have had an impact on those on the ground. Although there is not space in this book, or perhaps even in a series of books, to record all the aspects of the intervention, I increasingly felt that it would be useful to present several small pieces of the intervention in order to understand how different lives became woven together, creating a complex social, political, and economic landscape that was one part of the intervention.

Will's background as an engineer led him to see the issues of the intervention as a mechanical problem and, as we will see, probably led him away from issues such as funding that required different ways of thinking. Owen's training and general disposition drove him to approach the conflict from a tactical point of view. This thinking was not always as helpful as it could have been because much of his job was to forge relationships with Afghan Army officers. This forced Owen and others to try to think differently about what they were doing in Afghanistan. For example, in building these relationships in Afghanistan's patriarchal society, the fact that Owen was a father earned him respect and acceptance that his rank did not. Later he told me with a chuckle he quickly invented additional children and stories about his strong sons to impress the Afghan soldiers with whom he was interacting. Military rank was not enough in these situations; his ability to demonstrate his social status as a father mattered almost as much.

These and other seemingly trivial details about aspects of daily life—like the fact that during the surge the American ambassador was often required to participate in conference calls to the United States at 2 a.m. several nights a week, operating most days on little sleep; or the fact that far more time was spent by soldiers playing video games than fighting; or that many aid workers tried to drink away their frustrations at loud Thursday night parties—ignore what the experience was like for the individuals whose lives comprised this international presence in Afghanistan. If the intervention was ultimately the sum of these pieces, it seems only appropriate that we should study these pieces themselves. What an ethnography attempts to do is to explain how a society works, how it creates culture, and then look at the repercussions for those living in that society and how they make decisions.

This leads me to the second reason that I think the ethnographic approach is useful: It forces us to step back and look at the ways in which the hundreds of thousands of individuals and hundreds of billions of dollars that flowed into Afghanistan after 2001 created a new society, with new cultural norms (that was, admittedly, based on the emergence of other older cultural norms reconfigured). Although there was little thought before the American invasion about what would happen in Afghanistan after the Taliban were driven out, this first real act in George W. Bush's War on Terror would set the stage for America's presence internationally for the next generation. The successes and, more notably, the failures in Afghanistan shaped the way the American government and American people more generally thought about America's role in places like Syria and Yemen. Certainly there have been many internationally organized interventions over the past century, and it seems likely that there will be many more, but the U.S.-led effort mobilized troops, funds, and people on a level not seen since World War II. At the same time, the rise of Skype, video conference calls, and round the clock email connected those working in Afghanistan to their home countries in a way that had not happened in previous wars. All of these nuances have made this conflict unique and make it likely to continue to shape both how Americans see the world and how the world sees America for the next decades.

Part of the problem of looking at the dynamism of the intervention is understanding what its shifting goals were. For some it was a military operation, for others it was a humanitarian mission, and for others it was a state-building exercise. Even within these approaches there were subcategories that overlap but could also contradict each other, so that counterterrorist operations suggested the military quickly strike targets, while counterinsurgency demanded the military stay and develop relationships with the communities they were operating in. Part of the problem of any analysis that attempts to isolate any of these approaches is that the intervention was actually trying to do all of these things at once, ultimately doing none of them well. This makes assessment particularly difficult. Evaluating the intervention as a development operation ignores its military goals; looking at it as a counterterrorism operation misses its state-building mission. Statistics and maps of roads built and territory controlled ultimately mislead the viewer even further. And none of these approaches gives the viewer enough of a sense of the complex human landscape the intervention created.

An ethnographic approach, however, can move us past some of these narrow approaches and tell us a more complicated story about the past decade in Afghanistan. Particularly, as international troops began to withdraw and the intervention wound down, most in the media preferred relatively simple stories.[14] These were stories about money wasted and lives lost but also stories about girls going to school and successful elections. Simple stories make both politics and policy easier, but they are misleading. Suggesting that Afghanistan is the graveyard of empires and that the Americans never should have invaded tells us little. Even those supporting a more robust international presence relied on similarly simple clichés such as Afghan women as passive victims who need international assistance or Afghans as unruly tribes who are thoughtlessly willing to let terrorists set up training camps in their territory.

In most of these uncomplicated stories there was the tendency to blame the shortcomings of the intervention in Afghanistan on Afghans themselves. There was a focus on issues such as the effectiveness of the Taliban's tactics or the corruption of the Karzai government. What is missing from these explanations, however, is the role of the international community in these ill-advised adventures. In particular, these accounts do not look at how there was a certain logic within the culture of intervention that constrained the ability of individuals to think creatively and critically about the political world that they lived in. This created a world that was increasingly insular. It was a world of good intentions but increasingly contradictory goals.

Sometimes when complaining about Afghan politics and struggles with governance programs at the American embassy, I would hear diplomats and USAID officials grumble over beers about the inherent problems of the bureaucracy of the intervention. Similar complaints were voiced by military officers trying to organize missions and NGO workers delivering aid. "Bureaucracy" is often a convenient excuse and one that does help get at some concerns, but it is also overly simple. Bureaucracy is not always necessarily a bad thing, and, as Max Weber points out, it was at the very heart of industrialization and modernization and allowed us to begin to imagine notions like individual rights.

The problems with the bureaucracy of the intervention arose, instead, when it constrained individual action and when it prohibited the individual from choosing a course of action that he or she believed is right. People within the intervention could see the problem and, in some cases, could see the solution, but they were constrained by the structures of the intervention in such a way that there was little they could do to enact the solution. Bureaucracy tends to work "in theory," but, as we all know, life does not happen "in theory." That is the reason, when asking why parts of the international intervention worked (or didn't work), it is necessary to look first at the world the intervention created and then at what that world, its rules and regulations, tendencies and patterns, meant for those Afghans and internationals who lived in it or came into contact with it on a regular basis.

The lives in this book, I think, teach us three important lessons about what happened in Afghanistan and, perhaps, about intervention more generally. The first is that the intervention fashioned its own inward-looking culture, with its own language and way of thinking, composed of a wide variety of internationals and the Afghans who worked with them. Second, the insular nature of this community, as well as the logic and internal workings of its funding mechanisms and bureaucracy, made it particularly ineffective at looking outwards, engaging with the actual Afghan political world—in fact, the very nature of intervention's culture made intervention difficult. And, finally, those who could move across this boundary between Afghan communities and the world created by the intervention, oftentimes breaking the rules of each, were the ones who benefited most from the intervention, not ordinary Afghans.

The rest of this book is an attempt to look at the lives of a few people who were a part of the intervention and build an ethnographic account that suggests how the intervention built its own constraints, eventually crippling itself.

3 The Exotic Tribes of the Intervention

BEFORE LOOKING AT THE CULTURE CREATED within the intervention, it makes sense to ask to what extent the international community was actually a community. It was made of distinct pieces and subgroups that often seemed disparate and, at times, isolated. For example, many NGO workers, particularly those outside of Kabul, existed in a world that never interacted with diplomats, and during my initial research in Afghanistan I rarely bumped into international soldiers. Still, however, these groups cohered in several important ways.

Anthropologists, when looking at cultures, oftentimes analyze the ways in which various societies speak a unique language, live in unique structures, and have distinct cultural practices. If we are to try to take an ethnographic approach to the intervention, is it possible to pull out such pieces in a similar manner? This chapter tests some of the ways that we might be able to start thinking about what an ethnography of the intervention might look like and what it might tell us about the culture of the intervention.

Speaking the Intervention

At first it might seem simple to conclude that English was the language of the international community. There were 150,000 international troops from English-speaking countries, and donor money was dominated by the United States, Britain, Canada, and Australia. This, for example, meant that most NGOs, both international and Afghan, had to do their reporting in English. As a result, conferences, aid coordination meetings, and military briefs were almost all in English. A quick listen-in on one of these meetings, however, would show that this English was not the type of English that most Americans or British spoke. Instead, the international intervention in Afghanistan had its own distinctive patois that was marked by several unique characteristics.

The most immediately obvious of these linguistic oddities was probably the overwhelming use of acronyms. Terms that started in the military then often moved into conversations among diplomats and NGO workers, so that in 2013 everyone knew that Karzai needed to sign the BSA or Bilateral Security Agreement if American troops were going to stay. Similarly, just getting around required certain language, and you might have to bring your CAC (control access card) to enter the embassy or the CAFÉ (compound across from the embassy) before a meeting at the DFAC (dining facility) with a PolAd (political advisor) who has been told by the RSO (regional security officer) that only mission-critical movement was allowed regardless of whether the meeting is about AfPak (Afghanistan-Pakistan) strategy or simply recommendations for R and R (rest and relaxation) destinations.

For journalists or NGO workers working with the military or just trying to keep track of what was happening in the country, it became necessary to understand the nested military installations that spread across the country and the terminology attached to them. After the key bases like Bagram, PRTs or provincial reconstruction teams were generally the largest sites of an initiative to intertwine military and development work. They often had USAID and other civilian officers working in them. PRTs were then linked to FOBs, or forward operating bases, which could vary in size, and were generally surrounded by the even smaller COPs, or combat outposts. When referring to attacks, suicide bombings and roadside bombs were referred to as IEDs, or improvised explosive devices, but these could be broken down further to BBIEDs, which were bodily borne improvised explosive devices, as opposed to car bombs, which were VBIEDs, or vehicle-borne improvised explosive devices. Referring to any of these by their complete names would have instantly revealed one's newcomer status or have been met with a blank stare.

Even more mundane terms were often shortened, and people struggled to get their RFPs (request for proposals) submitted to the DC (District of Columbia) office before CoB (close of business). Groups and individuals were also acronymized, and local nationals working on bases were LNs, al Qaeda was called AQ, Osama bin Laden became OBL, and Ahmed Wali Karzai, the president's notorious brother and strongman of Kandahar, was referred to as AWK. Places also became letters, and Jalalabad Airfield was JAF (as opposed to KAF, Kandahar Airfield), whereas the key southeast provinces of Paktya, Paktyka, and Khost were referred to simply as P2K.

Other linguistic shifts were less formulaic and demonstrated the importance of insider knowledge. Sitting through the evening commander's briefing at a small FOB as the various officers ran through their briefings, the military jargon was so thick that I struggled to keep up with what was being said. Complicating the matter, the unit, which was patrolling an agricultural area with a large number of irrigation channels, had decided to name all of the channels after NFL teams to make discussing them easier. As a result I was distracted by talk of a CasEvac (casualty evacuation) at the intersection of the 49ers and the Cowboys, a couple of clicks over from the Bears in an area controlled by an important local elder. Of course, beyond the confusion for me as an anthropologist, we will see that this had more serious repercussions in terms of interactions with local communities because officers were not accustomed to local terms for landmarks used by elders who might approach the base, and the elders certainly were not versed in the hierarchy of NFL teams. All of this talk seemed to reinforce the odd mixture of Western words and assumptions that were being thrust onto this local context.

Language is of course deeply connected with knowledge and how we navigate and order our world. Anthropologists like James Scott have pointed to the way in which the rise of nation-states has simultaneously demanded a rise in the language that we use to order ourselves, from the use of last names or street names. Such use of language by the state renders citizens "legible," allowing the state to expand its control over the population.[1] Addresses may help the fire department find your house, but they also help the tax collector locate you. Afghans, living in a country with a historically weak state that had been at war for decades, resisted this process. One of the places this was more apparent was in the almost complete lack of addresses in the city of Kabul. Some streets had names, and, in later years, there were some attempts to put numbers up on buildings and street signs, usually funded by frustrated American officials. For the most part, however, directions were almost always relative to other landmarks and required a preestablished knowledge of the area to get around. My address in Kabul was "Behind the Old British Embassy," before I moved to the "Afghan Fried Chicken Street." In some cases these were simply translations of Dari or Pashto terms; the popular "Flower Street," for example, was originally the street in the center of the city where the florists were concentrated. In other cases the names said something about the history of the city, if you lived in Shar-e Naw, the New City, or simply referred to the nearest major intersection.

In the middle of the 2000s it was interesting to watch international organizations start to take on the Afghan practice of not labeling themselves, similarly trying to render themselves less visible to outsiders. This was primarily out of fear that having signs marking international offices would make them more easily targeted by attacks. Some suggested that, because many of the suicide attackers were young Pakistanis who had never been to Kabul before, such tactics could be used to avoid attacks on their compounds (though surely, if this were true, it led to an increase in attackers detonating in random intersections filled with civilians). Some organizations would replace signs with less clear markers that they would let you know about before visiting; one of the organizations down the street from my house was marked by a blue wall with white stars. Eventually, as with Afghan homes, you simply needed to know where something was, or you could potentially stop and ask someone along the way, with embassies' flags flying behind walls so high that they could be seen only from the inside.

As rents soared and properties sprung up, offices moved frequently, new buildings were built on recently cleared land, and it became even more difficult to find one's way in the city. So while one could still buy meat on "Butcher Street," it became increasingly difficult to find flowers on Flower Street, with those small businesses forced to relocate. Further complicating the matter, however, one of the most popular expat lunch spots was the Flower Street Café, often just referred to as "Flower Street," which was originally located on Flower Street but had moved to a more suburban neighborhood to the north. Thus, many newcomers could be excused for asking for an Afghan driver to take them to Flower Street, and ending up on a busy downtown lane with no sign of either shops selling flowers or an expat lunch spot. Confusing things even further, the owner of the Flower Street Café eventually got a contract to serve lunch at the Duck and Cover, the U.S. embassy bar. Thus, most American officials, who were not allowed to leave the compound except for official business, could also get Flower Street sandwiches within the embassy, blissfully unaware of the heaping side of confusing history that accompanied their wraps and salads. As a result, as with slang among adolescents, language and names became a badge of belonging, demonstrating that one was a truly a member of the international community, with the recently arrived scrambling to keep up.

Language also helps define and shape our opinions about the world, and much of the language of the intervention was deliberately manipulative, attempting to shape how events were understood. Thus, a military convoy might not be "attacked," but would "experience a kinetic provocation." The passivity of the phrase took away from the at times brutal reality of the battlefield, the same way that terms like *militia*, *insurgents*, and *irregular forces* ultimately suggest something very different from someone speaking about a "Taliban army."[2] As the number of international soldier fatalities increased from disgruntled members of the Afghan army, these became increasingly known as "insider attacks," reaffirming the line between "allies" and "insurgents." Such use of language could have serious consequences. On one level the insider-outsider language as well as ISAF's claims to be working *"shona ba shona"* or shoulder-to-shoulder with local Afghans reinforced the divide between "good guys" and "bad guys," and ignored the actual reality of the complex alliances and tensions that the intervention created. At the same time, however, these linguistic peculiarities also had more immediate results.[3]

One of the examples many Afghans that worked with internationals pointed to, in particular, was the challenges of grant writing. Grant writing in Afghanistan was a science, an art, and hard labor. NGOs and large contractors, in particular, would employ full-time writers. In smaller NGOs, these writers might be unpaid interns, but in bigger organizations, experienced writers who had won large grants in the past were particularly prized and well paid. They were often brought in from outside the organization, and it was not so important that they knew anything about certain programs as much as they were familiar with the grant-writing process and the linguistic idiosyncrasies that were associated with it. Forms would ask the writer to distinguish between the "outcomes," "impact," and "deliverables" of a project, and oftentimes those with the most experience implementing projects on the ground struggled with the linguistic rules of the intervention's bureaucracy.

These demands made it incredibly challenging for someone with no experience with the USAID grant submission process, which was particularly complicated, to obtain a grant. This created an almost closed loop of funders that received much of the international aid entering the country. Even highly efficient local NGOs well positioned to work on certain projects (as we will see Will and his associates at AWP were) would always be at a disadvantage to big DC-based firms that employed full-time grant writers. Against such competition, local Afghan companies rarely stood a chance. Later, around Bagram Airbase, several young Afghan businessmen complained about these processes to me. It was corruption, they said; otherwise how could you explain that the same few large American contractors seemed to win every grant and contract? Really, in most instances it seems likely that it was not corruption in the way in which they imagined, but the language of the intervention had the same effect: It kept certain groups out and others in, defining and regulating the international community through its rigorous use of these odd phrases and linguistic turns.

Living the Intervention

If language kept the local Afghan world divided from the international community by making communication difficult, more overtly, compounds and bases and their imposing walls did the same thing physically. Pockets of compounds around Kabul and other key Afghan cities and bases were linked together by the internationals who moved between them, creating a world that most Afghans could not access. The high walls helped mark these compounds, but there were other cultural traits and symbols that made these places distinct from the nearby homes of other Afghans.

A beautiful half–coffee table book, half–academic study called *An Atlas of Indigenous Domestic Architecture* (1991) by Thomas Barfield and Albert Szabo outlines the regional variations in housing in Afghanistan before the Soviet invasion in wonderful detail. In the book there are photos and illustrations of the various types of dwellings that different Afghans live in, along with descriptions of the arrangement of settlements that mapped the Afghan landscape by building types. After going through the book and then driving toward Mazar-e Sharif, you could easily tell when you were getting close to the bazaar town of Tashkurgan because of the increase in graceful, low-lying domed roofs. The book additionally contrasts the sprawling qalas or forts of the Pashtuns with the small houses along narrow lanes in a Tajik village not far from Bagram. Such distinction created certain social patterns, and the Pashtun compounds encouraged stronger family connections than the more urban Tajik residential structures. A similar study of architectural forms and the resulting social patterns could be done of the intervention, looking at how the sprawling international presence built and added on to their own forts, creating their own social and political patterns.

Of course, the most distinctive sorts of dwellings were the military camps like Bagram. Ranging from tiny outposts atop the mountains of eastern Afghanistan to the extensive bases of Bagram, Camp Bastion, Leatherneck, and

Kandahar Airfield, whose multiple layers of perimeter walls ran for miles in every direction, these camps looked fairly similar externally, just on different scales. Awash in barbed wire, built out of HESCO bags, burlap, and wire containers that were then filled with rocks and earth shoveled into them, many of the walls looked as if they might wash away in a strong rainstorm. The external walls, however, were often misleading, and at times the outer walls were just the first of many, with short breaks in between looked over by watchtowers: wall after wall, creating a labyrinth of concrete and mud.

These bases did not fit easily into the landscape—they contrasted starkly with other large Afghan structures. One of the differences was the fact that most Afghan compounds had large front gates. In contrast, it was common for bases to have no clear entrance. For the most part, they were accessed by helicopter, the main means of coming and going to many bases. The bases were designed to be linked to each other, not to the world outside their walls. This, combined with the fact that bases did not want to present easy targets for suicide bombers, meant that most bases had nothing that would resemble a "front door." Instead, there were often multiple breaks in the HESCO walls that surround the bases: one for deliveries, one for visitor traffic perhaps, but none was clearly marked in any language, making it obvious that visitors were not welcome.

On more than one visit to various bases I had no problem finding the base itself, but approaching on foot or by taxi it could be incredibly difficult to actually find the main entrance gate. The irony, however, was that those on the inside, who either arrived by helicopter or were driven there by lower-ranking soldiers in convoys, had little clue as to how to enter the bases either. The best I could do on a couple of occasions was to call on my cell phone to tell the person I was meeting that I was near the southeast corner of the base so that I could be directed to walk toward whatever side the entrance was on. Further complicating matters, the few pedestrian entrances oftentimes were incredibly narrow with sharp turns to ensure that any frontal attack on foot would be easily repelled, meaning that a visitor would have to peer down narrow alleys, unsure of where they would eventually lead. The nervous disposition of those working guard duty did little to help the situation: Once, looking for the entrance in Nangarhar and dressed in traditional Afghan clothes and with a thicker than normal beard, I was greeted by a Marine who pointed his rifle while telling me to "put the motherfucking cellphone down." I did, and he was clearly startled by my sarcastic apology in clear English.

Other Afghans who visited the bases reported similar welcomes or worse. On another occasion I was in the southeast of Afghanistan, waiting near the gate of a base for my car to pick me up and listening to a group of men trying to file a claim with the American guards for a car that had been damaged by one of their patrols. The problem was that the translator with the American soldiers was from the north of Afghanistan and spoke only Dari, and this was Pashtun country, so the elders spoke only Pashto. The translator, clearly embarrassed by his inability to translate, did not let on to the guards that he did not speak Pashto, and the guards grew more and more frustrated with the elders who seemed to actually have a reasonable grievance. What was clear from the encounter was that the walls of the base were virtually impenetrable for those living outside.

Despite the thick walls, inside the bases themselves the world was not necessarily very comfortable. Most slept under heavy cloth tents, sometimes augmented with plywood walls. As the intervention went on, larger bases like Bagram became increasingly built up, adding buildings and headquarters quickly and cheaply constructed, with troops sleeping no longer in tents but in modified shipping containers. Often all of the ground inside the area was covered with large gravel chunks that makes walking in thick military boots difficult and impossible in the thin sandals favored by most Afghan men. Most of the Afghan translators working on bases adapted by purchasing some of these boots themselves; in the bazaar outside Bagram, an Afghan in such boots was suggesting to those nearby that he worked on the base or visited regularly. Most often, however, the occasional Afghan laborer working on the base or elder visiting for a meeting struggled along the rocky paths.

Although most of the bases looked similar at first, the soldiers inside would quickly point to the nuances and reputations of various posts— Leatherneck was unbearably hot and dusty, the German base in the north was a terrific place to visit because it had a bar, and as long as the Canadians were in Kandahar there seemed to be a line at Tim Horton's regardless of the hour.[4] Conversations comparing the DFACs at various bases could stretch on and on, as could debates over the best gyms and recreational facilities. At first some of these conversations were perplexing to me, but after comparing the MREs (wrapped in thick plastic, just shake!) of the most basic outposts with the burgers of ISAF headquarters, I began to pay more attention to what type of food I could be expecting wherever I was headed next.

Figure 3.1. Helmand PRT housing from above. Photo by the author.

Yet soldiers were not the only ones living in shipping containers. Both the American and British embassies, caught up in the waves of expansion, were unable to keep constructing at a pace sufficient to house their staff. As a result, the far side of the U.S. embassy, referred to as CAFÉ, became a maze of bunkers and containers. Particularly at night (and especially after a few drinks at the Duck and Cover Bar located in CAFÉ) it was easy to become lost in the narrow alleys that separate the containers. Here, to fit even more people into a smaller area, the containers were stacked on top of each other, forming a honeycomb of low-level diplomats, each with his or her own cell—one bed, one desk, one chair, one bureau, so narrow that you could touch both sides with your fully extended arms at the same time. Packed with DVDs, paperback thrillers, and often video games, these containers ended up looking more like tiny dorm rooms than anything else, and in some cases diplomats would pass films back and forth in collegial fashion. In other instances, however, neighbors glanced at each other more suspiciously as competition for promotions and other perks increased.

In contrast with the military installations across the country and the diplomatic quarters in Kabul, packed together in the more affluent neighborhoods of Kabul and a few of the other large cities were a series of houses, compounds, and guesthouses where NGO workers, journalists, and a handful of other internationals resided. Instead of guards with guns, these guesthouses often relied simply on maintaining a low profile to avoid unwanted attention. (Though, as will be discussed later, many did have armed guards later in the decade, particularly those on USAID contracts who could use security as an excuse for increasing the value of their contract more generally.) Behind the walls of these compounds, the quality of the living spaces varied dramatically. Some had pleasant gardens and large windows. The worst were dull concrete affairs that were difficult to heat in the winter, with pipes constantly freezing.

During the 2000s, there was also a building boom of "narco-palaces" or "poppy palaces" in the Sherpur neighborhood, just north of many of the embassies, which created office-residencies for many of the large contractors. These buildings were so dubbed because of the assumed drug money involved in their construction, and the odd architecture of the area made it distinct. As Tom Freston described in *Vanity Fair*: "'Narco-tecture' takes classic design elements from ancient Greece and then goes psychedelic with them, adding touches from Mexico and Pakistan."[5] Often painted in pastel colors with gaudy garnishes, inside some had concrete fountains and other water features. Wide central staircases made the places impossible to heat, whereas poor ventilation and a lack of windows made them incredibly damp.

Not simply flamboyant, these buildings were also politically contested and became symbols of the corruption that came with the intervention. Most of them were built on government land from which officials had evicted poor squatters. Real estate agents connected with the officials then began selling the land illegally not long after the initial American invasion. In particular, the United Nations complained of then Defense Minister and later Vice President Marshall Fahim evicting families to seize land as early as 2003.[6] This led to several embarrassing episodes for the international community, such as one European mission renovating a large compound to turn it into an embassy in the neighborhood before being forced to abandon it because it was on illegally seized land.[7] Over a decade later, however, the exploitation of these properties continued.[8] The instability and lack of rule of law made landlords concerned about potential legal action against them or simply someone stronger coming along and seizing the property. This meant that, instead of investing in

Figure 3.2. Poppy Palace under construction. Photo by Casey Garret Johnson.

the property, they tried to make as much as they could as quickly as possible, cutting all sorts of corners with construction costs and placing buildings a couple of feet apart with no space for parking. As an engineer pointed out to me, "They mix so much sand in with the concrete, the entire place is going to come down in a medium-sized earthquake." International contractors, however, continued to move into the area. They were not there for the long run, were willing to take the risk, and were less concerned about bad press locally. Afghans driving through on one of the city's main thoroughfares, however, watched in disgust as poorer homes were torn down and new buildings were squeezed in to house foreigners. Soon, in what had been a lively Afghan neighborhood, the only Afghans who remained appeared to be private security contractors protecting the compounds, and a handful of Afghans who scurried in to work in them, glancing over their shoulders, concerned about the rise in kidnapping of Afghans who worked with internationals.

These contracting firms would put offices on the lower floors and then provide bedrooms for their international employees on the floors above. As security tightened, the employees often found no reason to leave these walled compounds, which increasingly took on the closed-off feel of military bases. As contractors won more contracts, they would often expand these compounds by renting the houses next door and cutting strategic holes through the walls to allow pedestrians to pass through. Some of the biggest firms closed off entire streets on the east side of the neighborhood. This created more isolated pockets of internationals, who might zip off in armored SUVs to the U.S. embassy or perhaps the occasional Afghan ministry but rarely left for any other reason.

The only really livable homes were usually rented by internationals working for smaller NGOs or journalists who had been working in the country for multiple years. These were often located near Shar-e Naw Park or one of the adjoining neighborhoods and were built in the 1970s when a certain amount of care and attention had been given to them. For those in Kabul for the longer term, rooms in some of these houses were highly coveted. My own house during the second half of my time in Kabul was run by Heidi Vogt, a highly efficient journalist from the Associated Press, who liked to organize dinner parties. There, one was likely to bump into UN officials, human rights advocates, and magazine journalists working on in-depth feature pieces, always making for interesting dinner conversation. An invitation to Heidi's house for dinner was prized in the constricted social circles in which internationals moved.

The rapid turnover of internationals, however, and their relative ignorance of the housing market led in many instances to massive price gouging. As security worsened, the United Nations started demanding that all of their staff live in homes that met certain security standards (for example, razor wire on all the walls, house walls that did not directly abut other house walls, and so on). Other NGOs and contractors took on these regulations to save time and soon, "UN-compliant" houses were in high demand even by those who did not work for the United Nations. Afghan landlords, of course, knowing these systems were in place, cornered the market on such places. Soon prices for a small room in Kabul were no different from rents in Washington or San

Francisco, and my own rent decreased significantly when I moved from Kabul to upstate New York.

As the decade wore on, many of the larger organizations like the United Nations and World Bank further tightened housing requirements and soon mandated that their employees live in houses that the organization owned or rented. With these moves, entire blocks of the city, particularly those around the Canadian, British, and American embassies, were shut down to through traffic. Although the designation was never formalized as it was in Baghdad, internationals in Kabul increasingly referred to this area of connected compounds and virtually no Afghan residencies as "the Green Zone." Barriers blocked the entranceways, and guards searched vehicles passing through. Oftentimes simply looking foreign and charging through could gain you access, but other times access was tightly controlled by rosters. Getting past required having your name "on the list," and, with communications between offices and the guards outside often haphazard, it was common to be left standing outside on a cell phone trying to reach someone inside to check to make sure the list was up-to-date. Forget trying to take your car inside.

Once past the barriers, however, this was a strange world of concrete streets, with blast walls on either side that, in contrast with the rest of Kabul, were eerily empty. With many UN and other officials working only six weeks at a time and then taking two weeks of R and R, and with other people occasionally being evacuated due to security concerns, the buildings rarely felt full to capacity. Inside the houses themselves, flat-screen TVs and brand-new gym equipment attempted to recreate the comforts of home, but the walls still felt narrow, often with additional layers of concrete lining the initial walls. It was rare to look out a window and see anything other than concrete.

The international community, however, was linked geographically in other ways as well, with certain streets and neighborhoods being points of intersection. For those looking to bring Afghan souvenirs home for friends and family, Chicken Street, the main backpacker street in the 1960s, was still the place to go if your security restrictions were not too tight. Similarly, a range of restaurants that were opened and closed and reopened became known for serving Western meals and perhaps, for foreigners, alcohol. Some of these, like the Flower Street Café, catered to upper-class Afghans as well, though most, like Peter Jouvenal's Gandamak Lodge, were shut up behind multiple layers of blast walls and accessible only after showing a passport (because it is illegal for Muslims to drink alcohol in Afghanistan, the few bars in Kabul often simplified the enforcement of the law by admitting only those who had passports from non-Muslim countries).

Outside the compounds where the internationals lived and worked, there were certain routes inside and outside the country that become important migratory paths. Most international flights into the country came through Dubai, also a place where people would leave for a weekend away or to renew a visa. It was unusual to take a flight in or out of Kabul and not know at least a couple of fellow passengers. Similarly, for the military, Manas Airbase in Kyrgyzstan was a frequent stopping and refueling point before flying on into Bagram or Kandahar.

These pathways also reinforced the fact that the international community had certain hubs in the country. The international military was concentrated on large bases in Kabul, Bagram, Jalalabad, and Kandahar, with a network of smaller bases (PRTs at the provincial level, then FOBs and COPs) that spread out primarily across the south and east. NGO workers, journalists, and others tended to be concentrated in Kabul, but there were similar smaller communities in Herat, Mazar-e Sharif, and other cities, linked both by daily flights and by the regular flow of visitors and new employees from Kabul and farther afield. Traveling to any of these places also gained one status; a Kabul-based official who had recently been down to Kandahar was given certain status in meetings back at the U.S. embassy, whereas, at the same time, D.C.-based diplomats who visited Kabul commanded a new authority when they returned to Washington.

While not geographically connected, these international offices, residences, and guesthouses formed a web across Afghanistan, where these strange tribes of internationals gathered, usually separated off from Afghans. Of course certain internationals, particularly those who had been there long-term and spoke Dari or Pashto, had close Afghan friends whom they interacted with socially, but even for those "old hands" interactions became more and more difficult. One Afghan friend whom I knew well began asking his international friends to drive their cars into his compound before getting out so that his neighbors would not see that a foreigner was visiting. Later, concerned that he was putting his family at risk, to his great disappointment, he felt that he had to stop inviting his international friends over at all. And so internationals became increasingly isolated in their different compounds and bases.

Although they varied in form, these dwellings possessed certain continuities that seemed to run through them—their impermanence, their insularity, their disconnection from the dwellings of neighboring Afghans. All of these contributed to the feeling that most of the internationals who were part of the intervention were cut off from the Afghans living in the communities around them. Beyond the ways in which these clusters of internationals were bound together by their separation from the Afghans around them, however, something deeper about how these individuals thought and looked at the world also tied them together.

Believing the Intervention

In the case of the international community in Afghanistan, thinking about religious beliefs might seem odd. Religion was not an overt part of life for most in the international community. In fact, it seemed at first that much of the international community was not particularly religious. There were almost no churches and few religious gatherings among internationals. As with Afghans, Sundays were not a day of rest; the weekend tended to be Friday and Saturday, with the workweek starting on Sunday. Several members of the international community took pride in their rejection of traditional religious values, with one couple getting married in Kabul's tank graveyard with a friend officiating with credentials he had received online.

Of course there were exceptions, most noticeably the large, but often quiet, community of Christian missionaries, many of whom were associated with IAM. In addition to this, there was a Catholic church in the Italian embassy, and chaplains of a variety of faiths were important members of many military units. Beyond this, overt expressions of faith were rare. In fact, one got the sense that there were more atheists around than one would have found in a typical American or European city. Perhaps it was the harsh realism of war and exposure to the violence that groups like the Taliban were justifying with religious rhetoric that made it more difficult to think that God might have been involved in everything that was occurring.

At the same time, however, it would be wrong to say there were not some common beliefs about how the world worked and what was important. In fact, the strong whiffs of atheism among many suggested that some new beliefs had replaced traditional religious principles. The intervention in Afghanistan certainly did not have "the White Man's Burden" of the British Empire or the "God, Gold, and Glory" of the Iberian conquest of the New World, but the majority of those involved in the intervention still did seem to possess a common, though perhaps unarticulated, ideology or worldview. Although it is difficult to make generalizations, the majority seemed to be socially liberal pragmatists who believed in hard work and at least some notion of human rights and social justice. Put perhaps more directly, the vast majority of those involved in the intervention in Afghanistan believed in the notion of intervention itself.

Expressions of this belief could take several forms. For instance, the belief that development aid could make the lives of individuals better or the belief that, by building a strong state, services would be delivered more effectively to citizens was common among those working for NGOs and embassies. This was a belief set that did not come exclusively from one side of the political spectrum or the other. Conservatives who saw this process of state building primarily through the creation of a strong national police force were almost as common as liberals who were working to empower women by setting up shelters so they could escape abusive families and corrupt police officials. But what united these very different political views was the notion that the international community could come into a foreign country, intervene, and fundamentally make it a better place. Later, when I was giving talks in the United States, it was common to find audience members who wanted to know what America was doing in Afghanistan in the first place, and, when returning from long stints in Afghanistan, I would realize how much I had become socialized in a world that assumed intervention was a good idea. Such attitudes, questioning the intervention existentially, were rare inside the international community in Afghanistan. Even those opposed to the intervention seemed to primarily oppose it because it was "being done wrong," not because the international community should not have been there in the first place.

Other precise values and beliefs of these interveners were more difficult to pin down but still seemed to form deep undercurrents. Some of these were more obvious than others. The majority of Americans do not have passports, yet clearly all of the nonmilitary internationals in Afghanistan had one. Unsurprisingly, and perhaps in continuity with those visitors in the 1960s and 1970s, the country seemed to attract the young and the adventurous. For most, coming to Afghanistan was both a risk and an opportunity. For young NGO workers, working in Kabul was an exciting and lucrative alternative to an unpaid internship in Washington, whereas for the military it was often a helpful step toward promotion. Many might have been on track to climb the corporate ladder and still had to deal with the boring bureaucracy of career advancement the same way that they would have in their home countries, but most were doing this while discussing future postings in Kenya or Geneva, as opposed to transfers up a floor in the office building.

The result, particularly during the surge, was a group of ambitious individuals, most of whom came in with a sense that there was the possibility of creating real change in the country. In some cases this led many of the recent arrivals to charge into projects optimistically with a naiveté that those with more experience in the country grumbled about. At one international conference I attended during the early stages of the surge, bringing together civilian and military groups working in the southeast of the country, the host of the conference, an optimistic young lawyer, asked everyone in the room to think for a moment about what "their home run" would be during their time in Afghanistan. The room was filled mostly with military officers and diplomats who were there only on one-year tours, and one hardened veteran analyst of the conflict quickly retorted, "Maybe we should be thinking about hitting singles first." Such a jaded insight was rare, particularly during the surge years.

At another point, after I had given a presentation at the embassy, a junior official came up to me with a copy of a three-page white paper that he had drafted proposing a toll-free hotline where citizens could report corruption. This, he insisted, could be a "game changer" if he could only get it into the right hands. It was difficult to make him understand, particularly when stuck behind the embassy walls, that corruption was so endemic that if such a line were to actually work, it would be overwhelmed in minutes. Getting the line working was unlikely because who would respond to the call, when the government was so corrupt that the police just outside the embassy gates were shaking down drivers? No one could enforce it. With money and people pouring into the country, many, however, believed that anything was possible. Those with less optimistic attitudes were often dismissed as lacking creativity or an understanding of what a good counterinsurgency strategy could do.[9] With money to spend, international donors wanted to hear upbeat ideas and were happy to have grandiose proposals pitched to them. The more realistic, who believed in gradual approaches, were quickly marginalized.

Part of me as an anthropologist wants to put some overly idealized spin on this and say that this was an educated, idealistic, multicultural group who could see past national borders to the core of humanity's similarities. That, of course, was not true, and although the group generally had a broader view of world affairs, there were certainly many times I had to hide a flinch at cringe-worthy statements about Afghans as "backward," or how "all violence is based on religious fundamentalism." Yet there was an undeniably progressive attitude that was prevalent in much of the international community.

Ultimately, however, while most may have been broad minded, members of the intervention were increasingly limited by something else—the narrow world that they lived in. The surprisingly limited circle of people who made up the international community—particularly as security restrictions became tighter and tighter and fewer internationals actually socialized at all with Afghans—combined with a confining language and system of beliefs all made it difficult to think outside certain narrowing pathways. As the intervention seemed to progress, these closed circles were reinforced by a strict political economy, making it gradually more difficult for people to envision any other way of making choices outside the predictable constraints of bureaucracy. Whether it was the language of development "best practices" or military "mission targets," the international intervention's culture increasingly looked inward for answers, relying on limited thinking that ignored the shifting political and economic reality just beyond the walls of their compounds.

The Tribes Next Door

The increasingly insular nature of the international community during the surge also meant that these internationals interacted with fewer and fewer Afghans. Although Afghans in the south and east of the country complained about international patrols, the reality was that most Afghans, like those in the bazaar in Istalif, had no real opportunity to encounter individual internationals. Even those living in Bagram, watching planes take off on a daily basis, almost never had direct contact with the personnel on the base. When patrols came out of Bagram, even those on community-oriented missions, it was common for most of the men in the bazaar to back away as the ranking elder among them engaged the troops. Usually this elder would then speak to the translator of the commanding officer in the unit while the other soldiers in the patrol and the men in the bazaar eyed each other quietly.[10] This made the role of those who did have access to the international community even more important and meant that the interactions between internationals and local Afghans were mediated by a small group that would deeply shape the intervention.

So who were these Afghans who worked and interacted with the internationals? Many, of course, were translators who were employed on embassies or bases. Some of these were Afghan-Americans or Afghan-Germans who were returning to the country for the first time after years away. Some were even born to Afghan families abroad; this was their first experience actually in Afghanistan. Most, however, tended to come from more upper-class and educated Afghan families. Because so few internationals spoke Dari or Pashto, the ability to speak English was a clear advantage and meant that most of the Afghans working in NGO offices, embassies, and bases were wealthier and better educated than average Afghans.[11] Those with computer skills were also highly valued, as were those that had previous experience working with NGOs. This meant the pool of Afghans qualified for such jobs was very small, and they often rotated quickly among positions at various organizations, seeking higher salaries and longer contracts, closely mimicking the extreme turnover rate that internationals in these organizations also had. This group of Afghans who had access to internationals also often used their positions to their advantage when it came to working with NGOs and embassies, and, as the economy grew (albeit from a baseline near zero), many of these Afghans benefited far more than their neighbors.

One of the people who was a part of this growth was Omar Rassoul, a young man who ran what most in the international community would have referred to as a construction or logistics company that did much of its work near Bagram. Omar's father's father originally set up the company primarily to export fruit from the Shomali Plain. His small business was operating not far from Bagram when Ronald Neumann first visited the area in the 1960s. However, particularly since 2001, the business had adapted to the changing times and economic opportunities in the area and, as a result, had become tougher to label. By the time the surge began it included a variety of small-scale factories, an import-export business, and a construction branch, and it offered heavy vehicles for rent.

When I first met Omar in a small garden in Kabul, he was wearing designer sunglasses and a stylish white *shalwar kamees*. When he was introduced by a friend of a friend, it was a little difficult to tell exactly what he did. He handed me his card, written in English, which stated that he was president of the Insightful Approaches group of companies (IA), an "engineering, logistics and management company."[12] Omar also quickly mentioned that he was a graduate student in communications at a school in Europe, where he spent part of each year.

Similar to IAM, IA had been adaptable during the ongoing conflict and subsequent economic boom, adding a construction branch as building around Bagram grew and starting a brick factory to save on the cost of purchasing materials for their various projects. The website explained that at IA "customer is our king and quality is our wing," and that in addition to logistics and management, IA would rent construction equipment and generators; sell concrete, gravel, sand, and other materials; and construct roads, bridges, dams, container warehouses, and public buildings; as well as pick up, sort, and deliver materials in their "fleet of dry vans, refrigerated units, flatbeds, intermodal and specialized equipment which can transport materials of any size based on your specific timetable, efficiently, cost effective, and most of all, securely." Its listing on the Afghan Online Business Directory also offered services in "bathroom, kitchen fittings and pipe construction . . . renovation car sales" and auto rentals.[13]

The website was not simply about their services, however; below their mission statement, there was a value statement that emphasized several traits, such as fairness ("we treat others as we would wish to be treated") and professionalism and excellence ("we conduct ourselves in a manner of which we are proud; as individuals and as representatives of our company and industry"). Written entirely in English, the website had many similarities with the website that Will Locke had set up for AWP: It was clearly aimed at an international audience of contractors, and such appeals suggested not only that IA was an economically sound partner but that they shared values with those who were a part of the international community. The site gave the impression of a company that understood the international community and implied that it would be easy to do business with them.

Omar was in many ways the type of Renaissance man who excelled during the intervention. His wide range of business interests echoed his range of academic interests, including philosophy, literature, and poetry. While I was spending time with Omar and one of his friends who was then working on his doctorate in history, he reflected on several occasions about how enjoyable it would have been to have a simpler life where he could have devoted his time to reading and studying. With an easy smile, he extolled the virtues of higher education while berating his younger brother, who had been driving us across town, for his flawed English.

As a student at Kabul University, Omar became an active member of the international students' association in economic and commercial sciences, eventually winning the opportunity to study abroad in Germany. Even after returning, however, Omar stayed in close contact with many fellow members of the association, who had also studied abroad and now formed an ethnically diverse group of young people who gathered together often for meals and lively debates on everything from poetry to politics. On one level Omar seemed to represent an emerging class of young educated Afghans who, particularly in places like the U.S. embassy, many hoped would be the beginning of an emergent civil society that a democratic Afghanistan could build on. Omar's trajectory, however, was not that simple.

Although Omar had clearly benefited from these experiences abroad and although some of these inter-ethnic groups that he moved within seemed a break from the tribal divisions that drove politics in the area historically, family ties were still important to both Omar's business and his social world. This was clear in how he spoke about the area. While touring various villages around the base, he would point out "our lands," which often belonged to a distant cousin or other family member. He also relied heavily on the support of certain allies among his relatives; as we will see, many of his business deals built on these connections in tandem with his connections with the international community. As with most influential figures in Afghanistan during the past decade, much of his success came from both his ability to adapt to the evolving political and economic changes brought by the intervention but also the deep family connections he had in the Bagram area. It was this ability to deal with both the past and the present simultaneously, particularly in his interactions with the strange world of the international community, that helped make him wealthy. To understand how this happened, however, we need to first turn to the ways in which Bagram's past continued to shape politics and economics around the base.

4 Before the Invasion

Sometimes Russian soldiers would come here to our village and play volleyball with the villagers. At night they asked people to stay at home and told us that if we were moving from one village to another or were checking on the irrigation systems that we needed to have lights with us.

—Bagram villager

Living in the Graveyard of Empires

History looms larger around Bagram than it does in other parts of the country. Here the histories of various groups in the area continue to shape current political tensions. Questions of landownership, political leadership, and even marriage are often deeply connected to when and how various communities came to the area. Much like America, only with more layers, Afghanistan is a country of immigrants. Some, like the Greeks, largely passed through. Others stayed. The Hazara are said to be soldiers left behind by the armies of Genghis Khan; the Pashtuns all descend from Qais, one of the followers of the Prophet Mohammad; many Tajik communities, like the potters I had worked with in Istalif, tell stories about moving south into Afghanistan from the fertile plains and valleys of Central Asia and its khanates like Samarkand and Bukhara.

In Bagram, one of the most ethnically diverse rural areas in Afghanistan, these ancient names and histories did not feel very distant as they slipped into daily conversations. Mohammad Yunus, a history teacher at the local high school, but also the uncle of Haji Zia, a key economic and political figure from the area, described the textbook history of the place to me: "In the past the Silk Road passed through Bagram. Because it was a safe, open area, with good weather, the caravans stopped by, rested, and carried on their way to Europe or China." When I asked people to reflect on the surrounding area, residents routinely praised the fertility and lushness of the irrigated fields. Not everyone, however, had a positive view of the landscape; in the same breath as pointing out to me how beautiful the hills around the base were, local residents would lament the rockets that the Taliban fired from certain picturesque vantage points.

Similarly, the influx of trade and wealth came with certain consequences that deeply shaped the character of Bagramis, the schoolteacher continued: "The people are brave, warriorlike and hospitable. Any sovereign who has wanted to dominate Afghanistan first has had to try and capture Bagram. Most of the powers who have come to the country, the British, Russians, the Taliban, have been defeated in Bagram, and none was able to conquer it completely. For example, Alexander the Great failed to conquer Bagram. The only way that he could finally subdue the area was to marry the daughter of a khan from the area."[1] Of course, this version of history is clearly idealized, and Alexander's army did eventually subjugate the area. Despite this, the theme of local collaboration in the schoolteacher's story reflects much of the area's understanding of history and their relationship to these outside forces. His mention of the Greeks, British, and Russians also suggests the ways in which certain historical eras have left an imprint on local understandings of international politics more than others.

In particular, this blending of history and myth was used to explain the cycle of boom and bust economics, closely tied to conflict and the presence of outside forces. Outsiders brought wealth but also turmoil to the region. By the twentieth century, archeologists were sifting through debris left by Alexander the Great's army from the fourth century BCE, which had been piled on top of Greco-Bactrian remains and were eventually added to by wealth from the Kushans, who built their capital in the area in the second century CE. All of this left deposits with a rich array of coins, delicate statues, and broken vases. The objects, mostly looted or excavated by DAFA, found their way to Kabul and farther abroad to museums in Paris and private collections in the West. Omar pointed to the site of many of the excavations as we drove by, where the French archeological federation dug starting in the 1930s. By the time of our visit, only the occasional looter still dug in the area. Because these looters were afraid of being caught, they dug at night and had no real incentive to dig in a methodical manner. As a result, they would quickly dig straight down before moving on to another area. This left the field potholed, strewn with dozens of haphazard piles of dirt and unsellable clay shards.

In the early nineteenth century British adventurers, scholars, and spies began crossing the area, leaving behind a series of well-read adventure travelogues about the simultaneously hostile and hospitable tribes they encountered in the area. These accounts were published in London with unwieldy and exotic titles like *A Personal Narrative of a Journey to the Source of the River Oxus by the Route of the Indus, Kabul and Badakhshan, Performed under the Sanction of the Supreme Government of India in the Years 1836, 1837, and 1838 by Liet. John Wood of the East India Company's Navy*. The British army, worried about the Russian advance into Central Asia, was quick to follow these adventurers, capturing Kabul in 1839; they would not remain in the area long.

Although the British were primarily based in Kabul, Bagram still played an important role in the story of their defeat. The siege and destruction of the British outpost in Charikar, just to the west of Bagram, was one of the omens ignored by British officers in Kabul of what was to come a few months later. It was soon clear that the British had overextended their reach in the Shomali, and it became difficult to determine whether the British were occupying the base or whether they were being held prisoner. Locals cut off water to the base in an attempt to slowly starve the British out. Eventually the remaining soldiers made a run for it, but only two of the British survived the flight from Charikar to Kabul.[2] Despite the story of their frantic retreat, once in Kabul no officers of consequence heeded their warnings. Afghan troops continued to mass in the Shomali Plain; after pushing on toward Kabul, they forced the British troops out of their cantonment in the city, the beginning of their disastrous retreat to Jalalabad.

During the Civil War of 1929 the area again became a strategic focal point as the Tajik bandit Habibullah, commonly known as Bach-e Saqao, or son of the water carrier, from Kalakan, a town just a few miles south, gathered much of his support from the region. Later, when Nadir Shah, the king's cousin, reasserted Pashtun government control, he attacked Kabul through the Shomali Plain, heading south into Kabul. To punish the supporters of Habibullah in the area, he later allowed the Pashtun tribes to extract revenge by ransacking nearby communities. In other instances he continued a centuries-old practice of Afghan kings and gave away land to entire tribes who had supported him.[3] The various mountain passes in and out of the area, from Kapisa in the east to Ghorband in the west, that Nadir Shah's allies rode through continued to be key points of control and have been contested in recent years by both the Taliban and local criminal groups looking to exploit their strategic position.

Accounts, however, that focus on Afghanistan as the graveyard of empires, looking at how the geography eventually defeated the British, the Soviets, and numerous others, ignore the fact that Afghanistan actually had years of stability between these momentary violent interludes. A more accurate history of the area would look at how local communities dealt with what these occasional disasters left behind.

The Sharp Shards of History

The map of ethnic groups in Afghanistan is often overly simplified with an orange Pashtun belt in the south and a green Tajik triangle toward the northeast with another circle around Herat, an oval of purple Hazaras in the middle of the country, and various pockets of smaller groups scattered around. On the ground in Bagram, however, such simple maps did not apply.

For the international military convoy on the main road from the airbase, the villages and mud walls that line the fields blended together, blurring the amazing social diversity of the area. In reality, the history of the area and the struggles between various groups created a social map that resembled gerrymandered congressional districts. Heading north up the main highway from Bagram, one first went through Rabat, a primarily Tajik town with pockets of Pashtuns living nearby. Next was Deh Misken, which translates as "the village of the unfortunates" and was primarily composed of Hazaras, who until recent decades were essentially a slave class in much of the country. When I asked locals about how this town of Hazaras came to be squeezed between Tajik and Pashtun communities, some in the town told me that it had been founded by slaves released by the king, something that also explained the Hazara neighborhoods near the former king's palace in Kabul. The next town was called Laghmani, or "those from Laghman," a province in the east of the country that was heavily Pashtun and had been gifted to the easterners in return for their support of the king. Then, just before entering Charikar, the provincial capital of the Parwan district, there is a village primarily of Sayeds, who were an exception from the ethnic organization of Afghanistan. Instead of using one of the more typical ethnic identities found in most of the country, they defined themselves as a group by all claiming descent from the Prophet Mohammad.

Afghan rulers in the nineteenth and twentieth centuries, concerned about external pressures from the British and Russian Empires, needed unity among the ethnically fractured population. To prevent one group from becoming too strong and threatening the central government, they made it a practice to resettle troublesome populations in the midst of other areas that the government was trying to suppress. Ideally, from the government's perspective, these two groups would then be at odds with each other and, instead of resisting government rule, would spent their time fighting each other. To further bedevil local politics, even when two adjacent communities are from the same ethnicity they are often from different tribes. Thus, the Pashtuns living in the Tajik town of Rabat are from the tribe of the Alikozai, who had previously lived around Kandahar. They were given their land by Abdur Rahman Khan, ruler from 1880 to 1901, who was attempting to simultaneously weaken the Tajik communities living in the Shomali Plain while undermining the unity of the Alikozai Pashtuns from the south of the country. This strategy of giving away free land to create social fractures appeared to have worked, and the era of Abdur Rahman, who initiated much of this social engineering, is looked back on as a time of brutal enforcement of state rule but also stability. Abdur Rahman, however, was also the last Afghan ruler to die peacefully.

Although many of these groups have lived together for over a century now, there were still serious divides between them, and old tensions could spring up quickly. In the area, interethnic marriage and the establishment of alliances between the groups was certainly not unheard of, but it was considered far from the ideal. It was better to marry someone from one's own community or do business with a distant cousin than to trust the neighbors who still might have ties to the communities that they emigrated from over a century ago.[4] This attitude kept the communities fairly socially distant, and relations between many of them were cool during times of peace but could be outright hostile during times of strife. In particular, local non-Pashtun groups accused Pashtuns in the area of aiding and abetting the Taliban in the area during the 1990s, whereas the Pashtuns blame these groups for reprisals that followed, even though in both of these instances most of the egregious crimes seem to have been perpetuated by groups from outside the area. This also created a social divide within groups, where the older generation remembered years before the war when the groups intermingled more frequently. Young men who had come of age since the American invasion tended to sympathize with these ideals of men who were typically their grandfathers because they were eager to start businesses or marry, regardless of the ethnic tensions. Their fathers, however, who had spent many of the years in between fighting for often ethnically based militias, were much more reluctant to trust their neighbors.

This separation was maintained in part by a local informal ban on the purchase of land within a village by members of other groups in an attempt to keep a community homogeneous. And yet there was some flexibility in these rules, which were far from static. In particular, young people in the communities subtly advocated for more leniency, whether it was having fathers arrange marriages outside the family or exploring business opportunities outside the family. Omar and his family, for example, purchased land recently in a village a little way down the road from his own. Such a purchase was not common, with community members far preferring to sell to fellow community members first. His family, however, was able to purchase approximately a hundred acres in the village for a garden by approaching an Alikozai Pashtun, whose family had migrated there in the nineteenth century. Still uncomfortable with many of his neighbors and less invested in preserving social bounds within the community, he was willing to sell to Omar's family. Many of the man's other neighbors, who were primarily Tajik, refused to sell to someone they considered an outsider (even though his family's home village for the

Figure 4.1. Unrenovated bazaar near Bagram. Photo by the author.

past hundred years was just a few miles down the road) and would sell land only to other local Tajiks. All of this greatly complicated the way that land was bought and sold and businesses were set up, meaning that young entrepreneurs had to take into account social and political relationships almost more than they thought about issues of supply and demand.[5]

Within an already fractured social landscape, the founding of the base in the middle of the twentieth century had added a new wrinkle, particularly in the relationship between the local communities and the government.[6] On one hand, it was a stick because it provided the national government with the ability to quickly put down any rebellions in the area (such as Habibullah Kalkani's uprising, which had toppled the government in 1929, and numerous other smaller upheavals that had sprung up at other moments). On the other hand, the base was also, perhaps unintentionally, a carrot, and it provided economic resources and jobs in the area, rewarding the tribes and ethnic groups in the area as long as they remained loyal to the national government.

Although the fertile lands and strategic location of the area had ensured a steady growth, they also encouraged certain levels of tension that had gradually become embedded in both the land and the social relationships in the area. Complex to begin with, these tensions and social relations grew only more complicated after the American invasion as the shadows of the expanding international military presence lengthened. While the base may have brought in new resources to the area, as Omar described the tensions associated with the contracts, hiring practices, and communication between local leaders and those on the base, he sighed and shook his head, unsure where to begin when explaining how the international intervention had complicated local relationships. To understand the political landscape in the area, one had to sift through these complex layers of history. Of course it was even more difficult for internationals working in the area to begin to understand the area, even those who had significantly more experience than most, and few American government officials had more experience than Ronald Neumann.

A Diplomat by Birth

Ronald Neumann did not visit the base itself, but he did drive past it when he first visited Afghanistan in 1967, traveling through the country with his new bride. He arrived, not unlike Will, to visit family. At that point his father, Robert Neumann, was the American ambassador to Afghanistan, a position that his son would also hold thirty-eight years later. The younger Neumann had just finished graduate school and, as he puts it, "had gotten carried away" and enlisted to serve in Vietnam. With three and a half months free before he was due to report, he thought "what better thing to do" than to take his wife to Afghanistan.

The newlyweds spent their time there traveling to almost all corners of the country. They took trips that over forty years later were impossible, driving to Kandahar as well as taking the epic mountain road from Herat through Hazarajat, back to Kabul. Later Neumann's wife went with friends to the Khyber Pass while he took a car as far as it would take him north to the Amu Darya, then the border with the Soviet Union. Here he arranged for horses, riding a few more days before trading the horses for yaks as he trekked into the Wakhan Corridor, the narrow sliver of Afghanistan that divided Pakistan from the Soviet Union. Here he camped in tents at 13,000 feet.

Neumann had already passed the Foreign Service exam, and this time in Afghanistan was also his first real look at the workings of an embassy. Reflecting back on the trip later he wrote: "For me, the trip began a cultural love affair that laid the ground for a career spent almost entirely in or working on the issues of Muslim countries."[7] Years later he would revisit the former ambassador's residence and reference his father regularly in speeches that he made at public events, a practice that Afghans, with their emphasis on patrilineal inheritance, understood and appreciated.

At first glance the ambassador appears to be more an academic than a diplomat. This is partially because of his owlish glasses but also has more to do with his thoughtful manner. During our various conversations, he had the tendency to slip in references to Shakespeare's *Henry IV* almost as regularly as references to recent diplomatic approaches and military history. He also always took care to remind me that he was "no expert on Afghanistan" and often prefaced his replies with "you would know more about this than I would . . ." But at the same time, he spent almost his entire career in the Middle East and spent years working specifically on Afghan issues. This was a concentration of experience rarely seen in the Department of State, which has the practice of regularly moving diplomats around to different regions of the globe. (In contrast with this, a friend of mine from college whom I spent time with in Kabul had been in the State Department for only a few years but had served in Venezuela and Bulgaria before arriving in Kabul, where he was considered particularly knowledgeable because he served a two-year tour in the embassy instead of the typical one.) In managing the embassy, Ron also had a strong preference for old Afghan experts and had a tendency to hire and promote individuals who had experience in the region or whom he knew personally, as opposed to making what might have been a more politically expedient selection. This reliance on personal connections and selecting colleagues he trusted innately was another trait that made him more Afghan in his approach to politics.

I first met Ambassador Neumann after giving him a briefing on some of the elections research I had been doing. His questions had a thoughtfulness to them, and he was remarkably open about what he did and did not know. His straightforwardness and humility were something that I was not accustomed to finding in embassy briefing rooms. I mentioned that I thought American officials had underestimated how seriously Karzai's honor had been offended when he was accused of corruption following his reelection. The ambassador nodded vigorously at this example of the international community's underestimation of the role of culture in politics. For most Western diplomats the notion that accusations of electoral corruption and honor might be linked seemed odd, yet for those attuned with the culture of Afghan politics, in a place where reputation was a man's greatest weapon and greatest vulnerability, such a connection was logical.

In our later conversations after his retirement, Ron often would reflect on how the Foreign Service needed to do more in its training of young officials on the local political and cultural context in which they were going to work. Language skills, he suggested, were not just about communicating but were about showing respect for one's diplomatic counterparts. This ability to think more reflexively both about his time in the Foreign Service and in the ways in which the Foreign Service shaped their younger officers was perhaps due in part to the fact that he had retired and was no longer a part of the bureaucracy, but it was also because he had remained engaged in Afghan affairs. As the president of the American Academy of Diplomacy, he followed developments in the country closely, traveling to the region to consult on American-sponsored projects such as the development of the Afghan Local Police (ALP). His forty years of experience gave him a depth that others lacked.

During their visit during the 1960s, which set all this in motion, the Neumanns were far from the only visitors to the country, and Afghanistan was experiencing something of a travel boom with young people on the "hippie trail" heading overland from Europe to India, stopping by to take in the beautiful scenery and cheap narcotics. Beyond these travelers, however, there were enough internationals working in embassies in Kabul to set up an international school. Accounts from this bygone era were captured in memoirs with titles such as *Land of the High Flags: Afghanistan when the Going Was Good* and in pictures of American children attending the international school and picnicking in the countryside. Farther south in Helmand, a massive USAID project brought together American, international, and Afghan experts on irrigation to make irrigable the sparsely settled area around the Helmand River. The town they set up to house these engineers became known as "Little America."[8]

This was also the golden age of anthropology in Afghanistan, with works such as Robert Canfield's detailed accounts of religious conversion in Bamiyan and G. Whitney Azoy's use of *buzkashi*, the game in which horsemen attempt to drag off a goat carcass, as a lens for local political analysis.[9] Many of these studies focused on Afghanistan's array of small minority groups in areas like the remote Wakhan Corridor and Nuristan, while others looked at a variety of Afghanistan's nomad groups.[10] In Kabul one could find these anthropologists mingling with Peace Corp workers, diplomats, aid workers, and tourists. For the young anthropologist working in Afghanistan, Louis Dupree served both as a mentor and as the host of frequent gatherings. His wife, Nancy Hatch Dupree, was author of the definitive guidebook for travelers in Afghanistan during that era, suggesting a visit to the zoo and a meal at Sitara with "elegant décor, quality + quantity at reasonable prices."[11]

In the guidebook, visitors were "urged to travel outside the city of Kabul and enjoy Afghanistan's magnificent countryside," particularly in the Shomali Plain. For those traveling into the foothills, however, she warned that "the road is deplorable, and meanders around quite haphazardly." She remarked that a trip to the archeological site at Bagram was well worth it but was poorly marked. She suggested for those lost in the area "on the whole, when in doubt, bear left."[12]

Although some of these elements seem far removed from the Kabul of today, other echoes still remain. (This is not to mention the fact that Nancy Dupree and her guidebook were still Kabul staples after the American invasion. While Louis had passed away in 1989, for the latter half of the 2000s Nancy was the director the Afghanistan Center at Kabul University, and many internationals noted that her guidebook's maps were still far more reliable than the error-prone piece put out by Lonely Planet in 2007, which, people complained, was more a novelty item than a useful reference.) An international school, primarily serving the missionary community, had been reestablished in Kabul, with, of course, a new generation of teachers, but one still occasionally met former teachers who had come back in other roles, whether as NGO workers or more occasionally as tourists to see firsthand what had become of the country. As one such returnee who had spent years away suggested to me, Afghanistan "gets its hooks in you." Sometimes, the recollections of those travelers who visited the country on the hippie trail were a little less consistent. One former traveler, working as a volunteer at an NGO in Kabul, suggested to me that this was not because travelers did not eventually wind their way back to Afghanistan, but the easy access to hash on his initial trip meant that "I can't recall all the details of my first visit here, but I sure did love it."

The details remained clearer from Neumann. After serving in Vietnam and formally joining the Department of State, he was assigned to a series of posts, beginning in Senegal but then getting sent to Tabriz in neighboring Iran, where he worked on his Farsi, a close cousin of the Dari spoken in much of Afghanistan. This was the first of a series of postings that would eventually help make Neumann something of a diplomatic specialist in the Middle East and North Africa. In the meantime, Afghanistan remained a part of the Neumann family dinner table conversation, as it did for the Lockes. Robert Neumann remained the ambassador to Afghanistan until 1973. Later, as a part of the Kettering Foundation, he was a key member of the Track II diplomacy that shuttled midlevel diplomats and other members of civil society between Washington and Moscow to discuss key disengagement agreements. One of the most important of these agreements was, of course, the Soviet withdrawal from Afghanistan. Although both Robert and Ron eventually had other focuses in their careers, the family continued to track the developments from afar, as Afghanistan entered a new, tumultuous era.

As Robert Neumann left his post in 1973, what had been a quiet mountain country of only 12 million, developing slowly and uneventfully, had, once again due to its geostrategic positioning, been pulled into global politics as it had in earlier times during Alexander the Great's campaign and in the struggle between the Russian and British Empires in the nineteenth century.

The Bad Old Days

The history of Afghanistan and the Bagram area following the Saur Revolution, the Soviet invasion, and the massive, CIA-funded resistance effort has, of course, been told ably by numerous others.[13] With the Soviet-backed government in Kabul, Bagram became a key installation for the Soviet troops supporting the communist regime. In the meantime, however, although many international journalists and others after 2001 seemed to assume that the international presence in Afghanistan simply emerged on a blank slate, in reality, this community of aid workers, diplomats, and reporters continued to morph and evolve in interesting ways during these turbulent years.

The sense of security that enabled visitors like Neumann to use Dupree's guidebook to roam the Afghan countryside in the 1960s and 1970s eroded rapidly for internationals in 1978, particularly following the death of Adolph Dubs, the American ambassador to Afghanistan. Neumann had worked for Spike, as he was called, in one of his earliest postings. The ambassador was killed during a botched rescue attempt at a Kabul hotel after being kidnapped. The details of his death remain murky, and this sparked a debate over the role of Soviet agents in the incident and the potential complicity of Afghan government forces they were advising. All this further increased the distrust between internationals, particularly those from the West, and the government. In the years that followed, especially after the Soviet invasion, international interest and the actual presence of internationals in Afghanistan were uneven, and the community fractured but never disappeared.

Following the Soviet invasion, although there was a great influx of Soviet civilians and technical advisors, most of the Americans and Western Europeans relocated to Peshawar, with several million Afghan refugees. Later referred to nostalgically by many who lived through it as "the bad old days," for relief workers, journalists, and arms dealers this was a time when money, adventure, and political espionage all seemed to mix easily together. It was the land of Charlie Wilson's War, and, at Dean's Hotel in Peshawar, young journalists like Peter Jouvenal mixed with aid workers and spies.[14] For others who were mingling over cocktails at the Pearl Continental Hotel, the focus was on supplying arms to jihadi fighters, reporting back to the world on their progress, and, to a lesser extent, providing aid in the massive refugee camps, which had grown up as replicas of Afghan villages, albeit displaced by several hundred miles. Although many of the internationals there had relocated from Kabul, Peshawar still had more of a Wild West feel to it. While there, Peter supplemented his income as a journalist by dealing in antique British rifles, and footage from inside Afghanistan was treated almost as bounties to be claimed, with Peter demonstrating one of these badges of honor when describing on his website how he was "the first cameraman to film Stinger missiles in Afghanistan."[15]

Here international journalists and relief workers negotiated with warlords leading ethnically based political parties to be escorted across the border into Afghanistan either to find a story or to continue relief projects. The Pakistani government's careful manipulation of the situation, and the guarantees they secured from the U.S. and Saudi governments, meant that funds could be directed only to the parties that the Pakistanis thought would be most useful to them in the long-term. The most notable recipient of these funds was the radical Hizbe Islami party headed by Hekmatyar, who for a while was the focus of American support despite his antiwoman, anti-Western rhetoric. This would have serious repercussions because it continued to promote a radicalized political ideology and violence between the groups receiving American and Saudi funding that would eventually lead to the rise of the Taliban and made the area increasingly hospitable for Osama bin Laden and other international supporters of militant Islam.

At this point, Bagram became home to a very different type of international, the Soviet advisor, many of whom worked around key centers, such as Kabul and Bagram, rapidly building Soviet-style factories and housing. These new developments, particularly around Bagram, where fighters could hide in the mountains before emerging at night, attracted a steady stream of attacks by jihadi fighters, most of whom had been rearmed in Pakistan. Western adventurers, usually reporters there to document the attacks, tagged along. These reporters, however, like the mujahideen fighters they accompanied, lived primarily in Pakistan, making only quick journeys into Afghanistan.

Although the conflict was primarily between the Soviet Union and the United States with Afghanistan in the middle, the international presence in Peshawar took on an increasingly multinational feel. This was in part because, even though the United States was spending more and more money on the conflict, Pakistan had pressured the American government to impose restrictions on agencies receiving USAID funds so that they could not send Americans into Afghanistan. This meant plenty of other jobs and grants for non-Americans and Afghans who spoke English, creating a cosmopolitan mix of internationals from various home countries all working in Peshawar during the height of the jihad period. As the fighting turned against the Soviets, most of these internationals were initially optimistic as the Soviet Union negotiated the withdrawal of their troops.

The departure of Soviet troops was expected to quickly trigger the collapse of the communist government in Kabul, but this did not happen. Najibullah, the communist president thought to be primarily a puppet, brokered deals with various local commanders and used militias to maintain his grasp on the major cities. With the regime proving scrappier than expected and the mujahideen more divided, international groups were conflicted. Figures like Hekmatyar, Rashid Dostum, Burhanuddin Rabbani, and various other ethnic leaders who had largely been armed with American and Saudi funds turned the fighting toward each other rather than the Soviet-backed government.

The United Nations continued to have an active presence, but, as the Civil War was primarily perceived as an Afghan conflict, Western interest in the region waned, as did funding. Few protested when the Pakistani-supported Taliban started consolidating territory that had been disputed during the country's chaotic Civil War. Although many of the internationals working in Peshawar remained, focus shifted again during the 1990s as the Taliban began their rise. There was still a group of international refugee workers with groups like the Red Cross, but the end of the Cold War stopped the flow of American funds; with less money from arms dealing or trade, international attention waned. Those left on the frontier, making occasional trips into Afghanistan, depending on security conditions, were a hardier bunch. Much of their work revolved around informal negotiations with an opaque Taliban bureaucracy, attempting to bring aid to the country despite the repressive and unpredictable rule of the Taliban regime. The romance of the resistance period of the 1980s faded.[16]

By maintaining a low profile, some relief groups like IAM were able to continue working in more secure areas, such as Kabul, and some groups found it simpler to maintain a presence in more remote rural provinces like Bamyan that the Taliban paid little attention to. This presence, however, was much more limited, and the groups' ability to work and remain in the country seemed almost entirely at the whim of an elusive and unpredictable Taliban government. At the same time, however, when the September 11 attacks suddenly thrust attention back onto the country, it was this group of experienced aid workers who were the first to begin the work of reporting back on this new war, while organizing the distribution of aid and the rebuilding of the country. And so, by October 2001, while waiting for Kabul to fall in Jabal-e Seraj, just to the north of Bagram, Peter Jouvenal found a sign in English advertising "Room with hot bath—foreigner welcome," suggesting that the life of the international community in Afghanistan was entering a new era.[17]

Uneven Layers

History around Bagram is indeed many layered, but these layers were rarely even. So while the Soviet period destroyed villages in the hills around the Shomali Plains, particularly during a series of brutal attempts to take the Panjshir valley to the north, from Ahmad Shah Masood's fighters, other areas were benefiting from the influx of Soviet aid. In telling and retelling stories about this era by local residents, a strange mixture of seemingly contradictory accounts arose.

Although the Soviet period was remembered by many around Bagram as a period of building and growth in the area, there was not a clear divide between those who supported the communist regime and those who supported the jihadis. In fact, most in the area had relatives who fought against the Soviets, even while working with elements of the Soviet-backed government. More recently, contrasting with other areas, it was common in the town of Bagram to hear the Soviets spoken of favorably in comparison with the current American tenants at the base. In particular, the Soviets were remembered as having made serious investments in the infrastructure and development of the country both before and after their invasion. On the national level, this included the building of several impressive feats of engineering, including the mile-and-a-half-long Salang Tunnel that cuts through the Hindu Kush about thirty miles to the north. At the time of construction in 1964 it was the highest tunnel in the world; currently in a state of disrepair, it has become a striking reminder of the useful projects done by the Soviets that the American presence has failed to maintain.

Locally, the most telling reminder of the Soviet presence was a set of approximately thirty Soviet-style block apartment buildings, located just outside of the main gates of the airfield. Several people familiar with the area suggested that the apartments were built by the Soviets primarily for the young Afghan Air Force, though most people when telling the history of the area said simply that they were built for workers on the base during the Soviet period, perhaps to emphasize how well the workers were treated in contrast with those on the base during the American period.

Although by 2012 the buildings had turned grayer and informal extensions and repairs had alleviated some of the oppressive uniformity that marks this type of apartment style in other parts of the post-Soviet world, the buildings were still remarkably distinct both architecturally and in how they were discussed by local residents. Utilities, particularly heat and electricity, were much more consistent here than in the traditional mud compounds just across the fields. One man standing by a well-maintained water pump described how, while originally meant for those workers on the base, most of the apartments had now been passed down, bought and sold, so that they had become an Afghan village, not that different from its neighbors. The sprawling social and family networks so visible in the mud compounds in the surrounding areas existed here as well, just jammed into square, ugly blocks.

The fact that these apartments were highly coveted was remarkable when you consider the aversion that you find among most Afghans to apartment living. Most nice Afghan homes have small but beautiful inner courtyards with gardens, even in the heart of the city. Such architectural elements provide flowers and sometimes vegetables, but, more important, they also provide the family, and the women in particular, a place to gather that is outside and in the fresh air but still private and away from the prying eyes of outsiders. Even without these gardens, however, local residents still considered the rows of apartments as prime real estate, a testament to Soviet engineering but also, in the minds of many, the investment that the Soviets had made in the area.[18]

The Americans, they suggested, invested less, and their presence was more temporary. This, local workers pointed out, was clear in the fact most of the translators and skilled workers on the base who were not from the area lived in a row of rundown temporary structures just to the north of the base. These hostels were made of a combination of mud walls and rusting metal scraps from the base, where the workers would sleep during the week, most returning to Kabul on the weekends.

One local resident reflecting on the architecture told me: "Look, the Soviets built with concrete. The Americans build with containers," referring to the shipping containers that serve to transport goods but also as temporary housing and offices that could be seen poking up over the walls at several points in the area. When the Americans leave, he suggested, these containers would simply "blow away." Furthermore, when the Soviets were in the area, gas and other materials that trickled off the base were inexpensive, and one of the perks of living near the base was that the cost of living was reasonable. After the American invasion, the man described, goods were stolen from the base or simply given away to certain groups, but this was not the same as during the Soviet period, when (as he recalls) they were distributed rather uniformly among the local communities.

These current opinions, of course, take a rosy view of history that forgets the atheism of the Soviets and the havoc helicopters taking off from Bagram wreaked on villages across the region. But this shift in perspectives since the Soviet period actually tells us much about how the communities around the base have come to understand America's presence since 2001.

5 A New Era?

WHEN AMERICAN BOMBS STARTED FALLING on Afghanistan in 2001, already in place was a dedicated group of aid workers and humanitarians, some of whom, like the Lockes, had already devoted decades of their lives to the place. With the rapid collapse of the initial Taliban resistance, many of those located in Pakistan or elsewhere abroad returned to Afghanistan. On November 12 Peter Jouvenal, who had been staying just to the west in Charikar, was there taking video when the Northern Alliance recaptured Bagram Airbase from the Taliban. The back-and-forth nature of the Civil War and Taliban eras meant the fall was quick, and David Loyn, in describing Peter's impressions of the fall of Bagram, pointed out, "There was not much retribution against captured Afghan opponents. The commanders and many soldiers knew each other well across the front line, and they had often fought alongside each other during the shifting alliances of Afghanistan's long war."[1] In the area around Bagram this was not a war with clear sides as much as it was a series of messy family feuds. Most of the Taliban fighters were allowed to quietly switch sides or return back to their homes, and it was only the foreign "Arab" fighters assisting the Taliban, many of whom had bounties placed on their heads by the American Special Forces, that the Northern Alliance seemed to pursue with real zeal. Such facts should have warned the international community about the complex political landscape they were entering.

Instead, however, for the diplomats arriving in Kabul and the press secretaries back in Western capitals, this ushered in an initial era of euphoria and optimism about Afghanistan's declared transition to democracy. In part due to the "light footprint" approach the Bush administration relied on initially, many of those organizations and individuals returning most quickly to Afghanistan were the ones that had previously worked there or in Peshawar in the interim. At first there were relatively few newcomers, in large part because few relief workers in other countries were ready to head to Kabul. Others in the diplomatic community were sent there because they had experience in the region or other connections. Zelmay Khalizad, the initial special presidential envoy and later American ambassador to Afghanistan, was an Afghan-American who had first come to the United States during high school and was the highest-ranking Muslim in the Bush administration. Many of these returning internationals had language skills and longtime Afghan friends and colleagues. What they lacked, however, was access to resources to help rebuild the Afghan state.

Although these returning individuals may have had experience with the country, for most U.S. officials—because the government had lost interest in Afghanistan during its years of Civil War—there was little sense of the history of the place. The attacks of September 11 were, for many in both the American public and those who eventually became a part of the intervention in Afghanistan, the point at which the story of the intervention in Afghanistan started.

Join the Navy, See the World

Owen's father was caught somewhat off guard by his choice to join the Navy. Even as a former Navy pilot himself, he thought Owen, who was a musician in high school, was perhaps too much of a freethinker to follow him into the military. Even after multiple tours in both Iraq and Afghanistan, Owen's appearance did not instantly suggest that he was a member of the military. He lacked the tattoos that were so present among members of the conventional forces, and, although his haircut was short, it was not remarkably so. Some premature gray around his temples made him appear older than he was. Even his build, a reminder of his days as a high school runner, was more subtly powerful than intimidating.

As Owen reflected back on how he came to join, he said, "My first interest was in the Naval Academy [as opposed to the Navy itself] . . . I liked the elegance of it, I liked the structure of it. There was a uniqueness to it that I really liked. Of course, you're foolish to have an interest in that and not understand that it also carries service with it later on. But I wasn't thinking about that in high school."

The expectations of those in the service changed rapidly following the attacks of September 11, which occurred a couple years after he entered the Naval Academy. They also changed Owen's goals as a member of the Navy. Not thinking about revenge as much as a deeper emotional change, Owen said, "I became much more purpose driven and patriotic; that drove my interest in becoming a SEAL and doing something that was specifically meaningful, as opposed to 'oh I'm just going to go hang out on a ship.' Not that that job is not important and that those people aren't serving, but [following the attacks] I wanted to go, I wanted to serve specifically in a role that would take me to Afghanistan."

Despite that, after the initial invasion of Afghanistan and the rapid scattering of both al Qaeda and Taliban forces, the Bush administration's interest in Afghanistan waned, and almost ten years passed before Owen was actually sent to Afghanistan. Instead, as a new SEAL he joined the invasion of Iraq and served two tours there in the interim: "For a long time the more elite teams went to Afghanistan, and, if you were a SEAL like any other SEAL, you went to Iraq. Everyone went to Iraq; only the elite guys went to Afghanistan. That's how I viewed Afghanistan. I viewed it as a place where you really had to do well in your field in order to have the privilege to go there." Owen paused, clearly aware once he had put it into words that some of this might have sounded odd to a civilian. "It's a really interesting thought to think about going to war as a privilege." Although he almost always kept politics out of the conversation, for Owen, Iraq and its unclear connection with the terrorist groups that had organized the September 11 attacks did not provide the same sense of purpose, and the tours felt more like a requirement of his job than anything else.

Inside the country, the Bush administration's "light footprint" approach toward Afghanistan, along with the switch in focus toward Iraq following the 2003 invasion, meant that much of the original momentum of the invasion was lost as the American military, and relief groups following its lead, chose to remain primarily in Kabul. The senior command that replaced the initial deployments to the country were much smaller, as the Department of Defense concentrated financial and personnel resources toward Iraq.[2] The decision not to consolidate positions in the provinces meant that opportunities for quick and effective aid projects were lost. Harder to perceive and measure were the ways in which the expertise of the international community was also wasted. Some of the old guard, particularly in the diplomatic world, moved on after the early years, and they were rapidly replaced by a newer generation, usually with less experience in the region. At the top of the diplomatic chain, two of America's most experienced people left, with Khalizad moving to Iraq where he was appointed as ambassador and then with Neumann retiring in 2007 from the foreign service. In sharp contrast with these first two American ambassadors to Afghanistan, the new ambassador replacing Neumann, William Wood, had previously been ambassador to Colombia, and his experience had primarily been in Latin America, the thought being that his experience dealing with narcotics would be helpful.

In the meantime, when Owen arrived in Afghanistan after two previous deployments to Iraq, he was surprised by the state of affairs: "When I got to Afghanistan, you could immediately tell that it was the neglected theater. Even in the bases, even in the little pockets of the country that America had made American, there was almost a Third World quality to the bases." This was particularly striking when compared with his experience in Iraq: "You could tell all the money went to Iraq. The military infrastructure was vast . . . we're talking permanent buildings. In Afghanistan, not so much."

Even the biggest airfields, like Bagram, were "disorganized in terms of how [they were] put together." There seemed to be little planning in how the new buildings sprawled. Many structures, barely a year or two old, had to be pulled down to make room for even bigger buildings. This was opposed to Iraq, where they carved out a piece of the Baghdad Airport and "made it a piece of Little America. Apart from the fact that everything was dusty, you couldn't really tell the difference between that and Fort Bragg [in North Carolina]." In these disorganized, ever-expanding bases in Afghanistan, young officers were expected to pull together battle plans quickly while engaging and supporting the communities they lived alongside. The demand for more space on the bases created tensions as local landlords charged more and more. Disputes broke out over unclear land titles, and soldiers like Owen, who clearly had other priorities, were frustrated by some of the delays and slowdowns. On more than one occasion I heard exasperated American officers who "just wanted to know who owned the land that the base was on." Of course, they were unaware of the fact that much of the land was likely to have been left by refugees leaving the country, taken by some local commander, sold, and resold, perhaps half a dozen times. The military would then pay rent to someone who held the land title, not realizing there might be multiple other titles that had simply been issued under different regimes.

Other international groups worked under similar haphazard conditions. Diplomats had their offices in modified shipping containers, and houses in the nicer sections of Kabul were rapidly converted to NGO offices. The research organizations I worked with moved on an almost yearly basis as rents increased, and it became difficult to locate these constantly shifting offices. As NGOs expanded, neighboring compounds were rented, with new structures hastily built or old ones renovated. Everyone seemed to be building haphazardly up from the ground. Even the ambassador initially lived in a container, and Neumann seemed to enjoy the way it made him more approachable to lower-level staff members. As he wrote in his memoirs of his time in Kabul:

> Home was two and half containers strung together in the shape of an H . . . Often I was asked how I liked my "doublewide," as my abode was called. The questioners usually seemed to expect some complaint, as the dwelling was of somewhat less than ambassadorial proportions. I think that they were often surprised when I told them it was positively palatial next to the one room in half a trailer with a shared bathroom that I had lived in for sixteen months in Baghdad. Besides, I had a small garden of grass with roses growing around the fence.[3]

Eventually two apartment buildings were built in the embassy compound across a small courtyard from each other where the more senior staff then resided. Designed originally to house the entire embassy staff when the planning had been for a limited number of diplomats, the narrow hallways, lit by fluorescent lights and lined with closed door after closed door, still gave off the feeling of a recently built college dorm. Such construction, however, never seemed to keep pace with demand, and soon the embassy was putting bedrooms in what had been designed as living rooms, and those living in one-bedroom apartments found themselves with roommates, furthering the college-like feel and the sense that little in the intervention was planned or stable.

Surging toward Nowhere

Despite the strong rhetoric of the Bush administration, the strategic approach of the international community was muddled in the early years of the intervention as the international forces continued losing ground in much of the country. In contrast with this, the speech made by President Obama at West Point on December 1, 2009, marked the real turning point and provided a sense of hope for many on the ground. At the same time, however, it was a change that did not surprise many people. The security situation in Afghanistan had been worsening since 2004; in response to this, donor dollars had increased slowly and the number of international troops had crept upward, but it was not until Obama declared that "the status quo is not sustainable" that genuine change in America's commitment to the conflict was widely acknowledged by both Afghans and those in the international community.[4]

Obama had already promised in his campaign the year before that Afghanistan was the "right" war, and once in office he had commissioned a study by General Stanley McCrystal, then the American commander in Kabul, to assess the troop levels in the country. The choice of McCrystal was telling because McCrystal was a well-known disciple of General David Petraeus, author of the recently revised counterinsurgency handbook and key figure during the similar troop surge in Iraq. While Vice President Joseph Biden and others favored a more limited counterterrorism approach, it was clear that many of the leaders of the U.S. military favored the COIN approach, and Obama's choice of McCrystal as author of the report essentially allowed the momentum of the perceived success of the COIN approach in Iraq to spill into the debate over troop numbers in Afghanistan.

Although the surge was announced as primarily a military shift, it had repercussions on all aspects of the intervention. Military spending leapt upward in support of the new troops, but so did civilian spending (albeit at a slower rate). With most of this money coming from Americans, the center of political gravity in Kabul could be felt moving firmly away from UNAMA (UN Assistance Mission to Afghanistan) headquarters and over a few blocks to the U.S. embassy and the neighboring ISAF headquarters. Perhaps unsurprisingly, at around this time the gate in the wall between the ISAF headquarters and the embassy was opened, so that officers and diplomats could pass through without even stepping outside their secure compounds.[5]

With this surge in spending, newly built offices at the embassy and at NGOs around the city quickly filled with a new younger generation of journalists and aid workers who flocked to the country. Books like *The Kite Runner* and *The Bookseller of Kabul* painted a romantic picture of the place, while the prospect of jobs, dramatic landscapes, and the potential of making a difference lured others. This new generation had little previous experience in the region but plenty of enthusiasm. This shifted both the economics of the intervention and the demographics of the international community. While many projects and sites remained neglected, money now poured in to support specific projects that appeared to fit the rhetoric of COIN strategy well. This made growth haphazard and, at times, seemingly random.

Job postings were filled in a similar way. With so many positions being created and with security increasingly becoming an issue, working in Afghanistan became less appealing for established diplomatic or relief workers. Many of those with experience in the region were of an age where they were more likely to be married and have children. Many of those with significant experience in Afghanistan had already served a term or two in the American embassy or in the UNAMA headquarters and decided they preferred returning to their families rather than facing the lonely struggle against both the Taliban and an increasingly corrupt Afghan government in a job that did not allow them to bring their families. In some cases, couples might try to find ways to skirt security regulations while working for two different international organizations—one woman I knew had to take a car to a security-approved restaurant to be met by a taxi which would take her to her husband's organization because she was technically not cleared to visit his compound. At the end of the day, she would then have to take a taxi back to the restaurant where she would be met again by a car from her organization. It was hard to tell why no one at her office questioned her desire to spend eight hours in a row in a restaurant on a Saturday. Managing such an arrangement in the long term was difficult for a couple and for those with children was nearly impossible.

As a result, Afghanistan increasingly became a place for young aid workers or journalists to cut their teeth. For those interested in a career in development, a masters in international affairs or international relations, or any of the other fairly vague advanced degrees in the field, was increasingly necessary. In Washington, even with one of these advanced degrees, it was not uncommon for individuals to be forced to work initially in unpaid internships, the supply of enthusiastic young people was so great. With the surge funding in Afghanistan, however, there were many more opportunities with funding attached. For many young people interested in development or policy, the choice was between working in an unpaid position, primarily getting coffee or organizing talks, in Washington or going abroad to a hardship post in a place like Afghanistan. For those willing to take the risk of hopping on a plane to Kabul or Kandahar, not only could someone with limited experience get a paid position, but there was also a definite opportunity for advancement.

For someone like Will Locke, with limited postcollege professional experience, such a situation presented an incredible opportunity. Simply by showing up at an organization like IAM, where there was such a demand for skills of all types, he took only a couple of months to turn an unpaid internship into a real job, and soon after ended up owning a large piece of a start-up company. For others, moving from organization to organization could make this even easier. At the restaurants frequented by internationals, people were always discussing potential job openings. One of Will's better friends in the country went from working as a volunteer grant writer for a small NGO, where he was raising funds for a jewelry school, to running the operations for a large security company, to a prestigious position at a demining organization, all in the course of a couple of years marked by savvy, well-timed jumps.

At the same time, however, moving to Afghanistan for a significant portion of time was not a decision to be taken lightly. Although most of the old-timers pointed out that, once they knew their way around, security risks were minimal, Afghanistan was still a risky place to take up residency. For some, like the military, such risks were part of the job; with over 3,000 coalition soldiers killed by 2013, young men and women in the armed forces paid dearly.[6] As the insurgency grew, however, so did risks to other members of the international community in Afghanistan. When I first arrived in Kabul in 2005, I wandered the streets fairly freely, taking taxis with other internationals who lived in an unguarded house next to the Ministry of the Interior. Things, however, changed quickly in the years that followed.

A major turning point for many was the January 2008 attack at the Serena Hotel. Six were killed in the attack, including one man in the hotel gym. This was an important shift for many in the international community because the majority of attacks up until that point had targeted military compounds, convoys, or large embassies. The Serena was a particularly vexing target for many in the international community because it was started with money from the Aga Khan Foundation, the large Ismaeli religious foundation. (It was also built on the site of the old Kabul Hotel, where Ambassador Dubs had been killed.) Additionally, it was one of the more culturally sensitive places where internationals hung out. By not serving alcohol, it deliberately catered to the Afghan elite and government officials as well its international clientele. Various embassies would hold conferences there, and it was a convenient place for internationals to meet with Afghan colleagues. Rumors circulated later that the gym had been specifically targeted because of the indecent dress of women exercising or lounging by the pool there.

Suddenly, places that had seemed secure were now targets, and internationals began to avoid public places. Soon it became apparent, however, that even private residences were not safe. This was made clear by the October 28, 2009, attack on a guesthouse used by internationals working to support elections. In addition to leaving five UN workers dead, the prolonged shootout between insurgents and guards kept much of the international community locked down. Building on this incident, a series of other attacks by groups of gunmen seemed aimed not at maximizing causalities as much as simply shutting down parts of the city near the embassies. Under such conditions, it was difficult for anyone to get any work done. In the days that followed the guesthouse, rumors swirled about a withdrawal of all UN workers except those who were absolutely essential. Some organizations even began sending their international employees out of the country for mandatory leaves around critical events, like the presidential election, when there were increased fears of attacks.

As more obvious targets, members of the diplomatic community were generally kept under tighter security restraints. Even the State Department's rather extensive precautions were not foolproof, and diplomats too were rattled when in 2012, a young female American State Department official was killed in Zabul while delivering textbooks. During such attacks, I, like many in the international community, would try to keep up with the flurry of texts from around the city suggesting which areas were and were not safe. Internationals working for NGOs would attempt to get intelligence through informal channels from the U.S. embassy or the United Nations because they provided very little formal information for their citizens living in the country. (The American embassy was one of the worst at keeping their citizens informed, sending out information about Labor Day closings but nothing in response to security episodes. In recent years, however, they have slowly begun releasing more information.) Slightly better information came from ANSO, the Afghanistan NGO Safety Office, which provided security reports, cobbled together from a variety of sources, to member NGOs; ANSO briefings were often packed with representatives from various organizations after these attacks. All this contributed to a sense of internationals closing ranks, interacting increasingly with each other and not necessarily with their Afghan neighbors.

By 2009 or so, kidnappings in the capital and around the country were occurring with some frequency, although they were often not publicized in the
media because the general consensus was that publicity would only encourage the practice. Most of the targets of these kidnappings were upper-class
Afghans, but internationals were increasingly grabbed as well. Many of those
kidnapped were released following the payment of ransoms, and the delicate
negotiations surrounding these exchanges meant that few outside those directly involved in negotiations knew whether money had changed hands or
if other concessions had been granted. Gangs of kidnappers quickly learned
that by asking for reasonable amounts but demanding the ransom in a very
short time frame they were more likely to get paid. Stories circulated about
young Afghan elites grabbed off the streets and driven around for a couple of
hours while their families had four hours to pull together a couple thousand
dollars. Given the lack of security, these kidnappers were able to threaten to
return if the families reported the incident, making it impossible to know how
truly frequent such incidents were. These approaches did not offer great rewards but were low risk for these growing bands of kidnappers.

These shifting economic and security conditions meant that, at the height
of the surge, toward the end of the first decade of the intervention, the international community was a hodgepodge of old-timers and recent arrivals.
There were those who spoke Dari fluently and those who were still shocked
by the five daily calls to prayer, relief workers and mercenaries, those there to
make a quick profit and those who had devoted a good part of their lives to the
country. But the international community was not a chaotic, eclectic group
with no ties. In part, common concerns such as security held them together.
Many in the international community also shared a common background in
the simple sense that they came to Afghanistan from elsewhere. On the military and diplomatic side of things, many Americans like Owen had served
previously during the war in Iraq. Many in the UN and EU contingencies had
spent time in the Balkans in Kosovo or Bosnia in the 1990s. Others had been
in East Timor. In contrast, the development crowd often had experience in
Africa: the Sudan, Rwanda, Kenya. In some ways this created a shared frame
of reference; people swapped suggestions about both the most effective literacy programs and the best beaches in Thailand to visit while on leave.

At the same time, however, this could also sometimes bring misplaced
assumptions. For example, after several small uprisings against the Taliban
in provinces of Ghazni and Logar, many in the media and the military were

quick to compare these uprisings to the Anbar uprisings in Iraq in 2006 where local tribes turned against al Qaeda. The hope was that this would similarly mark a turning point, where local populations would turn against insurgents. Of course, it quickly became apparent that the two events had little in common and that these Afghan communities were as angry with the Karzai government as they were with Taliban fighters, and such comparisons died down. At other times, development projects were derailed by assuming that "best practices," often drawing on lessons development workers had learned in sub-Saharan Africa with little real relevance in Afghanistan, would work. It was also increasingly difficult to determine whether such best practices were actually working in the Afghan context, because security made visiting projects increasingly difficult. This meant that conversations among decision makers were increasingly circular and less informed. As a result, certain projects that were favored flourished, while others languished, oftentimes with little regard to their actual effectiveness.

Million-Dollar Ideas

Part of what made Will's work with Alliance Wind Power so appealing to both donors and those interested in helping local Afghans was the sheer economic logic of it. In the early years of the intervention, Afghanistan was a country with a serious rural electrification problem. It wasn't until about five years after the initial American invasion that Kabul's electricity became somewhat predictable, but most businesses, offices, and embassies still had generators that they used part- or full-time to make up for the unreliable power supply. In a rush to fix these problems quickly, short-term solutions were often chosen over long-term effectiveness. Afghans and internationals alike were accustomed to frequent power cuts, and everyone kept a flashlight next to the bed. This also resulted in an emphasis on unsustainable household and office diesel generation on a large scale that rattled the windows of offices and contributed to the thick winter smog.

In response to the power problems in the capital, huge stanchions were being built around Bagram to connect Kabul to more reliable power sources in the former Soviet states to the north. As this system came online, power became more (though still not entirely) reliable, though most still hung onto their generators. In Kandahar, the issue of electricity generation was felt even more acutely. With electricity problems in Pakistan as well, there was simply no reliable source of power within a reasonable range. In the search for a sustainable solution, the Kajaki Dam, which held back the Helmand River to the northwest, was often pointed at as a potential solution to the project.

Originally constructed in the 1950s, this project had sentimental value for many of those working for the American government because it had originally been build with USAID funds. One of the upsides of the project was that it also had the promise of providing sustainable energy long beyond the potential end of the intervention. Initial attempts to refurbish the dam had faltered and demonstrated some of the challenges the various pieces of the international intervention had in cooperating together effectively. Ambassador Neumann had made it a priority for State Department funds, but a lack of coordination had slowed the project. The dam needed engineers and laborers paid by international donors, but, situated in a dangerous corner of the south, it also needed international troops to protect them. Neumann, in reflecting on his visit to the dam, concluded: "Conversations with ISAF were frustrating. ISAF fully understood the importance of the project, but it became apparent that we had different appreciations of the security situation." After visiting the dam in August 2008 he decided, "The need to get more ISAF troops was clear. So too was the need to inject more local Afghans into the fight on the government's side, but without additional foreign forces to back them up, this was unlikely to happen."[7] As a result, the project continued to move forward in fits and starts, but, due to the difficulty of getting funds from USAID, security from ISAF, and support from the Afghan government to come together simultaneously, little serious progress was made. And before the surge, there was simply not enough money or political will to make these various pieces come together at the same time.

In 2009, the surge swung into high gear, and the American military began to prioritize missions that would benefit the civilian populations in ways they had not previously. Electricity was no longer simply a development objective; it was a military mission in the counterinsurgency drive. In Kandahar they decided that one of the key ways to win hearts and minds would be to provide the city with around-the-clock electrical power. With power, businesses could stay open longer; streetlights would discourage crime and the movement of insurgents. This would spur rapid economic growth and increase security. The problem was that the only immediate solution would be to provide the city with costly and unsustainable diesel generators. The military favored this approach, which they felt they could get off the ground in a matter of months.

In the meantime, the State Department remained convinced that improvements to the Kajaki Dam, north of the area, would prove a sustainable long-term approach with more substantial economic benefits.[8]

Eventually, a compromise was reached that seemed to favor the State Department. New generators were built in Kandahar's power plant, but they were smaller than the military had requested, and major renovations at Kajaki were to be ramped up as a more long-term solution. Eventually, however, by choosing both approaches, the American government spent more money and got less than they should have. The generators in Kandahar cost $106 million to build, providing the city with only 60 percent of its electrical demand; in the meantime, the electrical plant housing the generators ate up $100 million a year in fuel and maintenance costs. The city's old distribution system also meant that much of the electricity being generated was lost in delivery, and government subsidies left residents paying one-tenth of the actual cost of electricity generation.[9] Raising prices was not an option because increasing household bills was clearly not a part of the counterinsurgency approach, and the general consensus was the security situation in Kandahar was delicate and could be easily upset by negative public sentiment. Furthermore, as Neumann pointed out to me, while some might grumble about the rates, there was no system in place to collect the electrical bills even if the government had wanted to begin charging (something that had also been a major problem in Iraq). The military "listened respectfully, but clearly didn't pay any attention."[10]

At the same time, however, by 2013 results from the renovation of the Kajaki Dam were increasingly being questioned. The project proved more expensive and challenging than had been predicted even by those who were most cynical about the project. It had taken 4,000 troops and 100 vehicles with coalition air support to deliver a new turbine to the site.[11] Already $500 million had been spent on the project, but because the Obama plan had always been to limit the duration of the surge, U.S. troops were already withdrawing from the area around the dam. This made it increasingly difficult to maintain security around the dam and on the crucial supply route to the site. Costs continued to rise as the project continued with a turbine originally expected to cost $18 million ending up costing $85 million. Tens of millions of dollars worth of equipment was sitting unused in Kandahar, and the number of Afghan workers on the project continued to dwindle as fewer and fewer were willing to take the risk of working in the volatile area.[12] Some analysts were also suggesting that the dam's watering of insurgent-controlled areas, such as Marja, was fueling poppy production and funding the Taliban.[13]

The subsequent audit of the project was scathing even though couched in bureaucratic language. The report from the American government's auditor cited a range of missteps big and small. These ranged from the fact that USAID "was not able to track implementation and financial progress adequately," code for the fact that officials had a limited sense of what stage the project was in or how money was being spent, to the fact that the subcontractor had charged $164,000 in first- and business-class flights that were not allowed under the standard rules stating that American contractors must fly economy class. Most important for the long-term life of the project, however, was the fact that the audit found that USAID "had not completed a plan for sustaining the benefits derived from the project," citing both financial and security concerns.[14] Several years into the project, it was still unclear, the report concluded, that refurbishing the dam was even viable.

Although numerous other studies have gone on about the waste in these projects, most of these accounts of gross negligence and misuse of funds do little to assess why they actually occurred. Why, for instance, did the U.S. government and many of the other members of the international community continue to emphasize such large-scale projects, particularly when small-scale electrification projects have become increasingly seen in the development literature as a more sustainable approach to infrastructure development? Why were small-scale, flexible projects like Will's going unfunded while hundreds of millions were being spent on large-scale projects with limited results?

In the mountains above Bagram, it was clear that the cost of such projects, along with the challenges of extending the grid, particularly into rural areas, was prohibitively expensive. With a smaller population that was more resistant to the insurgency, such large-scale funds were not likely to be dedicated to an extensive electrification project in the area. There was simply not the same need to win hearts and minds. This not only created resentment in rural communities that lacked electricity but also created some odd contradictions and tensions among local communities, the Afghan government, and those internationals sponsoring development programs. Soon governors of peaceful northern and central provinces were complaining that their provinces were receiving much less in funding than those in the less stable southern and eastern provinces where most of the funds were being directed. It was as if the intervention was deincentivizing stability.

On a smaller scale around Bagram, a place that was more stable but also received a healthy amount of funding, the uneven distribution of funds for development sometimes presented itself in vivid fashion. For example, the towering stanchions that brought electricity from Uzbekistan, rich in natural gas, south to Kabul, were a dramatic addition to the landscape. Paralleling the main road north, these were much discussed on car rides with my Afghan friends. These huge power lines, however, made no stops—the communities that lost farmland as these high towers had been put up had received financial compensation but did not actually receive any electricity from them. Although the economics of the situation might not have made it reasonable for there to be local substations along the route that would electrify these semi-rural areas, this provided little comfort for those forced to look on a daily basis at the metal giants lurking above their homes while filling up containers with diesel for smoky, aging home generators or simply going without power at all.

So how then could power be brought to those outside of the biggest cities? As an engineer and self-described "tinkerer" with a libertarian bend, Will was immediately attracted to the conundrum of getting energy to rural communities. It was a classic engineer's problem—with limited resources, how do we build a system that sustains itself? How could we empower individual communities to generate their own energy and not rely on either a corrupt government or the largesse of the international community?

Will immediately began drawing sketches, building wind blades, and talking to anyone who would listen about some of the opportunities of wind power and the challenges of designing an effective system. Of course, this was not simply an engineering puzzle; it was also a question of funds.

Hope Is in the Wind

Will's wind project began with support from IAM, which had done extensive work with small-scale community hydroelectric plants in the past. Their design was well suited for the many small villages in the valleys of the mountains that made up the center of the country; even during the earlier fighting, teams had been able to set up small stations in these quiet, hilly valleys. In the town where I had lived previously, this had been done by altering one of the several irrigation channels that ran through town. The program was designed to be as technologically simple as possible, so setup was easy, but, more important, repairs could be done by those living in the community. (This was in sharp contrast with larger projects such as the work on the Kajaki Dam, which constantly required the assistance of outside technical experts.) Especially during the years of intense fighting, when certain areas could be cut off from the cities for long stretches of time, dependence on technical support from outside a community or complex replacement parts could sink a project. Villagers were already skilled at the physics of irrigation, so keeping the mechanics of the turbine fairly simple was key. Even though it was often difficult to find replacement parts for all sorts of types of machinery, in small towns there were often mechanics who were incredibly creative when it came to jury-rigging the cars, tractors, and small generators they worked with regularly.

IAM also attempted to engage the community for other reasons. Although there were a variety of donor schemes used for the different sites where this program worked, an important component of each was that at least a portion of the cost as well as the manual labor needed to be provided by the village. The motivation for this was less financial than it was designed to increase community investment in the projects. IAM felt that, through community participation in its setup, the project was more likely to be maintained and protected by those community members. This was in contrast with later schools and clinics built without community involvement by USAID or the international military that were targeted by insurgents and often not closely guarded by the communities they were in precisely because they were symbols of the international presence.

Looking to branch out and build on the approach used in these successful hydroelectric projects, Will began working with IAM, but he eventually broke off to form an independent company with his three Afghan colleagues—a development practice encouraged by IAM, which felt that such small businesses were more likely to be successful in the long run. This approach was in line with much of the neoliberal thinking among development groups at the time, which argued that projects independent of government structures and motivated by individual profit were most likely to effectively assist in development. Thus, with an initial subsidy from IAM, Will and his partners set up their small shop on the western edge of Kabul, not far from the parliament building.

The shift from hydroelectric work to wind energy, however, was not seamless, and there were several key differences Will's team had to confront as they moved away from some of the hydro projects the group had been working on. Micro-hydro plants, for example, usually worked well in villages of a couple hundred homes, where a decent-sized turbine would have meant each home could have one or two lightbulbs. They were also labor intensive, initially demanding that the men in the community work together to reroute the irrigation channel. Wind turbines of the scale that Will could manufacture initially, however, were much smaller and demanded much less heavy labor in their setup, meaning that there was less opportunity for significant community involvement.

Another of the issues was simply the peculiarities of geography in Afghanistan. For one thing, wind in most parts of Afghanistan was not consistent year round. In particular, in many areas the wind was least reliable during the winter when electricity was most in demand. This meant that any charge the battery received would be quickly drained. Will explained gloomily how "this kind of cycling greatly reduces the batteries' lifespan." One of the appeals of the hydroelectric system was that costs were minimal once the organization had set up the project. For a wind project, replacing these batteries frequently was costly and changed the economics of the project. As Will tried to address some of these issues, he became convinced that he needed to make a paradigm shift away from the practice of electrifying entire villages. Instead, wind turbines could be constructed with slightly different goals in mind. In particular, wind turbines were effective when wind was at its most consistent and when energy demand could be regulated. Will began to think that given these constraints, his system might be best suited for pumping water in flatter areas that were not connected to the irrigation systems coming down the hills. This would serve fewer homes but would ultimately be more sustainable, making more land cultivable and potentially still providing some household electricity. Furthermore, during the growing season when there was the most demand for water, the wind was at its most reliable.

Such an approach seemed particularly well suited for southeastern sections of the Shomali Plain, just to the east of Bagram, as well as certain areas farther west. The fringes of the plain, to the north, received abundant run-off from the Hindu Kush mountains, but the flatter sections in the east and south were more difficult to irrigate. The area was appealing because there were a large number of communities, including numerous returned refugees, with farming experience in adjoining areas who were eager to have more cultivable land.

For Will, however, the greatest benefit was that the area was just about an hour north of Kabul. This was an easy and enjoyable day trip Will could take on his motorcycle, cruising around scouting out locations. The people in the villages where he worked were for the most part perplexed by the bearded American hopping off his bike, looking up at the sky, and testing for wind, but because much of the area's development relied on international support, they were somewhat accustomed to seeing foreigners and rarely bothered him. Finally, as the home of Bagram Airfield and a place where numerous other groups were working, this was an area that had received a good deal of funding that Will hoped to build on.

As a result of some of his initial explorations, Will came up with a short proposal and convinced the UN High Council on Refugees to give AWP a small grant. They used this money to build a wind turbine that provided electricity and a water pump for a village clinic on the Shomali Plain. Despite the fact that this was not exactly the type of project that Will had in mind initially, he thought it would give the team experience and a chance to try out their approach, and for the most part the project was a success. Although the batteries at the clinic needed to be replaced after three years, this was still much more efficient than paying the costs for the fuel that a generator would consume over that time. Will also continued playing with AWP's approach in the hopes that they could prolong battery life and make the entire system more effective.

A video that Will later posted on YouTube shows the setup of this wind turbine on a field north of Bagram. At first there is no breeze, and the group waits anxiously looking up at the blades. As the breeze picks up, the camera, which is being held by Will, moves over the voltage meter, which suddenly jumps. Suddenly, there is laughter, and the wobbly camera jerks around to catch one of the workmen, who had been looking up the hose attached to the pump, sprayed with water. With a shout, two young girls run out of the compound behind with empty buckets.

The video, however, was not simply for Will to record what was a nice moment of optimism in what could be the frustrating work of a development worker; it was also an important piece of advertising. Particularly as security worsened in the area and representatives of donors, like USAID, were less likely to get into the field to actually observe the projects that they were funding, this shaky amateur video was not only a testament to the work that AWP had done but also a way of generating interest and, they hoped, more funds. And Will increasingly realized that if he and his partners were going to stay in business, they were going to need bigger and better sources of funding. Luckily, in his speech announcing the surge, Obama promised exactly that.

Funding the Dream

In many ways Will saw the challenge of setting up a wind energy industry as both a moral imperative and as an interesting conundrum he enjoyed grappling with. As a response to some of the challenges of wind energy in a developing country, where the wind is not as steady as one would like, Will, who still relishes talking through the technical aspects of many of these issues, went looking for outside technical advice. He saw chatting with those who had grappled with similar problems as a way of getting some useful ideas, but he also saw creating a community of engineers committed to helping establish sustainable energy as an important aspect of development. He had already been in contact with Hugh Piggott, who had cowritten a book on wind power in the developing world called *Small Wind Systems for Rural Energy Services*, put out by Practical Action Publishing, that spoke to many of the issues Will was struggling with. Not everyone, however, was as interested in such a collective approach.

Partially as a result of some of these positive conversations with Hugh, Will was very willing to talk with anyone who swung by his workshop about their current projects or what he was working on at the moment. Thus, in 2009, Will was excited when he was approached by James Heiland, who was heading up a $22.5 million USAID grant to develop renewable energy in Afghanistan. The $22.5 million was a part of the surge spending and a drop in the bucket compared to the Kajaki Dam initiative, but it could go far in establishing some renewable energy initiatives, and Will was happy about the new international attention to sustainable energy. As a result, when James asked Will to present at a conference in Kabul meant to showcase the potential of renewable forms of energy in Afghanistan, Will was more than willing. Will's presentation was so successful, and his project so much further along than other international efforts at encouraging sustainable energy, that, as a follow-up to this conference, attendees then visited AWP's workshop, a rare trip outside international compounds for some of the participants.

As USAID officials discussed some of its plans for sustainable energy in Afghanistan, Will became increasingly convinced that water pumping for agricultural use was the ideal intersection of sustainable energy and some of the key demands of rural agricultural life in Afghanistan. Will tried to explain

Figure 5.1. Wind turbine installation. Photo by William Locke.

to USAID how these pumps would allow communities to expand their agricultural production at minimal costs and would "much better fit the annual wind power profile" than previous schemes had. However, his conversations with James, who oversaw the distribution of most of the USAID funds for these types of projects, continued unevenly. The way the funds were earmarked unfortunately meant that James and those above him at USAID in Kabul, who were so enthusiastic about AWP's work, really had little say over how the funds were distributed. There was still open bidding for contracts, and USAID in Washington was technically open to different approaches, but, in essence, USAID already had determined what type of programs they were interested in and how much they were willing to spend on them. In particular, officials in Washington had little interest in breaking the large grant into smaller pieces, which would take more effort to oversee. Ironically, one of the biggest problems was that Will was not asking for enough money; USAID wanted to hand out all its sustainable energy support in one contract.

As a result, James encouraged Will to submit a proposal not to further develop some of the ideas that he had about water pumps but instead to propose a project that would monitor wind levels in the west of the country. There seemed to be the belief higher up at USAID that the long-term future of wind energy in Afghanistan was in building large-scale wind farms primarily in the west of the country around Herat. This meant they would be willing to give someone a smaller grant to test the feasibility of the idea. This could potentially be a pilot project that would give Will enough time to hire a grant writer and a series of international consultants, which would enable him to compete with some of the larger international contractors. James felt like this was something feasible that he could pitch.

Although perhaps not illogical, such an approach took on many of the assumptions of projects like the Kajaki Dam. To be successful, it would need long-term international investment in alternative energies in Afghanistan, as well as the implementation of such projects presumably by international technical experts. It also assumed other things, for instance that security would continue to make working in the area feasible and that residents in Herat would support such a large-scale project brought in by outsiders. Going into a country that had previously had no wind energy and setting up a massive wind farm seemed like a rather large leap.

Will saw this and was frustrated. His approach was more small scale, very likely to work, and built from on-the-ground knowledge that Afghans in his company already had. The technical aspect of the project they could teach to local communities fairly easily. It could start small, but then it had the real potential to grow. Will, however, realized that USAID was willing to significantly overpay for their wind-monitoring project and that these funds could keep the company afloat while it continued to experiment and refine their approaches. Grudgingly, he pulled together a proposal for the wind monitoring. Beyond this project, however, Will's ideas about expanding AWP were simply not fast enough and would not spend enough money to make them attractive to USAID or most other donors. Some of his friends and associates encouraged him to seek support in grant writing, but Will could not bring himself to pay thousands of dollars a month for an international grant writer who knew nothing about wind energy when he was running a shop with only four workers. As a result, as the amount of money in various forms of aid entering the country increased, Will and the rest of the AWP team found it harder and harder to compete as large international contractors started swooping in to make quick profits. These larger competitors might not have had much on-the-ground knowledge or experience, but they did have full-time grant writers who had contacts with USAID officials and knew how to put together winning bids.

Eventually, a group with more international experience (though little experience in Afghanistan) received funds for the monitoring project. In retrospect, however, what annoyed Will most was the fact that the grant writing and proposal work ended up pulling him away from much of his other work, and this key moment, when Will had the ear of USAID officials and the possibility of scaling up AWP's work was within reach, passed by.

In the meantime, with the team members at AWP having failed to secure any larger contracts, relations among them began to fray. The ethnic diversity of the group, which had been part of their initial potential, began to create problems. Without funds coming in, the group were less willing to tolerate their differences. They faced generational tensions as well. Amir, whose father had initially opposed his work on the project, had returned on a part-time basis to school. With so many jobs available and many requiring some sort of degree, his experience working in a small and not well-known workshop seemed to now have less potential. Better to go get work at a bigger firm. Similarly, the others began to look for work elsewhere. The group did not necessarily resent the international community, but their experience of it was clearly discouraging, particularly considering the initial promise their work seemed to present.

While AWP did not die quickly, and Will and his partners continued working on smaller projects for a couple more years, the dream that it might grow and reach out to communities on a wider scale faded as the surge rolled on.

Contracting the Intervention

The USAID of then is not the USAID of today. Today it is a contract-management agency.[1]

—Ashraf Ghani, president of Afghanistan, anthropologist, and former World Banker

The Contracting Model

As Will's case suggests, the funding of development and other projects in Afghanistan created a world that had an internal logic but not one that was always effective at helping Afghanistan. Although there are winners and losers in all funding schemes, in Afghanistan during the surge the winners tended to be international firms, while the losers were smaller firms and the Afghan communities they serviced. This created a growing disillusionment with the surge between those in the international community and the Afghans with whom they worked. Despite some parallels made by politicians between the Marshall Plan and efforts to rebuild both Iraq and Afghanistan, in the sixty years between these efforts, the structure of the U.S. government and how it distributes aid had changed radically. As already made clear, the contracting model that was at the heart of the political economy of the intervention was far different from the model used to rebuild Western Europe.

These differences were exacerbated by the twin forces of a growing insurgency and a rise in international funding that made the work of USAID much more difficult. The increased threat of attacks meant that officials were less able to travel outside the embassy or a few other isolated compound walls, while, simultaneously, the surge brought in millions more in funding and demanded an immediate increase in both projects and oversight. Instead of relying on international soldiers or government employees to work on these projects, the outsourcing of aid to international firms became the single dominant mode for funding development projects.

Essentially the job of most USAID officials and, on a smaller scale, officials working for the Department for International Development, the United Kingdom's version of USAID, the World Bank, or any other large donor was not to actually do any sort of development work but to monitor and evaluate the work being done by contractors. With the surge in funding, the reliance on contractors became more pronounced, with less and less oversight of projects. Eventually, almost everything officials at the various embassies knew about the projects they were sponsoring was being told to them directly by the contractors themselves, who clearly had an incentive to describe their work in optimistic terms. With little sense of what was really happening on projects and pressure to spend budgets as quickly as possible, projects like Will's were unappealing because they were too small and because officials were making few field visits. Although Will's amateur YouTube video was a good start, it was less convincing than the glossy reports produced by writers working for large DC-based contractors.

There was no simple solution to the problems of the contracting model. Both government officials and the contractors implementing projects complained regularly of flaws in the structures. Ambassador Neumann, for example, knew that much of the money leaving the embassy was not being spent effectively, but there was no clear alternative. At the heart of this was the fact that the fixed-price contract model did not give contractors any incentive to learn or to adapt. It simply pushed contractors to spend what they were given and then apply for more. He reflected on this to me: "The contractor model is a problem, but I don't know if we're ever going to get out of it."

He continued, "First of all, look at how the model works: You see a problem, so you go out and ask contractors to give you a proposal, your RFP [Request for Proposal]. Once you fund them, the contractor is then hired to do the project. The contractor is not hired to come back and tell you that 'upon further consideration or knowing more, we actually think there is a better way to do it and that we are doing it wrong.'" There were few mechanisms for providing more funding to projects that were particularly effective or conversely to provide less funding to those that were failing. In each case a reduction or increase of funds required vast amounts of paperwork and at times was simply impossible. In such a system there was no incentive to learn or to adapt to shifting conditions, and in Afghanistan, in the middle of the surge, the conditions were always shifting.

In fact, government contracting officials, whose work was often primarily judged by their "burn rate" or ability to spend funds, also had no incentive to attempt to save money by adjusting a broken program. Such changes mid-contract would have meant more work for them and, perhaps, a reprimand for not spending all the money they were allocated. When projects were not going well, Neumann suggested, "A lot of contracting officials wouldn't thank the contractor for coming back; they're administrating the contract. The contractor has no incentive to tell you that you ought to do it differently and has no incentive to tell you about problems outside the scope of the contract."

This frustrated the ambassador as he toured the country trying to gauge the work that U.S. funds were doing:

> I remember Eikenberry and I used to go around, when he was the general [and commander at ISAF; he later became ambassador to Afghanistan two years after Neumann], and we would stumble on problems. This one time we were down in Kandahar, and we were looking at police training, and we realized that they were doing no live fire training, so they had no particular feeling of confidence in their weapon. They weren't doing live fire training because the ammunition was not being delivered, but the ammunition was not the contractor's responsibility, and the contractor was not particularly [bothered by this]. The people on the ground were very frustrated, but that word was not coming back up through the chain to Kabul. They weren't responsible for that.

As Will had experienced with the embassy's interest in sustainable energy, the increased funding and contractors that poured into the country created a class divide. Those at the top of the contracting food chain rented huge compounds, many in the Sherpur neighborhood of Kabul. These compounds were heavily fortified and protected by security contractors. Many of these were Afghan, but it became increasingly common to have Nepalese or other South Asian security contractors as well, who were unfailingly polite and well-trained in contrast with many of their Afghan counterparts.

In part this security was in place because the area was dangerous, but most small-scale NGO workers actually lived in much more modest homes without guards and encountered few problems. In truth, there was a significant economic incentive for such fortifications. USAID contracts allowed implementers to automatically tack on up to 30 percent in fees to pay for security. With this regulation, a $100,000 program was entitled to an extra $30,000 just for security, which could further add to administrative costs. So contractors had an incentive to maximize security up to the allocated 30 percent regardless of the actual risk. Having Nepalese security guards was thus, in some instances, not about increased protection but was actually a way for the firm to charge more. There was no incentive whatsoever to save.

All this security had the unfortunate effect of distancing those overseeing the projects from the actual work that was being done. Many young NGO workers who were friends with Will made the switch to the increasing number of contracting firms during the early years of the surge. Fresh off projects where they were involved in a more hands-on manner, they were enthusiastic and devoted to their work. Working under new security regulations for contractors, however, they were unable to visit the schools that were being built, the roads being paved, or the clinics being opened. One engineer I spent time with had originally worked on construction projects as an architect, climbing around the building sites, getting his hands dirty with the Afghan engineers he was working with. A couple of years later, he moved to a much better-paying job with a contractor paving roads in the south of the country. In this position he actually had to use a U.S. helicopter to fly over the miles of road that he was paving because it was deemed too dangerous to drive, never setting foot on most of the road he was constructing. Furthermore, although these lower-level contractors were often aware of the large amounts of waste taking place on projects, their supervisors, who were interested primarily in maintaining the contract, did not want to hear about these issues. It became almost a game among some internationals, discussing whether friends of certain personality types would be able to last in contracting positions. Bets were made on how long it would take individuals who were too freethinking to get chased out of their well-paying positions.

Especially as the media got a hold of several high-profile and highly wasteful projects, USAID officials were forced to respond to increasing criticism of their work. On one level, this made them more conservative and unwilling to fund projects they felt could have any negative repercussions in the media. No longer was the worst-case scenario a failed project with money wasted; the worst-case scenario was a write-up in *The Washington Post*. Another way officials responded to these issues was an increased focus on developing monitoring and evaluation tools (M and E in intervention speak) that could better measure performance. The problem was, however, that this evaluation was often done (or at least overseen) by the contractors themselves, meaning the methods of M and E become less about measurement of social or infrastructure change and increasingly about justification of the money that was being spent. At times, local research firms, including one with whom I worked on some joint projects, would be paid by contractors to do a monitoring and evaluation report on the contractor's project, which would then be submitted to USAID or other donors. The Afghan firms conducting these audits, however, wanted repeat business from these contractors, so it was not surprising that all of the reports I saw were much rosier than the projects seemed to me. Sometimes the contractor would even come back with "suggested" revisions of these audits.

Such manipulation of how projects were being monitored was not just misleading but could eventually distort a project and its goals. In some instances, monitoring tools themselves reshaped a project's approach. For example, when I was conducting research on some access to justice issues, there were a series of ongoing justice projects sponsored by the international community, including one overseen by a major USAID contractor. The stated goal of almost all of these projects was to improve access to justice for all Afghans. To evaluate the project, however, this meant asking, what does access to justice mean, and how do we measure it? These questions were not easy. Some of the smaller projects attempted to track disputes within the community, but this was challenging, required extensive on-the-ground knowledge, and did not yield nice quantitative results that could be charted. Some of the small Afghan NGOs running these programs were able to do this type of fairly accurate grassroots monitoring, but the international contractor with less of a local presence could not.

Instead, early on, the large contractor decided that one measure for success was simple attendance at the various training sessions on justice it hosted. As a result, reports were filled with numbers of participants at training sessions the contractor had run, as well as some nice photos of the event. However, none of these numbers actually addressed whether participants knew more about justice when they left the sessions or whether the training sessions were at all likely to increase access to justice locally. Moreover, to improve the contractor's results, the only real incentive was to get as many additional attendees into the next session as they could. This could include having participants attend repeated sessions or having daylong sessions that participants checked into in the morning, but then left—this was an approach, we will see, that was used by the Afghan Local Police as well. The only thing this incentivized the implementers to do was to hold more and more and bigger and bigger training sessions, with little regard to the outcomes of these sessions.[2]

Eventually the contractor on the justice program did hire some more thoughtful monitors who designed complex schemes for measuring the number of disputes in an area and how those disputes were being resolved both before and after the training sessions occurred. They even developed a comparative analysis by measuring the disputes in neighboring districts where the project was not active. This, however, required several iterations and sustained monitoring. By the time these mechanisms were developed and Afghan researchers were trained to work with them, the contract with USAID was almost up. Furthermore, while some of these approaches eventually made progress, often those higher up at the contractors had little interest in actually improving their data collection methods because this was costly and slow, and if the results actually did not demonstrate significant change in access to justice, funds were likely to get cut in the future.[3]

Part of the disconnection among what programs were designed to do, what they said they were doing, and what actually happened was probably unavoidable. At times this led to rather extreme strategies for circumventing the challenges of security. In discussions in Washington before the 2014 presidential election, some in the international community proposed using drones with heat sensors to monitor polling stations. The argument was that these polling stations were so far removed and dangerous that international monitors could not visit them. By using heat sensors, however, they could at least determine whether people had actually gone to the station or not, in an effort to catch some of the "ghost polling stations" from previous elections where ballot boxes seemed to appear from thin air. In the meantime, however, such approaches were costly, unsustainable, and subject to numerous loopholes. (What if commanders simply gathered a large number of their men at stations so it seemed as if they were voters? Even if there was suspected fraud at a station, how would anyone get there to prove it if security was already too bad for monitors to travel there? Was it legal to discard ballots just because a heat map suggested a low turnout?) Such ideas seemed workable in a Washington boardroom but had little likelihood of success on the ground in Afghanistan.

More concerning, however, was the way such ideas seemed to suggest the ever expanding distance between funders and implementers. And this was not simply the distance between offices in Kabul and headquarters in Western capitals. Members of the military complained that no one at Bagram ever really knew what was going on in the PRTs, that the PRTs never really knew what was going on at the FOBs, and that the FOBs never really knew what was going on at the outposts. A similar chain of disconnected and gradually more misleading information was found in NGOs that had their headquarters in Western capitals, national offices in Kabul, and then, more rarely, field sites in the provinces.

At each step along the way, however, officers and officials were encouraged to act as if they did know what was going on. This encouraged individuals to pass information along at each step, which almost always tended to be an overly optimistic interpretation of the limited view they had from the office in which they were sitting, further skewing the view of the conflict. As one man working for a contractor pointed out to me, "If you write enough glossy reports about how things are getting better in Afghanistan while sitting in an air-conditioned compound far from the projects that you are monitoring, you might actually start believing them."

Goats for Dinner: The Military Alternative

As the media brought forward stories of inefficient programming over the course of the latter half of the 2000s, oversight and applications for grants became more complicated and the review process longer. Fast-tracked programs were promoted, but, as the surge gained steam in the form of an increase in civilian spending, the constant tussling between funders and contractors seemed to slow projects down almost to a halt. In 2008, the Office of Special Inspector General for Afghanistan Reconstruction (SIGAR) was created, which audited a variety of U.S.-sponsored projects in Afghanistan, producing occasionally sensational and generally well-publicized in-depth reports that often revealed enormous amounts of waste. In Kabul, program officers increasingly feared the wrath of these auditors, making the process of putting contracts out for bid, reviewing them, and eventually funding them more and more laborious.

This could slow or derail projects in several ways. For example, bids for certain contracts would be submitted with the names of specific personnel included in project descriptions who had actually taken other jobs for other organizations by the time the contract had come through. In other cases, the need that the contract was addressing might have been covered by some other donor during the time it took for the project to be approved. (This led to the inverse problem of projects *not* starting because there was the belief that another donor might address the issue in the short-term future, which especially slowed down work by non-American donors who saw the United States massively ramping up spending during the surge and were frozen in part by the ambiguity surrounding where American funding was headed next.) Coordination of projects in certain sectors became almost impossible as donor countries would fund one aspect of a project; another donor funded another aspect but on a different time frame; and a third potentially had funds available but was waiting on the second to begin implementation. This frustrated many but perhaps none more so than the American military. With the surge ordered by President Obama, the top military leaders, led spiritually by David Petraeus, the architect of the updated approach to counterinsurgency, felt the need to "win hearts and minds" as quickly as possible. These delays in implementing crucial projects were no longer tolerable.

Of course, in addition to defeating the Taliban, counterinsurgency meant delivering services to recently "liberated" communities. This strategy was often referred to as "Clear, Hold, and Build."[4] The military was historically very adept at the clearing phase, which involved chasing out the insurgents, who were often all too willing to leave for safer areas once a significant international troop presence arrived. They were also fairly effective in many cases at holding territory once they had an active presence there.[5] These were the "kinetic events" that Owen was trained for. What the international military was less skilled at was the building process. This was a part of the military shift outlined in the *Counterinsurgency Manual*, the writing of which was led by Petraeus, who suggested: "By default, US and multi-national military forces often possess the only readily available capacity to meet many of the local populace's fundamental needs. Human decency and the law of war require land forces to assist the populace in their AOs [areas of operation]."[6]

Ideally, these tasks of addressing "the local populace's fundamental needs" were left to relief agencies, USAID, other large-scale implementers and international donors. In many cases, however, USAID programs and independent NGOs balked at going into recently cleared territory. On one level they did not have the security support in place to protect themselves; in some cases, particularly with small international NGOs, there was no real desire to associate themselves with the military. This was particularly true in areas where territory had passed back and forth from Taliban to American control and was still contested. Others protested that many development projects, like those

Figure 6.1. Weapon clearance area near a base entrance. Photo by the author.

focused on agriculture, demanded long-term investment and stability. Going in immediately after an area had been cleared was simply bad development practice and could damage an NGO's ability to cultivate longer-term projects.

The tension between the military who wanted fast-tracked programs put in motion and the more hesitant approach of some of the relief agencies in the country since before the U.S.-led invasion made relationships between civilians and military more complicated. Several times, when I was visiting areas that had seen recent insurgent attacks, lower-ranking officers in particular made it clear to me that they thought the area was too dangerous for civilians to be traveling in and wanted me to leave. At the same time, however, higher-ranking military officials in Kabul were quick to chide aid agencies for not working in some of the less stable areas where there was significant need for aid. Both of these conflicting messages particularly disturbed those NGO workers who had been in the country for a while and felt they not only knew local political conditions better than the military did but were better positioned to assess both community needs and how those needs were best fulfilled.[7]

The military, however, felt pressure to get projects off the ground immediately and to start delivering services to these areas they had recently seized.
As the areas across the country where ISAF was active increased and development organizations remained reluctant to work in them, the military looked
for ways to implement projects on their own. Although USAID led the charge
in terms of delivering development funds for the first four years following the
U.S. invasion, the balance soon shifted. By 2005 the Department of Defense
began outspending USAID on development, and eventually the surge moved
more and more money to military development projects. In the end, the Department of Defense was outspending USAID on development alone by a
margin of almost three to one.[8] The reliance on the contracting model meant
that this also signaled an increase in the number of contractors working for
the military in comparison with the actual number of soldiers deployed; between Iraq and Afghanistan, in 2010 the United States had 175,000 troops
deployed to war zones and 207,000 contractors.[9]

There were multiple problems with the military moving into the world of
development. Groups like ICRC complained in particular that blurring the
lines between development workers and soldiers put those working for aid and
development agencies at an increased risk. All of a sudden, they suggested,
everyone was a target. In Kabul this shift was visible on the vehicles that organizations drove. ICRC had professed their neutrality by drawing a gun with a
red X over it on their cars, as did some other development and human rights
agencies. However, it was not long before they removed this symbol as it became clear it did little to actually deter attacks, ultimately conceding that in
the conflict there was no clear line between international civilians and soldiers. Instead many opted for a lower-profile approach, leaving their vehicles
unmarked. For the military, which was more concerned about achieving its
own objectives, the larger issue became that disparate goals of development
and counterinsurgency could lead to approaches that undermined each other.

This was particularly true of one of the largest sources of funding for
military assistance with development, the Commander Emergency Response
Program, whose funds were often referred to simply as CERP funds. This program was designed to allow commanding officers to spend money on quickly
designed projects that did not need to go through the same channels of review
that other contracts did. The hundred-page CERP manual outlines twenty-
one different types of projects that range from health care and electricity
projects to paying for damages caused by the military to civilian property.[10]

The point of the funds was to allow commanders in the field flexibility in responding to the needs of the communities they were working in without being required to go through the normal process of securing approval from their higher-ups. The lack of oversight, however, had serious repercussions as the program evolved.

CERP funds were originally used in Iraq, and by 2008 $2.8 billion had been spent with minimal oversight, which launched a series of scathing critiques that often cited CERP's most outrageous projects. *The Washington Post* in 2008, for example, reported that $14,250 had been spent on "I love Iraq" T-shirts and $12,800 on pools to cool the bears and tigers at the Bagdad zoo, expenses that were difficult to reconcile with the stability strategy that was supposed to drive the use of CERP funds.[11] In Afghanistan, however, with better oversight, the U.S. military was convinced they could more effectively monitor the use of CERP funds and deploy them for development projects that would support the counterinsurgency strategy. Many CERP programs were aimed at agriculture, which drove Afghanistan's less industrialized economy, and so agriculture advisors were soon attached to many units.

Around Bagram, CERP funds were used on a variety of projects that ranged in size from supplies distributed to the local police to small-scale infrastructure projects. It was difficult for local communities, however, to distinguish these projects from projects that were run either with other military funds or even those run by completely independent NGOs. (This confusion was not limited to projects receiving CERP funds; in the small town where I originally did my field research, which had not received any CERP funds, locals could recount the various projects that had been done in the town but rarely remembered which organization had funded them, even though USAID and a few other major donors required their logo be stamped on any building or material they paid for.) The fact that CERP funds went, sometimes directly, to Afghan companies doing the work or even to Afghan NGOs further confused many people.

On the military side there was similar lack of clarity. When Owen made use of CERP funds, as was the case with many of the Special Forces soldiers, he was less focused on building long-term relationships with communities and more interested in making operations run smoothly: "The task force would send us into a village, and sometimes they would put up a fight. Basically we would round up all of the adult males, the kids would be running back and forth with bread, and it almost became a kind of community gathering by the end of the day." Because of the force that Owen and his men represented,

> We would receive no resistance whatsoever. We'd martial the men into the largest compound, and the women would hide. They would keep the kids. What we would do with the CERP money is that, we'd been in their village the whole entire day and by 4 or 5 in the evening, I'm pretty comfortable that this is what we call a permissive environment, you know, we're not going to get attacked; if there are Taliban fighters in this village, I have them here with me, right in this compound.
>
> A lot of times we would gather the elders, and I would have the senior Afghan [soldier] with me. I would gather that senior guy and say, "Hey, talk to these knuckleheads and tell them how important security is in their village, and if they want projects like schools and wells and things like that, the first thing they need is security, they need to provide their own security" . . . and they would get together and they would talk, and what I would do CERP-wise is basically buy them all dinner.

As an officer, Owen, who regularly voiced some concern about the role of SEALs in counterinsurgency, was primarily concerned about the safety of his men. Once security was ensured, however, the funds could also enable at least attempts at fostering better relationships between the Afghan government and the people in the village:

> I'd buy up to eight goats, and the women would cook up the goats, and everyone would eat, and I'd pay them the money for it. Sometimes they were pissed, and were like, "Hey, you're in our village," but a lot of times I think that they were just so used to it after ten years that they were like, "Hey Americans" . . . So that came from a CERP payment. "Dinner's on me, fellows, sorry for taking up your day."
>
> Occasionally I would get some adult males that would get all fiery and want me to pay them for a days' worth of work, and I'm like, "I'm not going to do that" . . . You couldn't be the guy they were going to walk all over, but at the same time I saw an advantage to being charitable or at least understanding of their inconvenience. Originally, when I landed in the helicopter that morning, me and my guys got off ready to shoot someone in the face, since we didn't know what the threat was . . . For it to turn into a community gathering, I saw it as me enabling the Afghan military to go into a village and talk

to them about security. . . . I'd always give the money to the Afghans and let the Afghans pay . . . To me, that showed the villagers that the government of Afghanistan was working and that they were paying their soldiers and had the money to give the villagers money in that sort of setting. I felt like when I couldn't do anything else, at least I could do that.

Owen saw both the upside and the downside to these temporary funds: "A project or contract has a permanent feel to it [as opposed to CERP funds], like I'm going to give you this amount of money every month, but the project is eventually going to become rubble, and they're going to keep asking for money . . . that's how I saw most of the projects going." CERP at least provided him with a way to give easy handouts. Still, it was clear that these odd community gatherings, in which Owen used CERP funds for the villagers to buy their own goats and cook them for dinner, were not exactly what the designers of the program had in mind when they thought about emergency relief and were a far cry from what most NGO workers in the area would have promoted as best practices.

At higher policy levels, CERP funds also received mixed reviews. The RAND corporation assessment of the program in Iraq found that the projects had been successful enough that the U.S. military should continue to use CERP funds as a central aspect of the national security strategy; these funds were particularly useful when paying to finish projects left incomplete by other donors, paying for battle damages, or when making condolence payments.[12] These strategies, however, still required skills that were not being taught in basic training. As a result, this left some analysts recommending that the U.S. military begin teaching courses in accounting and program management to prepare soldiers to run development projects more effectively.[13] All of these recommendations, however, pointed to the fact that the military, by taking on development projects, was moving dangerously out of its comfort zone, forcing it to rethink its approach to training and preparation for missions. Not all officers were eager to move the training of soldiers from the firing range into the accounting department.

The legacy of CERP funds in Afghanistan, however, ultimately reshaped the intervention simply by the sheer amount of money being dropped into the Afghan economy. Although in 2004 $40 million was appropriated to CERP spending, by 2010 that number had swelled to over $1 billion, or approximately 5 percent of the Afghan gross domestic product.[14] Both Kabul and Parwan were on the list of the provinces receiving a higher proportion of CERP spending, with numerous projects in the area around Bagram funded directly through these channels.[15] With $1 billion in flexible aid money swirling around communities like Bagram, there were sure to be both opportunities and economic distortions. Many of these distortions, however, were also embedded in how these projects fit into the larger military bureaucracy and the privatization of the conflict.

Stars and Six-Figure Salaries

Given their flexible nature, as Owen suggests, it was difficult to distinguish which CERP projects were actually effective and which led only to rubble. In part, it was challenging to assess the effectiveness of CERP funding simply because there were so many projects that were so different from each other. Supporters of the counterinsurgency approach found numerous anecdotes of successful small-scale projects. At the same time, critics, particularly from the development world, could respond with a similar number of stories of funds misappropriated and projects gone awry. As programming went on, however, it became increasingly clear that there were some major downsides to giving officers almost unrestricted access to flexible funding. As Owen pointed out to me, a decentralized program like CERP really ultimately relies solely on the officer who is in charge of it. And, for many in Afghanistan, the motivation was often less about the mission than it was about their own personal advancement, either in their careers or financially:

> Military commanders at the colonel level come into a place like Iraq or Afghanistan with a campaign plan or an idea, and they are only there for a year at most. And during their time there they shape whatever they want to shape. And maybe that means rebuilding a specific part of a base or building a specific structure for a mission that came up. So what you see are a lot of unfinished projects, and you see where people had a certain idea and were going in a certain direction, and then something changed national policy-wise and so we abandoned that.

In one case that particularly irked Owen, the U.S. military built a dining hall complete with deep-fat fryers for the Afghan national army. "The ANA soldiers looked at them and asked, 'What do we do with these? We grill our meat.' For me that's a great example of maybe American arrogance or maybe our own complete . . . [he trails off] . . . how could we be so unaware?" At the same time, however, he added, the officer in charge of overseeing the building of the dining facility had probably simply been following orders, and following orders was the best way to advance in the military.

As the surge went on, soldiers increasingly discussed officers who were "trying to get their stars" or move from the rank of colonel to general. Such moves could take years when in the United States or on a peaceful deployment in Germany or Japan, but in Afghanistan soldiers had the opportunity to distinguish themselves and advance in a relatively brief amount of time, in a manner that had many parallels with the opportunities that young NGO workers had. With Obama announcing a set endpoint to withdraw the American troops that had been added in the surge, this also put a limited time frame on the ability of many of these men to advance. This, along with the temporary end of the American presence in Iraq, created the sense that the U.S. military seemed likely to contract after the war, meaning that there would be far fewer opportunities to be promoted once units were rotated back to the States. Although this was a particularly powerful motivator for those looking to become generals, a similar logic about promotion applied up and down the ranks.

Owen found such issues were even more frustrating in areas where overlapping groups worked. It was one thing to waste money on deep-fat fryers but something different to run programs that interfered with other units' missions, particularly when personal motives were clouding the decision-making processes of many. As a member of the Special Forces, Owen primarily was assigned to assist in the "battle spaces" or AOs of other units. For a while, Owen's team was assigned to assist in an area where a particular colonel whom Owen had previously clashed with was in charge. "This guy was a piece of work. He held a *shura* [local council meeting[16]] with this village [that was under heavy Taliban influence], and he held his hands up and said, 'I have pacified the Taliban in this region,' and as soon as the words came out of his mouth, 82s [a type of small rocket] started coming over the walls, and World War III broke loose." Owen was standing in the back at the room at the time with a colleague. "We looked at each other and said, yeah, they seem passive."

In such instances, for the officer that Owen described and others like him, this was evidence of the lack of options and a sense that very little was possible. What could Owen do other than let such officers make ineffective decisions, even when he knew they were ineffective? CERP was still going to provide them with the funds to run these programs. For example, part of the colonel's mission was to set up the local branch of the Afghan Local Police. The ALP was a branch of the Afghan police set up during the surge years to essentially localize the police. The controversial program took local militias, trained them, and armed them to work in support of the ANA or Afghan National Police (ANP). Concerns had been raised about having what essentially were militias doing the work of the ANP. Others were simply concerned about the complex logistics of figuring out which groups should be trained and armed and which should not. Doing this incorrectly could have meant resupplying insurgents and possibly undoing the work of previous programs such as the DDR (or Demobilization, Disarmament and Reintegration Program), which had been designed earlier in the decade to remove guns from the hands of these militias.

This colonel, in particular, was not convinced that the ALP program would be successful in the area. Normally, recruitment was supposed to involve careful discussions with local elders and a vetting process for each individual fighter. Instead, as Owen describes this colonel,

> He held another shura and said, "We need to create ALP," and everyone said, "Yes, ALP," since these elders will say yes to anything that someone in the military says. And he said, "All right, here's what I'm going to do"; what he did was hold this meeting, and he paid all the military-aged males, I don't know what the sum was, but he paid them on Friday to show up to a training on Monday. Guess how many showed up on Monday? Zero, money gone. I don't know how much he gave them, but gone. It was CERP funds. That's a CERP project.

For individuals like this colonel, however, the ultimate impact of the project mattered little, it seems. Whether this was because he did not believe in the military's move toward counterinsurgency, which would have justified the arming of such militias,[17] or whether he was simply unconvinced of his unit's ability to contribute was not clear, but that did not mean his decisions did not have a certain logic to them. Although Owen was quick to point out that this colonel was much more the exception than the rule, he was still critical of officers who made decisions based simply on the appearance of good work, instead of really asking what it meant to perform a mission effectively: "People know exactly what they need to do to look good to their superiors, and they are willing to show you a façade, a façade that looks really good, but it's just desert back there."

Success was about the appearance of success. Partially this was some of the difficulties of metrics and measurements discussed earlier. How can you ensure that a counterinsurgency project works? How do you measure hearts and minds? It's difficult, so instead the military bureaucracy, like the M and E experts working on USAID projects, tried to find easier units to quantify. The result was that projects like the colonel's were judged simply on how many names were on the list of enrollees and how much money had been distributed. The program had expanded so quickly and was so large that it was too difficult to monitor whether the names on the list actually came to trainings and took part in ALP exercises. Even if attendance was kept, would this have also measured things like loyalty? How was that quantifiable? The problem in a hierarchy like the military, of course, was that the appearance of success had much to do with both those above and below one in the chain of command. Although the colonel in the preceding story, whom Owen did not report to, could be ignored, other instances were more difficult for Owen to deal with.

"I wrote after actions [reports] about missions that we had conducted, and I would send these up in my comments. I wouldn't get any resistance from the colonel I was sending them up to; instead, he would just change my briefs [before sending them to the general above him]." Here the colonel Owen was reporting to was more concerned with making the mission look like a success than in dwelling on the shortcomings and the potential for lessons learned Owen often focused on. "I took [the reports] to the major I worked with, and he was, like, 'just go with what he says.'" Owen considered filing a more formal protest, but ultimately he was not sure what would have been gained. The colonel was not radically changing information, just making things from Owen's most recent mission sound more positive and ignoring certain struggles. At the same time, however, one could imagine the colonel's sanitized version of Owen's report being doctored slightly more by his superior and so on, the actual account becoming more and more slanted as it traveled upward, increasing the distance between the reality on the ground and those in offices making the decisions. For Owen, however, it seemed much simpler to continue working at his job.

Having his briefs modified, however, meant lessons were not being learned and future missions were not adapting to the knowledge learned from the mistakes of earlier attempts. I had seen this before in the development world and particularly with contractors who actually had an incentive to guard the results of their work, particularly from other contractors who might eventually bid against them on contracts.[18] I asked Owen why the various branches of the military seemed to be ineffective at learning, particularly among the Special Forces, who were much more nimble than other parts of the military and who were less likely to feel competitive about their projects and battle spaces:

> We chose to learn the wrong lessons. What we chose to learn in the military is how the brief could have been better, how the staff could have been more efficient. When it comes to tactical things, we're better at that . . . We learned from lessons like *Black Hawk Down*, because people died [and it garnered significant media attention]. When it's just money that's just spent in the wrong place, we're less serious about that, and I think that's a problem. We spend a lot of money that ain't our money. But we should, we should spend it like it's our money, but we don't. We also kind of do things with the feeling that Uncle Sam will buy us another if we break it.
>
> The example of the deep-fat fryer, that briefed really well I'm sure. That got some colonel promoted to general, I'm sure it did, which at the end of the day is what matters to him. Does he care what the Afghans get? No, not at all. It makes a great picture, a nice storyboard and a promotion at the end of the day. But why would you spend the effort doing it? That to me is mind boggling; when you look at the dollar value of it, it's criminal, but no one is dying. Nobody dies when you order a dining facility to be built. It's only a good news story.

Sitting later in his new office in Washington, Ambassador Neumann was more generous to some of those whom Owen was criticizing, perhaps because his view was from the top; it was easier for him to see some of the challenges with trying to make all the various pieces fit together. Still, he often pointed to the struggles both the military and the State Department seemed to have making adaptive decisions on the ground: "Our biggest failure is that we do not build learning organizations, and we can't [build such organizations] the way that we rotate people. The organization adapts what they are doing in time on the ground as they confront local circumstances." The problem was that, by the time the surge came along, most in the State Department had limited on-the-ground knowledge despite the fact that this was when it was most needed. When they did see something not working (or even working), there was the tendency to veer wildly, making large strategic changes: "We just stand back and think that everything is a policy issue. It's an American [tendency], but I think it's a larger Western issue. Certainly Washington is a policy town, and we are very fixated on policy, and there is very little understanding of implementation. Often it's not about the policy, it's about the implementation." Gentle changes could have made a major difference, but, as with the colonel in Owen's account, careful alterations to a program were not likely to advance one quickly in a career. Instead, splashy policy papers that offered new, quick solutions were more likely to stand out to superiors.

For Neumann, however, it was not a simple question of how promotions were made; it became a question of how bureaucracies think and react. Implementation of all types of projects in Afghanistan was challenging during this period, and oftentimes it was simply easier to throw up one's hands and begin an entirely new program instead of trying to figure out what was going wrong with the current programs:

> Just to make up an example: You can have a policy where you use tribes to secure roads, and you could find, as we did in Iraq, with pipeline security, that you spend a lot of money—they fought with each other, they used the money to build up political positions, they made deals with the insurgents, and you got no security at all. You could find that if you did a better job selecting which leaders to work with . . . you backed them up when they were in trouble, and because of that you both got security and you got an improvement in government. In that hypothetical model, you can have big success or huge failure with same policy—it's all about implementation.

The way that contracting worked made adjusting projects once they were being implemented more difficult because it was relatively easy to write a call for proposals for a new project but it was much more complex to tweak a current project with a resistant contractor.

"When we don't have something going well, we tend to think that you have to change the policy, so you have long review, big muscle movements moving resources. Now sometimes it is the policy that needs to be changed, but a lot of time the problem is not in the policy, it's in how you implement it." Reflecting further on this in his memoirs Neumann summarizes:

> If we do not understand how critical implementation is, we are prone to starve it of resources. If we do not understand how much time is needed for

accomplishment, we are drawn too often to fire up ideas when we have only begun a process to put them into effect, and instead go charging off searching for new ideas whose realistic accomplishment time we do not understand. Divorcing high-level policymaking from implementation leads us to ignore information from the ground level necessary to make policies work and prevents us from learning how to adjust policies when they do not. In short, making policy without paying attention to implementation is a bit like sailing near reefs without a lookout; the compass and map are not enough.[19]

Hydroelectric power was not reaching enough people, and Will's wind project was not large enough, so USAID jumped immediately to a model of large-scale wind farming. If that failed, however, they were likely to step away from wind energy entirely instead of looking at ways it could be fine-tuned to adapt to the Afghan economic and physical environment. For many well-intentioned aid workers and diplomats, it was simply easier to return to the drawing board and try to start all over again designing a new policy.

Others, however, were less concerned with how lessons were being learned and quicker to embrace the potential ways of profiting from the intervention. This was especially true of those who had skills that were in high demand by the military contractors seeking contracts from the Department of Defense. Retired SEALs and other members of the Special Forces were often the most sought after, but so were those with more basic technical skills. Such contractors often worked rotations of eight months on and eight months off, as one of the gunsmiths that Owen worked with did, getting paid many times the salary that they would have earned with a similar skill set in America.[20]

While driving around the naval yard in Norfolk, I asked Owen how he felt about a gunsmith who was earning $200,000 a year providing support for his men. He was clearly conflicted and replied after a pause, "I don't remember being upset about it. I remember thinking that it kind of sucked. If I weren't in the military, there's no way that you could pay me enough money to go sit in Afghanistan, but I have a family; I have a life outside of the military. I suppose if I were a single guy [it might be different], you know?"

In other cases the motivation was obvious. Owen continued, "I had a guy I worked with; he was in the Navy and then got out. He was wildly in debt. He was in debt like $100,000: credit card debt. And he said, 'I have an easy solution; I'm going to go to Afghanistan for a year, and I'll make $200,000.' And he did. He paid off his debt, plus had $100,000 in the bank. He also took that at great personal risk." For private security contractors, the logistics of support were entirely different. In the case of Owen's friend, his job was to defend a private convoy, along with one other international security contractor and a team of Afghan guards. The problem, Owen continued, was that if "the convoy gets attacked, there was no one coming to save you. No one. They can't get on the radio and call for a CasEvac [casualty evacuation, that is, the international military would not extract them if attacked]. At the same time, he got himself out of credit card debt."

Further complicating the relationship between SEALs and the security contracting world was the fact that one of the marquee contractors was Blackwater, a firm set up by Erik Prince, who was a former SEAL. Blackwater provided much of the actual security in Iraq for the Department of State and other civilians, though it came under intense scrutiny after several instances when civilians were shot by the private contractors. Owen told me:

> When Iraq was at its height, this is when the Blackwater scandals were coming up, the contracting thing became really popular among some of the SEALs. I disagreed with it. I thought it was stupid. Because, one, why would you go to a combat zone without all the support that you need, like air support, medical evacuation, that type of thing? The second reason is, I saw it as a very troubling trend in the military. Guys were like, oh, I don't like the constrictions that are put on us in the military in terms of rules of engagement and that type of thing. So I'm going to join a company that operates completely under its own set of rules, and I'm going to do, basically, a military job.

The scandals that Owen referred to here, including the killing of civilians by Blackwater contractors in Iraq, forced Prince to relinquish control, and Blackwater became rebranded as Xe. However, other firms simply replaced Blackwater, and little changed in terms of the security contractor model on the ground in either Iraq or Afghanistan. In the meantime, SEALs who had been in Afghanistan were increasingly hired by contractors elsewhere; for a while, protecting container ships as they passed close to the Somali coast became another appealing destination for those leaving military service.

For Owen, however, former soldiers looking to use their training to make large sums through private contracting reflected more troubling trends generally about American priorities:

I may be biased, but I see military service as a noble calling, doing our nation's bidding, whatever that might be, ultimately a selfless endeavor. When guys go to the contractors' world, I see it as them using the job that I love and that others like me have dedicated their lives toward as a purely selfish end. It also highlights something that I think is really ugly about American culture these days. After 9/11 happened, there was a flurry of organizations, firms, companies, and wealthy individuals who used a national tragedy and a call to war as a means to profit. I remember hundreds of Ford trucks being shipped to Iraq to give to prominent Iraqis and some of the more elite security forces, but where is the Ford dealership in Iraq or the service centers to repair these vehicles when they break down? Because the dusty, dry desert environment that is most places in Iraq will render a Ford truck useless after a year or so. Somebody is living nicely in Malibu after selling the trucks to the U.S. government, but the end result of the money spent is unsustainable. Our government is more in debt, and the Iraqis have a few hundred really nice up-armored and broken Ford trucks.

Although some of these patterns of war profiteering might not be as new as Owen suggests, they did reach incredible new heights, particularly during the surge when there was pressure to accomplish things and spend money as quickly as possible. These economic opportunities only made it more likely that the private security and contracting models would continue to thrive well into the future. In the case of Afghanistan, mercenaries continued to be uncomfortably mixed with soldiers, not to mention diplomats and development workers, leading to more contradictions in the sense of what the intervention was actually trying to achieve.

Looking back on it, Owen continued his bleak assessment of what it looked like to many of those soldiers on the ground:

How did we allow that to happen? It still boggles my mind. I think that Cheney pushed those initiatives. I think it's terrible and un-American, kind of. Here's this nineteen-year-old private in the army, who joins because "by God, we were attacked and I'm going to pick up a rifle and go fight." And that kid goes over, and he's doing everything he can, and he's doing it for fucking peanuts; those guys don't get paid shit. And then he becomes this jackass . . . who's getting paid hundreds of thousands of dollars to ride around in little helicopters.

Another Chance for Funds?

These stories of projects and wasted money are easy to dismiss as tales of incompetence or a simple lack of effort. But the intervention was filled with men and women who were highly competent and still ended up in such situations, and much had to do with the incentives each individual was dealing with. Despite all of these criticisms, the one thing the small rapid-funding approach of the military did have going for it was that it lacked some of the onerous bureaucratic tendencies that funding from USAID and other large donors had. This created opportunities for small-scale projects like the ones Will dreamed of implementing. Hearing of an increasing number of small-scale projects funded by the military, Will's interest was quickly piqued, but how to proceed? The small-scale approach, of course, also meant that much of the information about the possibility of funding came through personal relationships and other informal channels.

The first problem with getting funds like this was the relative lack of communication between many in the development world and the military. As Owen put it, "I don't think either group really trusts the other." The military saw NGO types as a liability, people who were unaware of the risks and who might need to be rescued at some point, thus putting military lives in danger. At the same time, many of the NGO workers who had been around much longer than the soldiers saw the military as exacerbating the conflict, acting hurriedly and ultimately making things worse, not better. Both criticisms probably had some validity, but some individuals and organizations still did try to reach across this line. Nevertheless, the challenges of communicating between the groups were daunting.

Will attempted to overcome this communication hurdle by contacting the head of an international agricultural program whom he knew who had worked with the military in the past. This man encouraged him to approach the military working on PRTs, particularly those in the areas close to where AWP had worked in the past. The Parwan PRT was a few miles up the road from Bagram Airbase, and, for both Will and Afghan businessmen like Omar, it seemed to be more approachable than the formidable challenge of getting access to the enormous airbase. In addition, there were funds available on many of these smaller bases in lesser amounts than were available from USAID. The PRT's also had limited areas of operations and could better appreciate the gradual approach Will was advocating. The fact that he was asking for tens of thousands, not tens of millions, of dollars was actually an advantage in these situations. Could this solve the problem of Will's work being too small to get funded by other larger donors?

In many ways this too would have been an ideal source for contracts for AWP. PRTs and other small-scale military installations did not want to rely on local sources for energy, and running generators was noisy, smelly, and expensive. Although this was certainly not true of all members of the American military, Will found that many on these bases came from outdoorsy backgrounds and supported environmental protection. Others were simply fed up with the constant noise that the generators produced. Will's hands-on approach of building small wind turbines appealed to them.

Will's contact offered to help him get introduced to the military liaisons to the army corps of engineers, suggesting in an email that "those are the most likely and easy markets at this moment, in my opinion. Who knows," his contact's email continued, "you get some serious orders, can sale up and reduce the production costs as you move along. Oh, one more: also don't hesitate to ask the full price of a package. There's plenty of money around!"

Will, however, still continued to struggle to secure funds. The problem was that, because he was not a current contractor to any of the branches of the international military, he did not have contacts on the bases near where AWP had been working. With no phone number and strict security access, for Will and Omar alike, there was simply no way to get in touch with the right people inside. At the same time, it was rare for these bases to have much of a sense of the NGOs or other businesses working in their areas. Moreover, many were in more dangerous areas, and even those in stable areas were not in the type of place where one could simply walk up and ring the doorbell. Although Will had managed to get email addresses for some initial contacts, the problem was that most of the officers rotated through on one-year tours, and some of these officers had already moved on. The length of the average NGO project was too long to fit into the tour of a single military officer. In other cases, when Will had met with an officer, that person was already on the way out. In some instances he might get the name of the new person coming on board, but that person often took time settling in, and Will's effective, but not very splashy, projects would not have been at the top of the list of priorities of those officers looking to "hit a home run" during their tours. In retrospect, Will reflects that perhaps he could have done more, but ultimately the way that Will and his associates had slowly and carefully built their business did not seem to fit the model of how most of the contracts from the military worked.

This, we will see, created a problem not just for AWP but for anyone looking to run a business or make a profit near one of these bases during the surge. With funds like CERP supporting certain projects while ignoring others, personal connections became more important than actual good business models. Knowing someone on the base could lead quickly to lucrative projects with minimal oversight. This fed into a larger problem, in that, especially for Afghan businessmen, funding from the base was not the only winner-take-all large pot of funds in town. There were also large amounts of money to be made in the opium trade or by smuggling. Legitimate business growth takes time, and, during the surge, those who hesitated lost out. Even the labor market was skewed because jobs on the bases paid significantly more than jobs outside the bases. This gave young men less incentive to make choices like investing in a small local business or improving their farms because international donor dollars meant there was the appearance of many other lucrative opportunities. AWP was faced with a choice of unrealistic hypergrowth or gradual stagnation. Although good for some, the problem with windfall profits is the economic distortions they create. With such prizes to be had, people took risks and were less likely to invest—think for example of the California Gold Rush, when stories of quick profits were everywhere but neither political civility nor organized government services seemed to flourish.

Even for those not directly involved, this created large amounts of market volatility, which oftentimes created difficult to predict market discrepancies. For example, in the summer of 2013, at the local car market near Bagram, the price of a used Toyota Surf SUV (the vehicle of choice for many NGOs) had plummeted from $20,000 to close to $7,000. In the meantime, the price of a good used Toyota Corolla had remained fairly fixed around $5,000. The reason, I was told, was that NGO and international contractors, who tended to purchase SUVs, were decreasing their spending in preparation for the drawdown of international troops. At the same time, the local Afghans, who were more likely to purchase a Corolla, had yet to feel the economic contraction, which kept prices fixed. The car dealers, however, who had purchased a rather large stock of SUVs during the surge, stood to lose a good bit if prices did not climb. In such ways, the mismanagement and unpredictability of international funds leaked out into the local economy and shaped that as well. The consequences of these economic swings would become severe as relationships between those inside Bagram Airbase and those outside slowly deteriorated.

Although some of these funds did lead to useful projects, there was also concern that the military was getting involved in doing development work even though their aim was not actually to "develop" Afghanistan. The contradictions swirling around the goals of stabilization, counterinsurgency, development, and state building confused the ways in which projects played out on the ground level and the ways that individuals like Omar and Will made decisions. These distortions were even more extreme in areas like Bagram, where there were so many projects going on simultaneously.

7 Climbing over the Wall

The U.S. will never leave Bagram because they have paid so much to get into Afghanistan, so they will never leave it easily. The United States has some plans for Afghanistan, but two more years is not enough for them to achieve their goals. Even if they seem to leave Afghanistan, they will leave behind a figurehead president so that they can achieve their long-term goals, which they planned perhaps sixty years ago.
—**Afghan Bagram contractor, 2012**

The Weight of Development

On a warm early summer day, Omar and his brother drove me out to show me some of the work his family had been doing and some of IA's factories. We began at a small production yard that made ornamental bricks for paving things like walkways. The compound was just west of Bagram and doubled as a shady orchard. One minute we were sorting through the bricks as they were being pushed out of their molds, coughing on the cement dust kicked up from the floor; the next, we were walking beneath a tight, narrow, orderly row of heavy fruit trees.

As with many Afghans in the area, families like Omar's had been taught the value of economic diversification by years of instability. Thus, Omar worked with his father to keep their logistics business going, did some construction, and maintained the brick factory both for their own construction projects and occasionally to sell to others. At the same time, however, it was not surprising that the fertile land they had purchased around the factory produced a variety of fruits and in a pinch could be economically productive or at least sold for a good price to a local farmer. Such flexibility and economic diversity was not new around Bagram or unique to the strange hybrid companies that served the intervention. Among the potters I had studied, it was common for the eldest son and perhaps the second son to remain in the pottery workshop with their father. Oftentimes, however, the third and fourth sons might work in agriculture or even move to Kabul to look for a job in the city.[1] Such flexible strategies gave families multiple

Figure 7.1. Brick factory. Photo by Gregory Thielker.

sources of revenue, and, if the price of pots fell, the family had other sources of income to depend on.

Families around Bagram had similarly adaptable political strategies, and it was not uncommon to hear of families during the jihad who had one son who fought with the mujahideen fighters, one son who worked for the communist government, and one son who stayed at home tending to the fields. Such approaches were crucial in times of political instability. Many of these patterns remained the same after the American invasion, with just the sources of power changing. This meant that a family might attempt to establish ties with NATO forces, the insurgents, and the Afghan government simultaneously. With no way of really knowing who might come out on top during the conflict, having a son in each camp meant that regardless of how the conflict evolved the family was likely to have allies in whatever political order followed. Those living in the area dealt with the economic volatility the intervention created in a similar way. Omar's firm, IA, catered to the initial boom in building by the international community around Bagram, and then, as the international organizations in the area needed vehicles to travel in and other supplies, the company moved into procurement, and Omar, as we will see, was always looking for the next market that IA might need to move into if the economy of the intervention veered wildly again.

Despite some of these continuities in terms of the flexibility of economic and political strategies, however, Omar belonged to a new generation of Afghan merchant. Although he had childhood memories of the fighting, Omar came of age during the American invasion. Unlike the formative experiences of the generation ahead of him, who grew up amid more direct and constant conflict, the central theme of his political and economic experience had been growth. And growth, at least statistically, had been extreme; according to the World Bank's estimates, the economy grew by 800 percent between 2000 and 2012.[2] Such numbers, however, were often difficult to put into real terms. Much of the economic spending had been reckless and wasteful. Growth was also far more apparent in Kabul and other urban areas than it was in places outside major cities. Omar, however, still believed that this growth was meaningful and was cautiously optimistic about the future. He also realized that such growth was precarious, and he and other young merchants had learned to be as agile as possible on their economic feet.

Leaving the orchard, we headed north by car, looping around the base, past the former cement factory in Jabal-e Seraj to the north. Looking at the hulking decaying factory, Omar shook his head and lamented the loss of industry in the area. Although Afghanistan never developed much of an industrialized economy, what industries it did develop in the 1960s and 1970s tended to situate themselves in and around Kabul, as well as a few of the other major cities like Kandahar and Mazar-e Sharif. As a result, the Shomali Plain benefited in particular, and in 1967 cement production had peaked at 177,000 tons produced per year.[3] After that production had dipped, halting altogether during the Civil War and the years of fighting that followed.

Still, the factory at Jabel-e Seraj was a beacon of the hope for economic growth in the area, and, during the increase in spending brought on by the surge, there was new interest in reviving the few still operational parts of the factory. In 2009, the factory had received a visit from several American engineers and members of Task Force Warrior to assess what it would take to revive production. A press release from Bagram following the visit pointed out that the team had spent the previous three years working on a similar project in Iraq and claimed that the experts were impressed by "the relatively good working order of the plant and the level of expertise in management" despite the fact that the heavily damaged plant was able to function only one hour a day.[4] Such initial optimism was common in the military, whose can-do approach contrasted strongly with the slow bureaucratic turning of civilian agencies like USAID. Unfortunately, such optimism also often ended up being misplaced. Not long after the initial visit, a U.S. Geological Survey report raised serious concerns about the viability of restoring the plant and pointed out that such restorations would be pointless before an electrical spur line was built to the plant from the main grid.[5]

Under the weight of other failing infrastructure projects, such as the issues with the Kajaki Dam, it quickly became apparent that the cement factory, in what was considered one of the more stable parts of the country, would not receive much international donor funding. As a result, Afghan officials, looking to avoid the economic burdens of such projects, pushed for a more neoliberal model of private investment. Unfortunately, the estimated $23 million it would take to get the factory productive again was daunting to Afghan businessmen like Omar.

Even if he could pull together the necessary capital, the risks would have been enormous. What if the spur line to the main grid was never built? What if the Taliban returned? What if a new Afghan government decided to revoke the privatization? What if local communities did not feel that a new private company was using enough local labor and the police were not strong enough (or interested enough) to halt a violent protest against the privatization? What if things simply become unstable enough that construction projects froze and the demand for cement dropped? Such concerns meant that businessmen like Omar were far more inclined to take on short-term quick turnaround projects that could generate profits with minimal investment in serious infrastructure. Construction was ideal because a company could wait until it had a contract lined up before purchasing the materials, and labor was rarely a problem. Even IA's brick factory was fairly easy to turn on and off based on demand, and if it sat dormant for a few months it would cost little more than the salary of the guard (who was also watching the orchard).

The biggest concern about the concrete plant for most businessmen was the lack of assurances from the international military that they would at least be able to provide security in the region in the coming years. The Obama administration's strategy of first declaring troops would withdraw by 2014 and then extending a limited number of these troops to 2016 created firm deadlines for the departure of troops, which appealed to American voters but made Afghan businessmen nervous. As a result, the Afghan government had begun to look abroad for financing and listed the factory as an investment opportunity at a conference organized by the Confederation of Indian Industry in Delhi, which included investors from India, China, Iran, Kazakhstan, and Turkey.[6] Thus far, however, no one had expressed enough investment interest to revive the plant. Perhaps at some point such foreign investment would drive growth in the Shomali region, but Omar was not optimistic. For those living in the town adjacent to the factory, however, it was a sad and constant reminder of the unevenness of international assistance. It had become a symbol of the inability of the American troops on the plain below to generate real economic growth locally and made people increasingly nostalgic for the times when Afghanistan was peaceful.

As we drove back toward the base, new buildings became more common, and as we passed an abandoned dried fruit processing factory in Charikar, Omar grew more animated. The Shomali was known across the country for its fruits, and the array of fruits the area produced was one of the real pleasures of working in Istalif. My backyard had mulberry trees that tasted best when cooled in the irrigation streams running through the garden, and neighbors had everything from figs and sour cherries to persimmons. Something was almost always in season; in the fall, pomegranates and walnuts ripened and were stored to be eaten during the winter. The bazaars and roadside stands in the area were filled with these goods, all for low prices, and the possibility of moving them to the markets in Pakistan and India was on Omar's mind.

Of course, most of these fruits were fragile and easily damaged when transported on Afghanistan's poor roads. However, dried fruit, easier to ship, had been a growth industry in the 1960s and 1970s. During these years, close to US$20 million of dried fruits and nuts were exported a year, in contrast with less than $10 million a year for fresh fruits. Together these fruits made up a sizable percentage of all of Afghanistan's exports.[7] As a result of this history, forty years later, Omar thought there was the real potential to revitalize the industry. The risks here were also more minimal than with the cement factory—the fruit was already being grown in the area, so drying and exporting it would simply open it up to new markets, where they could find customers willing to pay higher prices. On a deeper level, it appealed to Omar that Afghanistan, currently importing plenty of cheap goods from Pakistan and India, could export something Afghans were genuinely proud of to those markets. Even if he failed, there were still plenty of local consumers who might not pay as much but would ensure that he did not lose too much money.

In the meantime, the roads leading out of the Shomali toward the border with Pakistan had been much improved, and demand for produce in both Pakistan and India was growing. Investment in such a small factory was well within the means of Omar's family, but they had yet to make any real moves in that direction other than his father's purchase of the orchard. The real problem at the moment was time and opportunity cost. With new buildings going up, built both with international money and by Afghans who had made money during the past decade of international involvement, there were many economic opportunities likely to produce higher returns in the short run than a dried fruit factory. So even while Omar dreamed of a fruit processing plant, he hurried back to Kabul to make some phone calls about a construction con-tract he was attempting to secure.[8]

Services and Security

After I had spent several weeks in the Bagram bazaar talking with people and conducting interviews, one of the more perplexing aspects of relations be-tween local communities and those on the base was reconciling the generally high levels of economic growth in the area with the growing resentment from the communities. This is not what counterinsurgency theory would have pre-dicted. Economic growth and better service provision were supposed to win hearts and minds. Although construction had boomed around the base and merchants like Omar had seen their businesses expand, there was, even at the moments during the surge when money was coming in the fastest, a sense of impermanence and a frustration with the lack of sustainable growth com-munities were experiencing. None of the local construction seemed to cause any of those flares of national pride that were clear when Omar discussed the potential for selling Afghan fruits abroad.

Most of the growth and investment by both international donors and local businessmen seemed to have a limited direct impact on the commu-nities around the base. Roads remained in terrible condition; garbage lined many streets in the center of town; unemployment and underemployment remained high, particularly among the youth population; criminal activity was common; and, while the schools and clinics in the area were certainly better than they were under the Taliban, many were still in questionable con-dition. Money was coming into the local communities, but it seemed to slip through the communities' fingers like grains of sand, leaving little lasting impact and ultimately dividing the community as frustrated residents argued over whom to blame. In the past, local leaders seemed to hold the community together. Now they primarily worried about dividing the spoils from the intervention.

Much of the confusion about what the results of the international presence should have been came through in interviews I conducted in the area. There was little agreement over whether it was the Afghan government, the international military, or NGOs that should have been providing services. What was clear was that communities did not feel as if they were getting what they deserved. One of the central complaints that emerged while I was speaking to those around the base was how, despite the constant reminders of the technological and economic might of the American war machine, services to the area had not improved as much as many expected. Furthermore, they simply continued funding and not demanding accountability from corrupt government officials in Kabul who meddled in local affairs but did not provide any real services.

An old adage about rural communities in Afghanistan was that what they wanted from the government was to see as little of it as possible. This presented some problems for counterinsurgency strategists, who were hoping to win the loyalty of communities through service delivery. A decade of intervention had also changed some of these attitudes as communities increasingly demanded services and had opinions about what types of services were being provided.

Around Bagram, expectations were, if anything, higher than in other parts of the country. The government historically had a more active presence in the area than other nonurban areas, and Shomali residents were accustomed to visiting their relatives an hour and a half south in Kabul and seeing the type of services that were being provided in the city. Others had been refugees in Pakistan or Iran and had seen what those governments provided for their citizens. Most of their desires seemed to revolve around security, health, education, and basic infrastructure. Although there were schools in the Bagram area and a hospital attached to the base, much of the development in the area was uneven. This led to disillusionment with the entire international project. As one local official complained just outside the base, "We do not have a well-equipped hospital in Bagram. Ninety-five percent of our roads and streets are not asphalted. Our agriculture and irrigation systems are medieval. There are no well-trained teachers in our schools. Security is not good, and, most important of all, we do not have electricity."

Some of the expectations were, of course, historical, and, as the years passed, the history of the communist period was increasingly idealized. As a result, by 2009 the American presence was constantly being compared to the Soviet presence, generally negatively. "The Russians were here to help us, the U.S. is here only to take our resources," one man stated definitively. Of course, further questioning almost always demonstrated some of the complexities behind what seemed like straightforward opinions, and, when I asked the man why the Russian presence had been so beneficial, he described how they used to steal gas from the base, and he later cursed the Soviets for their atheism.

Not everyone around the airfield blamed the international military for the ineffective nature of the distribution of funds. Many went out of the way to blame the Afghan government and local officials for allowing the corruption that undermined local development projects. Some primarily lamented the naiveté of the international military and how they appeared simply to allow government officials to steal from them. They also blamed the Afghan police for the lack of security. As one businessman complained, "The lack of security is the only problem in Bagram. We cannot run our businesses comfortably. There are robbers everywhere around Bagram, and we cannot travel outside of specific areas. Every day there is another robbery or kidnapping, but the police have done nothing about it so far." Although most of the attacks that followed the American invasion in the area seemed to be roadside bombs targeting international troops, civilians were increasingly targeted as well. Often, those working directly with the base were targeted, and stories of translators being robbed as they left the base were common. Demonstrating the ways in which common criminals and the Taliban both benefited from the presence of the other, the robbers would often then threaten their victims by telling them they would inform the Taliban where they lived if the victims reported the crime. The Afghan police were considered particularly responsible for not reining in this type of banditry.

The greatest frustration, however, that came up in repeated interviews was the way in which the international community was wasting resources. Sometimes this was news of another failed large-scale project. One local government official described how an official from the airfield had given him a nicely published report on the amount of aid that had gone to local communities. When he asked the official's translator to convert the amount in dollars to Afghanis, he said the translator could not because there were not enough digits on the display of his calculator to include all those digits.[9] Where, the official wanted to know, had that money gone? Why had the people not benefited more from it? What had happened to the promises that had followed the invasion?

Other times, however, the waste was smaller and more symbolic. This particularly undermined the reputation of the international community. As one teacher complained, "I believe that the people on the base don't have any humanitarian sentiments. There are hundreds of poor families who live just outside of the base, and yet they are burning their extra materials and food. We asked several times if they would not stop wasting those materials but rather help the poor and needy, but they acted as if they were deaf or emotionless." All of these pieces came together to make the local community feel isolated, unfairly treated, and resentful, emotions that increasingly boiled over in the later years of the decade.

Hire Local

Many of the officials on the base were at least generally aware of criticism from the community, and, particularly as there was an increasing shift toward reaching out to local communities, more of an effort went into improving relations by providing men in the area with jobs.[10] A central part of the reasoning here was not simply that hiring local labor would stimulate the economic growth but that, with local youth able to find steady employment, they would be less likely to join the insurgency. This, of course, also fits into local Afghan practices, and businessmen like Omar went out of their way to hire people from the area. Such hiring worked in two ways: Omar and other businessmen would hire relatives and other close allies to expand their patronage networks, but they would also hire allies of other well-known local commanders to avoid future problems. Having a few relatives of several different local commanders and other leaders was one way to avoid extortion later.

Such a careful arrangement of political alliances was, however, much more challenging for officials on the base who had less knowledge of the local political landscape. What they did have, though, that Omar lacked, was access to large amounts of funds. Simply hiring a large number of local young men to work on the base, however, was more difficult than it might have appeared at first. The contracting model that dominated how the military was doing business meant that most of the laborers on the base were not hired by NATO or the American military, but by contractors. This was often a hassle for these contractors who were based in Kabul and had little incentive to pay higher wages to local workers. These contractors were worried about their construction projects, not about base relations and security, so they would turn toward local labor only when pressured by the military or when it was directly stipulated in their contracts.

Another of the key challenges in actually trying to get money into the local economy was the layers funds had to go through before the funds got close to the ground level. The military contracts for large projects on the base went almost exclusively to large international contractors. These companies were usually American, though they would often subcontract to other international firms, and around Bagram several of these firms were Turkish. These firms would then often subcontract again to Afghan firms, and sometimes large Afghan firms would contract once more to smaller firms. So the money passed from the military to international contractors to local contractors headed by Afghans with contacts on the base, who often spoke English and were Westernized, and then, finally, to the local laborer. At each step, of course, contractors took a cut, and the pot of money grew smaller, with little left when it reached the local laborer. On occasion, a local commander or elder would be in charge of the hiring, taking a further share away from the laborers.

Omar was a typical subcontractor, who had never received money directly from the base but had done some building for larger Afghan companies one step up the contracting chain. He was, however, always striving to climb the contracting ladder where it would be possible to gain a larger cut of the contract. As work on the base expanded, the bureaucracy around contracting increased, making this even more complicated and difficult for officials on the base to track and caused Omar to hope that he might gain a point of entry into these lucrative practices.

For the most part, however, those living near the base were disappointed. The growing complexity of the process meant that locals perceived hiring as uneven and aiding only certain groups. As the owner of a tea shop in the bazaar said, "The base used to give priority to those who live in the area, but now you need to know a broker inside the base to get hired. Now you will see a job announcement for 100 vacancies, but when those positions are actually filled it turns out to be people from all over the country and not Bagram."

As one local teacher described the changing process, "Recently the employment process has become very complicated on the base; there is now even more bribery and corruption in the system." As the base attempted to institute new hiring practices, more paperwork was required and more accounting mechanisms, making the process even less transparent externally. One of the ironies here was that, while the military spent a large amount of political and economic capital setting up committees to stamp out corruption, the way in which money was ultimately distributed around Bagram led most Afghans to conclude it was actually various internationals who were responsible for most of this corruption. Ironically, smaller CERP projects that were later criticized for being unaccountable (perhaps rightly so) were at times perceived as more transparent by the communities because they tended to directly address a need, such as building a bridge, that the community had requested through an elder or group of elders. In such cases, there was more transparency simply because the money was going through far fewer layers before it was being spent, and the community could actually see the bridge being built and where the funds had gone.

As those outside the base watched certain groups continue to benefit from the intervention more than others, narratives about big companies simultaneously colluding and taking advantage of the neoliberal business model of the military began to circulate. As one man complained: "They have their own specific contractors for the big projects. They usually make these contracts with them without discussing them with people from outside [the base]. We know that the U.S is a capitalist government; they like to be in contact primarily with capitalists and make their contracts with them. There are only a couple of rich businessmen from Bagram who get the contracts from the base; apart from that, most of their contractors are foreign companies." International reports about American citizen concerns about big businesses after the 2008 financial crisis also circulated in local communities and were popular topics in the local media. This only further fueled these narratives and conspiracy theories about how funds were being distributed. We will see, however, that these stories became only more damning as laborers came out of the base complaining about conditions inside, eventually making some of the criticisms of ineffective spending secondary.

The schoolteacher continued describing the strange economic setup: "At least someone in each family works inside the base, and that has a direct effect on our economics . . . The bazaar has really developed since the international forces inhabited the base. Of course this benefit is for those who are employed there. I am a teacher and a farmer; personally I have not gained anything from having the base here." A district official complained about the lack of transparency in the various development projects in the area: "In general, they do not keep their promises. For instance, last month they promised that they would help our farmers financially, but after all these talks all they gave them was a pen and a notebook. This was their financial assistance!"

But if international officials on the base, many of whom were desperate to hire as equitably as possible from communities around the base, were not ultimately in control of hiring practices, then who was?

8 The Merchant–Warlord Alternative

IN JOB PROVISION PROGRAMS and other development projects created by both the base and the NGOs in the area, oftentimes the most important factor was not about how many laborers were being hired or how much was being spent on development but who was choosing the laborers and deciding what projects would be implemented where. As with the contracting model, neither the donor nor the intended recipients seemed to gain the most; it was the contractor in the middle who was best positioned. Around Bagram, the local leaders were also perceived as liaisons who gained much from the presence of the base, and these individuals gained status as rumors circulated about their ability to provide jobs and direct funds. The simple existence of rumors about these practices empowered these intermediaries and gave rise to a new generation of leaders. These younger merchants did not represent a purely new form of leadership, and they often used local traditions like deference to their elders to help them build allies, but they were simultaneously dynamic figures who took advantage of both the historical cultural tendencies of the area and the new influx of donor funds.

One of the most intriguing of these figures was Haji Zia.

A Young Businessman

When I first asked Omar about Haji Zia, he laughed, shifting in his seat. "Why do you want to know about him?" he responded slightly uncomfortably.

Questions about Haji Zia tended to elicit this type of response, and it was sometimes difficult to distinguish history from legend when people did start discussing him. For many young Afghan men, his story was something of a dream, and perhaps unsurprisingly it tended to get embellished. I spent numerous lunches with some of my younger Afghan friends listening to them speculate about Haji Zia's net worth, describing his latest business venture or foray into the media and wondering whether he was thinking about entering politics. Because these tales only enhanced his status in the eyes of many, there was also very little reason for him to attempt to clarify or set the record straight. Particularly after several unflattering pieces in the international press and legal troubles with the Americans, he became more hesitant to speak with the press, which in some ways encouraged more of these tales to swirl around him. By 2013 Haji Zia was half-man, half-myth for many of the young men in the communities around the base, which ultimately did even more to increase his shadowy influence on local business and politics.

The legend of Haji Zia went something like this: Zia came from a powerful family with an uncle who was an important military commander in the north during the Civil War and Taliban periods. His uncle rose very high in the National Directorate of Security (NDS), Afghanistan's intelligence agency, in the years following the U.S. invasion. He later became a regional police commander, still an important position but a more provincial one, probably, many speculated, because Karzai was concerned about him gaining too much power in Kabul. Zia's uncle, now a prominent national figure, had built a large mosque in his natal village, adjacent to Bagram, that stood directly across from one of the side entrances to the base. Larger than most buildings outside the walls, it simultaneously seemed to challenge the base's stature and was also a clear declaration to the community around him about the strength of his connections with those inside the walls. The mosque demonstrated his influence because the military perceived such looming structures so close to the base as threats, and at the time the military was still attempting to tear down most of the large buildings around the base that could serve as strategic positions for attackers.[1] For the most part, however, the aging uncle had become more concerned with national politics and left local issues to others, coming only occasionally to visit the area around Bagram.

Zia himself came from a poorer branch of the influential family and as a young man did not have much of a reputation at the time of the American invasion. It was said that he started as a taxi driver around Bagram. And, according to some of the more elaborate accounts, he had to borrow money just to buy his first taxi.

Here the story on occasion becomes more fanciful, with different exaggerations depending on the speaker. Some accounts describe how, while driving in the area, he befriended a translator on the base, and, about this time, with the base expanding, a small contract for razor wire came up for bid. The translator apparently had insider information about the bidding process but because he worked on the base could not bid himself. So he and Zia formed an informal partnership. Using the translator's knowledge and Zia's independent status, they were able to win the contract. They fulfilled the order and split the proceeds. Now, however, having delivered on the contract and with new contacts in the base, Zia decided to leave the translator behind and go out on his own.

Although the razor wire contract was small, there was at this point a set of more established Afghan contractors who were mostly splitting the large contracts from the base among themselves. However, when another, much larger construction contract came up for bid, Zia, using his uncle as backing, threatened the other contractors at the last minute, forcing them to submit high bids. It was not clear whether Zia's uncle was directly involved in this threat or whether Zia simply relied on his powerful name, but either way the tactic was successful and Zia secured himself his first large construction contract.

One of the other contractors was particularly outraged, complaining loudly in the community, but with Zia's contacts there was little that he could do, and he decided to let this one contract go. However, Zia's entrepreneurial mind was bent on rapid expansion, and he did a masterful job establishing relations with officials on the base. Early in the intervention, particularly, these officials had little knowledge of local politics outside the base. To them, Zia was an affable, enthusiastic young businessman who tended to deliver on his contracts on time. He was the same age as many of the men on the base, seemed more understanding of Western culture, and was a welcomed change from some of the older commanders, who were the main contractors. Young men in the community discussed how these older commanders might have been militarily powerful and not good men to cross, but they were not necessarily skilled at business. In this new world where there were cultural misunderstandings and goods were often not delivered in as timely a manner as officials on the base would have liked, Zia was a man, they thought, with whom they could do business. Initially, it seems, international officials had little knowledge of the collusion or other scams surrounding many of the contracts; as a result, for Zia, one contract led to another.

Soon, Zia's newly established empire was paving the runway and providing fuel to the base. He increasingly used his various family connections and his growing business network to keep the contracts flowing. In one instance, it is said that a Pakistani businessman who was less concerned about the danger Zia's uncle posed threatened to undercut him until several of his fuel trucks were mysteriously blown up. Even this, however, seemed like an opportunity to make a profit.

The companies supplying fuel to bases across the country were particularly notorious for the various opportunities for scams they presented. Contracts were lucrative, with Zia, along with other contactors, able to charge a significant markup by emphasizing the risk to fuel shipments. Another young man, describing the cunning of fuel contractors to me, explained how all large contracts from the base required the contractor have insurance. This was not common for an Afghan business to have at the time. This man suggested that when savvy businessmen learned about this, instead of complaining as many other contractors did, they used it to their advantage. One approach was to take the occasional truck and empty it before it reached the base and then blow it up. This allowed the owner to make money by selling the emptied fuel to those in the community and then make an additional cut by collecting the insurance money. Taking this one step further, when it was time to renew the contract, they could also argue that their shipments were under constant attack, allowing them to charge more for security. The general attitude was that demand was so high, the shipments simply had to continue, even if some were lost along the way. Despite rumors of corruption, for several years Zia was still happy to discuss aspects of his business with the international media, lamenting the loss of oil tankers in particular in a 2008 *Wall Street Journal* article following an attack on a supply convoy.[2]

Despite the fact that the details of these scams could rarely be confirmed, other merchants around the base believed them to be true, and the fact that Zia was eventually blacklisted by the base suggests that the military also eventually found the accusations credible. This occurred at a time when there was increasing concern about logistics companies actually in collusion with Taliban commanders, either paying them to provide safe passage through insurgent areas or, in some cases, paying them to attack on certain days so the contractors could then claim damages.[3] In the meantime, however, the amount of fuel demanded by the international military was so great that these attacks, although annoying, did not really cut into the long line of tankers queued up outside Bagram, waiting to be inspected.

Of course, in the unstable years around 2005 and 2006 in particular, with the insurgency gaining momentum and roadside bombs and other explosions becoming increasingly common occurrences, it was sometimes difficult to tell fact from fiction and discern who exactly was responsible for such explosions. Perhaps the fuel tankers were blown up by the Taliban, perhaps they were blown up by supporters of Zia as a favor, and perhaps Zia worked with the Taliban indirectly to make sure they were blown up. But, really, it did not matter much to those living around the base. Either way, it became clear that Zia was making vast sums through contracts from the base and was not a man to be trifled with. And for some of those young men outside the base, he was actually a figure to be emulated.

A Man on the Inside

Zia might have been able to manipulate some of the officials' lack of sophistication about the political and economic world outside the base, but he could not have made all these deals and complicated arrangements work without some support from someone inside the base. Particularly as the money began to flow into the country, U.S. auditors tried to keep up with the variety of scams and collusion that involved American soldiers and contractors who oversaw much of the contacting on the various bases. As they were going through the paperwork of the Special Inspector General for Afghanistan reconstruction and various Justice Department records and speaking with those who worked on the base, a picture emerged of a shadowy world of payments, forged documents, and dreams of boxes of cash that rarely worked out. In these accounts and documents, it became almost as difficult to determine the difference between fact and fiction as it was in the stories the communities outside the base told about Haji Zia.

Layers of bureaucracy were often intended to eliminate corruption, but the number of civilians, contactors, and military officials from different countries, all working on different projects using different management systems simultaneously, meant that figures like Zia could often find individuals who were willing to bend the rules or exploit certain loopholes in exchange for some sort of payment. In many cases, however, it was only those who made the most obvious mistakes who were caught. Rarely were those behind the schemes ever prosecuted.

In May 2011, for example, a military contractor and former member of the National Guard who had also served in Iraq was caught trying to ship $150,000 in cash to his ex-wife in a DHL box from Bagram. He was working at the time for a company that was actually a joint venture of two other large contractors that held multimillion-dollar contracts for "vehicle and equipment maintenance, facilities and supply management, transportation and other services in Afghanistan."[4] The Department of Justice claimed that he had arranged to receive $400,000 in kickbacks in exchange for favoring an Afghan subcontractor for the lease of heavy equipment, similar to the types of services that Omar's company provided. In this case, the Afghan firm was subcontracting from his firm, which was actually subcontracting from two much larger firms, complicating that matter.[5] Reflecting some of the difficulties of both stopping and prosecuting such corrupt arrangements, similar to Al Capone eventually being booked for tax evasion, the contractor was not actually charged with any crime related to his actions around accepting kickbacks or collusion on contracts but was convicted only of money laundering. It was the shipment of the money he was ultimately prosecuted for, not the manipulation of contracts. In his defense, the contractor claimed that the money was actually won while gambling on the airbase, but ultimately the court found this unconvincing, sentencing him to thirty months in prison and a $52,000 fine in addition to the forfeiture of the funds.[6]

In addition to collusion in bidding for contracts, when I interviewed individuals around Bagram, they were much more interested in discussing the series of smaller ongoing fuel scams that took place on the base and often claimed that one of the benefits of living near Bagram was that fuel prices were lower in the district than elsewhere in the country.[7] A common scheme was for Afghan truck drivers to empty or, more often, partially empty their trucks before entering the base. A prearranged employee on the base would then receive a cash payment to sign that the truck was full before it was emptied into a larger storage tank. After that, it became impossible to tell where the missing fuel had gone, whether it had been stolen from the storage tank or whether it had simply leaked out. The siphoned fuel would then enter the local market, driving down prices.

Figuring out the amounts stolen in such a manner was difficult because only the instances that were caught and reported came to light. However, over the course of just a few months in 2006, three civilian employees of a large-scale contractor on the base (with over $5 billion in total contracts) were reported to have falsified reception receipts of fuel from a secondary contractor, whose drivers had underdelivered on shipments. Prosecutors found evidence of falsification in forty-eight shipments of fuel worth $800,000 over these months.[8] By 2009, the three contractors, reaching different plea arrangements, were convicted of or pled guilty to charges of conspiracy and bribery. In this instance, again, prosecutors had been able to prosecute only those working on the base, lower on the chain of command, as opposed to arresting those who designed and profited most from the scheme.[9]

In response to some of these cases, the military designed more rigorous controls on fuel use and the reportage of use, aimed at detecting if and when fuel supplies had been illicitly depleted. In some instances, soldiers tried to work around these controls, and two sergeants running a similar scheme falsified deliveries by claiming the fuel levels were depleted due to increased consumption during colder weather. The men, who were receiving some $2,000 a day to let trucks leave the base with fuel bound for the black market, shipped the cash home in tough plastic boxes.[10] In general, however, the increased scrutiny and awareness of various forms of monitoring seem not to have stopped involvement of contractors in fraud but made it more complex. Several years later, in 2012, for example, another contractor at Bagram was convicted for her role in falsifying documents that reported the movement of various vehicles. In exchange for payments of $50,000, she allowed employees of an Afghan company that was subcontracting to the U.S. Army on a separate contract to bill for mileage they had not traveled.[11] In this case fuel was being paid for but not used. Such complex schemes now required collusion between workers on different contracts, not just an overseeing contractor falsifying documents. The woman, who pled guilty to one charge of bribery, also did not appear to be very high up in the scheme, and there were no further charges reported.

Publicity surrounding these cases led the U.S. government to take an increasingly active roll in trying to catch such deals as they were happening, as opposed to relying simply on audits. Hearing of a potential fuel scheme at a base farther south in Ghazni, SIGAR (the Special Inspector General for Afghanistan reconstruction) initiated a sting operation aimed at catching the drivers in the act. In this case, two drivers paid a coalition soldier to essentially leave 500 gallons of fuel in the trucks that they then drove off the base, so they could leave with "empty" trucks, selling the excess in the bazaar. In exchange for this, the soldier was paid $500. Afghan prosecutors brought in by SIGAR, however, were waiting and monitoring the transaction, immediately arresting the Afghan drivers after they left the base.[12] More than anything else, however, the brazen acts of the drivers and the relatively low amount of money involved in the transaction simply suggest how common such practices were.

Sometimes these scams involved working more directly with local Afghans and Afghan businesses. In one case, two employees of PAE, a subsidiary of Lockheed-Martin, worked with an Afghan associate to set up a fake Afghan uniform company. One of the men, who was in charge of purchasing on a contract training Afghan corrections officers, would submit purchase orders for twice as many uniforms as were actually needed. The Afghan associate would then purchase half the order number from a different, legitimate uniform supplier. The second American, who was on the training end of the project, would then sign for receipt of the original number of uniforms requested, and the three would then divide up the 50 percent profit they made. The Department of Justice claims they made between $120,000 and $200,000 in this manner.[13]

Overall, while the U.S. government has successfully prosecuted some of the Americans involved in a variety of scandals, they have had markedly more difficulty in prosecuting the Afghans involved. On occasion, those lower down, like the drivers caught with the stolen fuel in the SIGAR sting, were arrested, but particularly those involved higher up seem to have rarely been prosecuted, particularly if the scale of the fraud reported by those around the Bagram bazaar is to be believed. Such operations were costly, involving both U.S. and Afghan officials, and it seemed like an inefficient use of funds when you consider the fact that the bribe in the instance above involved was only $500. In the case of the uniform scam, it seems that the American contractors were eventually cheated out of $70,000 by their Afghan business partner. "I hope he's just late getting back from Pakistan But I think we got took," one said in an instant message to the other.[14] Certainly figures like Haji Zia complained about how increased scrutiny slowed their business ventures down, but they certainly did not seem very concerned about prosecution by American officials.

One issue, of course, was jurisdiction. Detaining an Afghan in Afghanistan would mean involving the notoriously corrupt Afghan justice system. In many cases those involved could walk after paying a bribe. This would have been particularly true of someone well connected, like Haji Zia. American officials had already been infuriated on several occasions when President

Karzai released several well-known figures who, with significant involvement of international officials, had been convicted of trafficking narcotics.[15] In other situations there were issues with evidence gathered by American investigators being accepted in Afghan courts.[16] In some rather extreme instances, to combat the corruption of the Afghan legal system, American investigators actually lured Afghan contractors to the United States to prosecute them or have them serve as witnesses in cases against American contractors.

In perhaps the most sensational case to receive international attention, three Afghan contractors from the Bagram area were lured to the United States with the promise that they were attending an all-expenses-paid trip to a conference on business in Afghanistan. Once arriving in Chicago, however, they were immediately detained.[17] The men were held in the United States and used as witnesses in a case against American contractors and soldiers who had accepted bribes while working at Bagram. In what became a rather embarrassing case for the American government, not only were the three men put up in a hotel for fourteen months waiting for the trial to get underway, but one of them was just a driver, who had no access to information about the company's wire transfers, one of the key elements in the case. Bagramis debated over whether this was a case of mistaken identity; many Afghans have just one name, they pointed out, and this was endlessly confusing to the Americans on the base. Others thought he was sent at the last minute in the place of someone higher up because his bosses had been tipped off. During questioning by the defense, prosecutors acknowledged that the driver had incurred between $60,000 and $70,000 in witness fees and housing costs over the fourteen months, even though he had not actually provided any useful testimony for the case.[18]

Although these events occurred thousands of miles away, it was interesting to see how the stories about these trials circulated and returned back to the communities around Bagram. In another case I was told about an Afghan businessman who had been lured to the United States to testify (it was never clear to me if he was one of the ones brought to Chicago, but the way the story was told led me to think that he was not). According to the story, this businessman served some time in an American prison for his roll in a kickback scheme. However, while in prison, he had his court-appointed lawyer help him apply for political asylum. His argument was that because he had assisted the United States and had in his testimony referred to other Afghan contractors who had the backing of dangerous commanders, he would be killed on returning home. According to the man telling the story, because the case occurred in an American court, the businessman's assets in Afghanistan were not frozen. As a result, he was able to have his family sell off his businesses while he was in prison, and on release he was granted a green card. The man telling me the story (the man in prison was his friend's uncle) assured me that the man was doing quite well and had bought a car dealership in California with the assets he had raised from selling his businesses around Bagram. He had brought his wife and children over to the United States as well and was living comfortably.

Unsurprisingly, in the eyes of many around Bagram, some of these attempts to clean up corruption failed to have their desired effect of making the finances of development and contracting around the airfield any less corrupt or more transparent. For example, after cutting out several of the local Afghan companies due to corruption, one local Afghan government official complained that this had simply led to more foreigners getting rich off the presence of the international troops: "In the first years they used to give some projects to the companies from Bagram, but now they are giving them only to foreign companies. For example, there is a street construction project going on in the bazaar right now that is being done by an Indian company." As the Afghan official continued to explain, "I am sure that most of that money has returned back to donor countries in different ways [particularly through private contractors]. Otherwise, if that money had actually been used in Afghanistan, our country would have progressed ten times as far by now."

Bagramis followed these stories in a variety of ways, reading news articles in the Afghan and international press, discussing the rumors they heard in the bazaar, and sharing stories of relatives who had been part of certain schemes. Ultimately, it was difficult to determine what had actually happened in many of these cases, but for many Bagramis the truth was secondary. The impressions and distrust that such stories created were the important residual aspects of these events. Ultimately the perception of corruption and the lack of transparency in business practices involving the base did much to damage the credibility of the coalition forces, exacerbating later violence.

From Contracting to Business as Usual

Eventually, several young men living just outside the base said, it was some of the simpler scams that got Zia in the most trouble on the base; the rumor was that one of his employees became too greedy when paying off contractors inside the base for fuel, which led them to tip off officials higher up. Despite this setback, the increased scrutiny that Afghan companies working on the base were under meant that it was likely Zia had been actively preparing for this eventuality and had set up businesses off the base as an extension of his work on the base. By the time Haji Zia was blacklisted from military contracts, it was, in many ways, too late. He already had established contacts both in the government and in such a wide variety of businesses both inside the country and abroad, particularly the United Arab Emirates, that it was almost impossible to do business around the base, legitimate or otherwise, without at least involving Zia or one of his subsidiaries or allies. Zia's chief business interest remained a transport and logistics company. The company was listed as Zia Ahmad (Mohammadi) Co. Ltd. but was also sometimes referred to in official documents as the Afghan International Transport and Logistics and was referred to by most in the area as simply "Haji Zia's company," demonstrating some of the issues with determining exactly where Zia's businesses began and ended, particularly because he also owned parts or all of numerous other businesses associated with construction, paving, and transportation.

In looking at the political and economic landscape around the base, Zia was clearly an emerging force to be reckoned with and a figure that young men like Omar viewed with a mixture of awe, fear, and envy. Zia was also the type of leader that military officers, like Owen, were trying to reach out to, both in their attempts to encourage business growth and because he offered an alternative to the insurgency. Oftentimes, however, the military looked first to the local elders and commanders who had been influential in previous decades. But Zia had not followed in the path of many of the earlier warlords and commanders who had been so influential in the country since the Soviet invasion.

Leadership in Afghanistan has historically been divided between the territory controlled by the national government and those areas left to the "unruly" tribes, sometimes referred to as Yagistan.[19] In these areas, local tribal leaders held sway. Unlike some conceptions of the noble savage, however, these leadership types did not represent an ancient, unchanging ideal. Instead, leadership and authority are dynamic concepts.

For example, in the case of Uzbeks in the north of Afghanistan, local khans have built their reputation based on their ability to command resources and exercise their influence among their followers. Historically, one of the places where this has taken place both metaphorically and in concrete form was during *toois* or circumcision and marriage festivals used as an excuse to hold the buzkashi matches studied by Whitney Azoy.[20] At these celebrations, men would gather to play and watch this game that involved horsemen competing to carry off a goat carcass, but, at the same time, the gathering also allowed them to demonstrate and reaffirm their political alliances. As Azoy argues, in the 1960s and 1970s khans demonstrated their strength and authority in part by owning horses and riders who won on the buzkashi field. On another level, however, real influence was demonstrated by the ability to host a large buzkashi match that was attended by a large number of followers. Conversely, holding a buzkashi match that was poorly attended was then a great mark of shame.

The politics of the game transformed, however, as leadership and the sources of authority changed during the jihad against the communist government. Forced into exile in Pakistan, khans had access to different resources that reshaped how buzkashi matches were held. Money and weapons from the Americans and Saudis, distributed by the Pakistanis, allowed leaders to reaffirm their positions while ignoring some of the rituals, such as feasting and visiting, that historically had reaffirmed alliances. Removed from the original context, buzkashi was still a venue to demonstrate authority, but the audience was different, as was the game itself. For example, one khan that Azoy refers to as Aid Khan hosted a buzkashi that he invited diplomats and relief workers living in Peshawar to, aimed at securing funds and prestige from the international community.[21] Now these displays of influence were used to gain international resources, rather than local reputation. They were no longer performed for the Uzbek spectators but for the few international dignitaries. As a result, there was less emphasis on the actual game itself, and the play deteriorated. Khans were left to make their mark by demonstrating their links to international funders and diplomats instead of on the buzkashi field.

Following these precedents, Zia represented a continuation of the ways in which leadership forms had been shifting over the past generation.[22] Particularly since 2001, for many commanders around Bagram, the locus of power had moved from the informal, kin, and tribal-based militias to the private companies, and Zia took advantage of this shift. In the community, Zia did more than just set up businesses, and he used his newfound wealth to establish a series of charitable foundations with a center in town that performed a range of activities such as distributing food to the poor on holidays (an activity often fulfilled by more traditional and older members of the community).

In addition, the foundation had built mosques in the area, and a new hospital bore Zia's family name.

Though the methods he used for achieving fame, such as honoring traditional Afghan values like feeding the poor, were not novel around Bagram, Zia represented a new generation of Afghan leaders. Many earlier anthropological studies of Afghanistan emphasized the different forms of leadership in rural Afghan villages. In the town where I had originally done my research, there was generally a clear divide between the *malik*[23] or khan, who were the traditional tribe elders; the mullah, who was the religious leader; and the state official, who had government power. These divides in leadership types were historically common in other parts of Afghanistan as well.[24] But, not really being a commander or a malik, Zia was a new hybrid of businessman-contractor-commander-elder figure that made him difficult to categorize but also allowed him to move through a greater number of political venues fluidly, profiting from all of them simultaneously.

This hybrid leadership did not necessarily sit well with everyone around the base. For example, when I asked about Zia in several of my interviews, individuals began with, "Initially, he was only a translator." This statement, however, meant different things depending on who was saying it. For young men in the area, this demonstrated that Zia had used his wits and connections to advance. It demonstrated for them the potential rewards of hard work and slick dealings in this quasi-neoliberal economic dystopia. For many in the previous generation, however, this statement reminded people of his humble origins, suggesting that Zia had risen above his place in society and that he had climbed too far and too fast. For them, his wealth and fame demonstrated how Afghanistan had lost touch with its traditions and culture.

Aware of this, Zia attempted to appeal to the older and more conservative in the community by establishing his religious credentials as well as his economic wealth. Amid all this expansion of his business interests, Zia found time to perform the hajj, the pilgrimage to Mecca. This is how he had become known as Haji Zia, instead of simply Zia (again, a practice more commonly found among older Afghans). This careful cultivation of his business interests and charities meant that Zia not only became well known around Kabul but also earned a reputation for himself in Herat, Mazar, and other major Afghan cities, particularly among other young businessmen.

Zia had also begun to intermingle much of his business interests with the politics of a new, more "democratic" government. The democratization process in Afghanistan and, especially, the rounds of elections since 2004 have created new opportunities for the political elite like Zia to consolidate their power.[25] Several key local leaders used provincial council elections in 2005 and 2009 and parliamentary elections in 2005 and 2010 to legitimize their importance through legal means and to expand their power. Parliamentary positions in particular provided local leaders with access to government resources in Kabul and contacts with international donors. This was the case for several former commanders such as Anwar Khan, from south of the base in Qara Bagh, and Haji Almas from the west of the base. Both men retained their reputations as commanders but also worked to bring international development projects to their areas.[26] Even simply having close connections with men such as these facilitated a wide array of opportunities for local residents, whether it was finding employment or using their connections in the government to secure a contract. As the intervention wore on, Anwar Khan and Haji Almas became known for having connections to a variety of resources as well as still possessing reputations as mujahideen fighters, and it became increasing difficult to do business in the area without working with them.[27]

Perhaps realizing that he would be considered too young or perhaps simply feeling that he did not want to commit the time necessary, Zia did not run for office in the initial elections following the American-led invasion. Instead, he encouraged his father to run for parliament in 2010. Using his family's financial success, his father's campaign leveraged many of the charities his son supported. His website noted the seventy mosques his family built in the Bagram area, as well as the hospital bearing the family name. This gave Zia close personal access to all of the privileges that came with the office but less of the scrutiny and fewer demands on his time. At the same time, many in the bazaar spoke of the son and father almost as a team (it was often said that "they decided" to run), which furthered the perception that Zia's father was something of a proxy for Zia's wider business empire.

Several people I spoke with near the base and in Kabul claimed that Zia was preparing to run for office himself when the time was right. He had already joined one of Afghanistan's more powerful business associations, and it was clear that his business connections would come in handy in the corrupt world of campaigns in Afghanistan where one needed vast sums of money both to mobilize voters but also to potentially purchase votes illicitly. With the economic opportunities brought on by the base, commanders were running for political office; young merchants like Zia were having an increased influence on local politics; and tensions were running high over the vast but limited resources available. All this meant that serious political shifts were taking place in the communities around the base.

Dream Big

In many ways, Zia's case is extreme: It is a rags-to-riches story of the coming of age of a businessman-politician-commander-contractor who triumphed over the haughty but simple-minded Americans on the base and, in fact, beat them at their own game. Zia, however, was far from the only young figure taking advantage of the variety of resources brought in by the intervention. On a higher political level, for example, Abdul Razziq, who was approximately the same age as Zia, had started as a local police chief at the border crossing at Spin Boldak. Gaining a reputation for brutal efficiency and loyalty to the communities he policed, Razziq used his renown to cultivate connections with the NATO forces in the province. Soon he gained so much fame in the international community that *The New York Times* and *The Atlantic* were writing articles suggesting that he might be the best way to stabilize southern Afghanistan. With this international backing he was quickly promoted to the position of police commander for the entire province of Kandahar, one of the most important positions in the ANP, and there were rumors spreading of his larger political aspirations.[28]

Although these tales of power, corruption, and fortunes being made using connections to the international military and involving huge sums of money circulated regularly among young men who lived in Bagram and farther afield, local residents were quick to point out that relatively few members of the local community actually benefited from these rapid ascents. Most aspiring young merchants who lived in the area were much more like Omar; they had never received a contract directly from the base and had benefited only by subcontracting construction projects from other larger subcontractors.

But, still, figures like Omar strove to emulate this new hybrid model of leadership that combined entrepreneurial business growth blending new and old interests with connections to the Afghan state and the threat of violence. Even this process on a lower level, however, was fraught with danger and political intrigue as these merchants attempted to navigate the new world of contracting and subcontracting, filled with the perils of corrupt officials and older violent commanders. In particular, when discussing local commanders and their roles in the area with me, Omar always spoke carefully. He almost always tried to gauge what I knew about these figures from other sources before revealing his own thoughts on them. Although he might not have relied on their protection, unwanted attention from any of them could seriously derail his business interests. Still, he tried to distinguish himself from the other warlord-turned-businessmen in the area who relied more directly on violence. He, like several others I spoke with from the area, pointed out that, despite being their home territory, the area was not safe for some of these more prominent commanders who now need to travel accompanied by numerous bodyguards. These commanders still owned land and exerted influence in the area, but, afraid of assassination, they mostly remained in their heavily guarded compounds in Kabul, ruling from afar and relying on allies to flex their political muscle in the area. In comparison, Omar noted after we met his father one morning, standing, chatting with several other men, on the street outside of his Kabul office, "Look at my father, he does not need guards," to contrast him with the commanders who could move through the area only in large convoys of bodyguards.

Yet even a good reputation in the community and among key commanders in the area did not protect Omar from every type of hazard in this unregulated world of merchants, contractors, and commanders. In some instances, it was the internationals who were the most untrustworthy because they did not need to eventually return to these communities, as Afghan merchants and commanders did who still had families in the area. Omar himself had been cheated while subcontracting from a firm run by an American. Omar had been given a small down payment, but halfway through the project the contractor took all the remaining funds and fled to Dubai. Omar was left having already completed much of the construction on the project, but he did not receive the rest of the payment that he was owed. Over a year after the fact, he was still bothered by the affair but did not feel he had any real means of recourse.

In more casual conversations with Omar it was clear that even while helping run the family business, under other circumstances, he would have preferred not to be a businessman. He could not help but to occasionally begin talking about his love of poetry. After returning from studying abroad he was one of the key organizers of Afghanistan's branch of the International Studies Union, which connected students from a variety of universities around Kabul to other universities abroad. Referring to the group's Facebook page, he suggested new ways for people of his generation to organize in the coming years, and he hoped that this would be a venue where Afghan literature and culture could grow. Civil society and student groups had grown, particularly in large urban areas. Even in Bagram and the districts to the south, I found soccer clubs, cultural magazines, and study groups all run by young people while investigating the ways in which youth were potentially mobilizing in the run-up to the 2014 elections.[29] Despite this, the economic opportunities present at the time still led many of these young men away from what they might have done otherwise: Who could resist the giant contracts, new SUVs, and free trips to conferences in America?

What the cases of Omar and Zia represent was how, as certain historical modes of authority were breaking down, a certain flexibility and hybridity were needed to navigate the complex realities created by the international intervention in Afghanistan. Although some, like Zia in particular, had learned to thrive in this unstable political and economic world, others, like Omar, were more slowly coming to terms with it. For many of the more ordinary citizens in the Bagram area, we will see, there was little to be gained from this opaque mixture of new and old politics.

9 Warlord Density and Its Discontents

Only those who work inside the base can get in, and the foreigners inside are not allowed to leave, so that we never actually see each other . . . The base and our area are like two different cities, separated by concrete walls.

—Bagrami elder

THE UNEVEN SPREADING OF DEVELOPMENT MONEY around the base gave rise to new figures, like Omar and Zia, while older figures were forced to adapt to the changing political economy of the area. Ultimately these shifts changed both how local politics were organized and also more generally how communities interacted with the base and viewed the international intervention. With the counterinsurgency model in full effect, soldiers like Owen were increasingly being pressured to work on the relations between the base and the communities around it as well as the various pieces of the international community and with the Afghan government that made up the intervention. In Kabul the talk was of "civ-mil" ventures, donor coordination, and synergy. On the ground, however, such cooperation was not as smooth as it might appear on a PowerPoint. Although Special Forces soldiers had originally been relied on to kick down doors and catch terrorists, now they were told they had to build relationships.

Owen reflected back on some of the challenges of trying to make this shift:

I had one commanding officer who used to say this: "Be the lion, because the most feared animal in the jungle is the lion, and guess how many friends the lion has? He's friends with everyone, because he's the most powerful animal in the jungle." It's an interesting thought that if you want to be the lion, you have to be friends with the ants. And they'll love you, and they'll respect you for it. My mission was always to show absolute respect. I trust my guys to be friends with the other soldiers and told them, "Let them shoot your M-4 [most army soldiers would have had less sophisticated M-16s], and don't be the asshole in the gym." They'll respect you so much more if you take the time to be friends with them. Just be a good dude.

Just being a good dude, however, was increasingly not enough in the complicating world of Afghan politics outside the base.

Warlord Density

As Omar talked about his business plans for the future, it was interesting how often a wide array of other political actors were mentioned—not just figures like Haji Zia but also local parliamentarians like Haji Almas and former commanders like Zia's uncle. The area was thick with political actors who all had some sort of interests in the area, not to mention weapons.[1]

One of the things that jumped out at me when I was spending time around the base, when compared with other parts of the country where I had done research, was the large number of different groups that moved around armed. Guns were not rare in Afghanistan, but they were certainly more visible in the area outside the base. Police checkpoints dotted the landscape, and people were frequently removed from their cars and frisked. Other men in local, informal militias moved about freely, the police waving them quickly through checkpoints. At one of these stops, while my vehicle was being searched, masked men careened by in green pickups, standing in the back of the truck and swinging from the handles of mounted machine guns. Their vehicles looked like Afghan National Army vehicles but without any of the usual formal markings, and there were few clues as to whether they were a part of the National Directorate of Security, Afghanistan's secret police, or whether they were members of a local militia.[2] The other drivers who had been removed from their cars and were being searched pulled up their scarves to avoid breathing in the dust the trucks had kicked up, with annoyed but unsurprised expressions. Such sights were common around the area.

It was not just the Afghans who were armed. Many of the international groups doing work in the area around the base traveled with weapons. Although most were American soldiers, it was often not clear to the locals what branch of the military they were affiliated with or why they were there. For NATO troops from other countries, flags might reveal country of origin but not their relationship to the base. Adding to this confusion, international contractors in the area would often move around with armed guards, both international and Afghan.

The legal status of these armed civilian security contractors became controversial at several points, and Karzai complained about these groups in Kabul, where they often drove recklessly and set up barricades stretching out into the streets. Their operating procedures often conflicted with Afghan law and were a point of contention between various foreign governments and the Afghan security forces. Sometimes there seemed to be a certain security logic behind this, and, for example, U.S. embassy vehicles refused to roll down their windows at security checkpoints because some of these had been set up by insurgents disguised as police. Because they were diplomatic vehicles, they would just press their identification against the window. Other cases were more extreme, and one logistics officer explained to me how protocol for hitting a pedestrian with a vehicle was to not stop but to drive immediately back to the organization's compound and then send an Afghan logistics officer out to discuss the situation with the police. Partially in response to some of these types of incidents, in 2010 Karzai declared that all non-Afghan private security firms needed to leave the country; they eventually compromised with international diplomats who argued that international development projects needed armed protection that the Afghan police were not providing. New regulations on international security contractors were imposed, but the issue remained a point of contention between the Afghan government and international diplomats.[3] The general rule at most of the checkpoints near Bagram or outside other major cities, however, seemed to be that if an armed international or Afghan seemed legitimate, it was wise to let them through.

Militias were not rare in Afghanistan. Many were left over from the jihad and Civil War era. A handful had been pulled directly into the Afghan army or police briefly after the American invasion, but the reintegration of these former fighters in the Afghan security forces meant to follow the demobilization of these groups had been minimal. Most local militias that remained were less formalized, simply groups of men who were not fighting but were prepared to follow their commander on short notice.[4] In some cases, the international community even encouraged the re-formation of certain militias. This was particularly the case with the Afghan Local Police, which was an ISAF-sponsored program that granted local militias some of the status the police enjoyed in order to fight insurgents more locally.[5] Other figures, like Haji Almas or Anwar Khan, would have a protection detail of armed men of varying degrees of formality. In most areas where I had previously traveled, even if a checkpoint was run by informal militia it was fairly clear who the military force was in the area. For example, when I was traveling in Kunar with a friend who was a well-known local dignitary, our driver was able to call ahead to the various groups staffing checkpoints so we would be waved through quickly. The Shomali area around Bagram was different, however, because there were so many groups active simultaneously.

One of the key differences between the Shomali and some other regions in Afghanistan during the growing insurgency was the fact that the area had not come to be dominated by a single commander or strong man. In areas like Uruzgan, commanders like Matiullah Khan dominated entire provinces.[6] In some cases, relations with the international military shaped the way in which these leaders came to power, with the British in Helmand initially supporting Sher Mohammad Akhunzada's control of the province and then later demanding his removal due to his involvement in the drug trade. In other instances, former commanders used government positions, particularly governorships, to assert their command over a province or series of provinces from a key urban center, as was the case of Gul Agha Sherzai in Jalalabad and Atta Mohammad Noor in Mazar-e Sharif.[7] In some regions, younger leaders, some with resemblances to Haji Zia, came to power, such as Abdul Razziq in Kandahar. In each of these cases, however, a single man or small group of men seemed to control large amounts of territory, population, and resources. Local politics were then shaped by the relationship communities and lower-level political figures had with these key commanders and warlords. This seemed to contrast with the Shomali Plain, where a variety of local figures held some power and were constantly competing with each other for more. If anything, however, the area simply seemed to be more densely packed with commanders.

What could explain this density of warlords? Partially, this was due to the fact that the area was more ethnically and politically heterogeneous than others, meaning communities were more likely to split with their neighbors over support of certain individuals. As discussed in Chapter 4, the area's unique social history created historical political divides that had only been exacerbated during the Civil War when political parties often divided up territory along ethnic lines. With no reconciliation process to speak of, local leaders were able to take advantage of simmering grievances from that era.

Beyond these historical elements, however, the presence of international troops also played an important role in this spread of power. Military officials interacted with a variety of these nearby local commanders but did not overtly support any single figure, contributing to the proliferation of lower and midlevel figures. Local leaders knew they could gain wealth and status by manipulating local political structures but could not act with complete impunity with international forces lurking by so closely. If commanders were perceived as contributing to local instability, they risked catching the attention of NATO forces. With so much money to be made, why take the risk?

As money came in from the international military and Kabul right down the road, many of the most important local figures turned their interests toward national politics, ignoring the happenings in their local constituencies. Figures like Karzai's chief of staff and later ambassador to Pakistan, Omar Daudzai, hailed from the region but had little interest in the day-to-day politics there, leaving their allies and relatives to fight over the available resources. For these leaders and others like Haji Zia, local political or economic disruption would simply distract them from their commercial dealings, which made them more likely to tolerate a politically divided world, as long as business kept growing and international funds continued flowing.

This led not only to a large number of influential commanders but also to a particularly factious political landscape, where individuals had a large number of political parties, patronage networks, and other local groupings that they could choose to support. These numerous factions led to more small-scale violence rather than less large-scale confrontation. As the insurgency went on, kidnapping became more prevalent, and certain areas were considered unsafe at night, despite the fact the Shomali was not one of the areas with a significant number of insurgent fighters. Instead it was mostly local issues that were being fought over.

One day in the bazaar, for example, the talk was primarily of a checkpoint that had been set up by a group of armed fighters the previous night. At first the claim was that they were insurgents, but it later turned out the armed men were trying to catch a man who was fleeing the area due to a land dispute. The police were not trusted to detain the man because they could be easily bribed, so local men took it on themselves to set up a roadblock. Similarly, another village had been in the midst of a protracted leadership dispute over which elder really represented the people, and a well-known parliamentarian eventually had to be brought in to resolve it. These types of low-level disputes were common and at least anecdotally seemed more prevalent than in other parts of the country. At the same time, however, most of these disputes remained small as commanders and businessmen like Zia, along with the international military presence, prevented them from growing too violent. Still, these occurrences presented a significant hassle for local residents who had to deal with almost continual small-scale instability. As one man put it to me, if these militias and political parties continued to encourage local fighting, eventually, "We will eat each other."[8]

The combination of the instability and abundance of resources also upset some of the traditional ways in which communities governed themselves. Afghan local leaders were historically expected to be more responsive to the needs of communities than tribal leaders in other Middle Eastern societies.[9] Although power was often inherited, it was possible for the community to reject the son of a malik or other leader for not possessing the right qualities (for example, a malik should be wise, generous, and just and possess a certain gravitas). If the community did not consider the malik's son an appropriate successor or if the malik did not have a son, a new malik would be appointed by the elders in the community. This meant that being a malik was both a position of power and a burden—the malik had to host feasts and funerals, travel to the district center to meet with government officials and resolve disputes.[10]

This quasi-democratic system, however, could be disrupted. An elder who had access to either guns or money could essentially declare himself malik and use his money or the threat of violence to maintain that position. In such cases, individuals in the community might grumble and say that he was not a "real" malik, but they did not have the ability to do much about it. Azoy's account of changes in leadership and in the meaning and purpose of buzkashi as khans moved to Peshawar and gained access to international funds and weapons demonstrated some of the ways leaders could become less responsive. Around Bagram, after the American invasion, both with the guns that militia leaders possessed, either left over from the Civil War or brought by insurgents, and the great amount of money that had entered the communities, either in the form of international aid or simply construction projects, similar changes became visible. Many local leaders suddenly had a variety of types of external resources, so they no longer relied on the community for their legitimacy. Instead they could simply buy or bully their way into positions of power.

This shift away from historical quasi-democratic leadership had created a good deal of resentment in the community. As one laborer described the recent changes, "There are no actual leaders in Bagram right now. Our representatives won the elections only through corruption and deceit . . . They think only of their own pockets." There was little that this laborer felt that he could do to change his circumstances.

As resentment continued to grow, some of these elders, particularly those who had fought in the jihad against the Soviets, became aware of the criticism that many in the community had of their leadership, and they tried to reach out in a series of economic and political initiatives. For example, in 2012, a group of these former fighters set up a mujahideen shura in the district. Shuras, or councils, were bodies of elders, ideally egalitarian in nature, that brought men from the community together to resolve disputes and discuss local political issues. In some parts of Afghanistan, they could be highly formalized, whereas in others they were more ad hoc.[11] Shuras could also range in size from small councils that gather at mosques to large tribal gatherings in which leaders represented literally thousands of members of a tribe.[12] In the Bagram area, shuras tended to meet regularly at both the mosque or neighborhood level, as well as more occasionally at the district level. Local communities supported shuras because they gave them a say in local issues through their leaders, and local leaders supported shuras because it gave them an opportunity to demonstrate their benevolence and leadership publically. However, when leaders who traditionally sat on such bodies found external forms of support, whether this was in the form of guns or international funds, they had less incentive to attend these meetings. As a result, some such consultative councils lost their utility. Instability and the presence of international forces providing security also meant that such communal bodies were less likely to hold the same sway they had in the past.

Instead of just disappearing, as many who saw them as tribal relics perhaps assumed that they would, shuras oddly began to proliferate. Leaders who felt left out from the development initiatives and interactions with the base were quick to join local shuras hoping to increase their influence.[13] Instead of there being one district shura, as was the model in many areas historically, the mujahideen shura in Bagram was far from the only council in the area. In part as a response to this, the shuras met regularly to demonstrate their effectiveness and vitality. Threatened by the growing influence of Zia and other young businessmen, these elders built a new building for the council and served lunch to those who brought disputes or other local issues before the council. They set up subcouncils, including one to support local cultural initiatives and another to reach out to the youth in the area. The elders hoped that by pooling their collective influence they could reestablish some of their importance in the area. However, the council faced significant challenges. In one recent case, a lower-level militia member had been arrested by the police for possessing an illegal weapon. The case was brought to the mujahideen shura, which sympathized with the arrested man but said that because the weapon was already in the hands of the police, there was little they could do about it. Previously, when there was only one main district shura, it would have been more likely that the police would have listened to their petition. In a seemingly parallel case in the district next door, the district shura had pressured the governor to allow elders and their supporters to carry weapons into the district compound. In Bagram, however, with power divided among many councils, the police had less reason to pay the councils heed.

Not to be outdone, however, Zia set up his own council that met at his foundation's headquarters in town. The elders on this council helped to distribute funds from the foundation but also attempted to become involved in some of the same political issues that were being addressed by the mujahideen shura. Although this collection of elders whom Zia was connected to might not have been as established or reputable, they benefited greatly from Zia's financial status. Zia also had these elders help him distribute his money, making him appear to be less of an upstart to some in the community. Furthermore, the mere existence of another shura undercut the authority of the mujahideen faction that could no longer claim to be the only shura to represent the people in town. As a result, young men in particular had a wide array of merchants, commanders, and councils, all of whom they could approach in times of need, which deepened the political factioning around town.

Although this local political intrigue may have seemed far removed from the security and development concerns of the base, in many ways, they were intertwined. The widespread funds, distributed through an opaque bureaucracy, created the economic conditions that gave rise to figures like Haji Zia but also encouraged other traditional leaders to cooperate with each other less and less. In turn, the factioning and tensions over resources and the local balance of power created opportunities for insurgents as well as simply entrepreneurial criminals to spread instability.

Many of the Afghans living nearby were aware on a certain level of the connections between the uneven distribution of funds, the increasingly distorted nature of local politics, and the small-scale skirmishes and violence it created, but there was little that they could do to stop this violence. On the other hand, for many of the internationals working on the base, this instability simply looked like insurgency, despite the fact that the instability had much more to do with the local economic and political arrangements in the area than with any sort of ideological opposition to the Afghan national government. Insurgency, instead, became a umbrella term that covered all manner of crimes and instability, most of which had very little to do with the Taliban or other organized insurgent groups. This was particularly the case in areas like the Shomali that had been heavily damaged during earlier fighting between the Taliban and mujahideen factions and had little desire to see the Taliban return.

Of course these factions and the near constant low levels of violence and tension created opportunities for some who were willing to take more flexible paths on the road to power and wealth. Because many of these shuras were particularly looking to reach out to a younger generation of political leaders, those leaders could play the shuras against one another. In one instance, a youth soccer club in the area was able to take funds from multiple shuras simultaneously because the shuras wanted to have their names connected with the club.[14] In other cases, someone like Will simply benefited from the fact that most of the key actors in the area were too preoccupied with their own feuds to worry about him. Will, who usually drove up to the area on short day trips with a couple of his partners, visiting the various sites where his wind turbines were being installed, did not attract the attention of other large-scale projects, like the massive Kajaki Dam or more local highway paving projects. In a more insurgent-filled area or even simply an area were there were fewer other political issues constantly being debated, Will might have encountered more resistance. Because his project was so small and the funds being used were fairly limited, Will was able, for the most part, to fly under the radar of local feuds and tensions. This allowed him to set up a wind-powered pump in one area without worrying about upsetting those in another.

The unevenness of the opportunities the instability and lack of transparency around Bagram created an increasingly complex political-economic world, making life difficult for those living around the base. For young people looking to get ahead, like Omar, there were numerous leaders and organizations with whom they had to cultivate relationships, but it was rarely clear which of these leaders had access to the base or other forms of contacts. Oftentimes those who appeared the strongest lacked real connections, whereas the strong could afford to appear weaker (or at least less publically visible) to avoid unwanted scrutiny from the authorities. Figures like Haji Zia often downplayed their connections in an attempt to avoid jealousies and open competition with the mujahideen council. At the same time, other young, less influential businessmen might exaggerate their connections to the base in the hopes of attracting business with those outside the base. In a world without transparency, appearances were everything. Appearances, however, could also be highly deceiving. All this led to a proliferation of rumors and stories that circulated in the communities around the base, which created resentment and a simmering anger directed toward the international intervention, occasionally with horrible consequences.

The Incinerator

Although many of the complaints about the shortcomings of local leadership did not directly involve the base, its presence still cast a shadow on almost all local political issues. When I talked with locals around the base in 2012, it was clear that concerns were not simply about services, economic inequality, and the increasingly fractious nature of local politics but that a more psychological divide had grown up with the walls around the base. Despite the initial welcome by most, any trust between local communities and the international military there had vanished. Instead, it was replaced by a rich set of conspiracy theories and tales told by the people around the base.

These rumors grew as laborers reported back to local communities from inside the base. Some of these reports and stories seemed plausible, such as accounts about troops, on short rotations, burning their old supplies and equipment when they left the base. A significant amount of material was burned on the base rather than being shipped out, and this was a task performed by Afghan laborers, though it certainly seemed unlikely that material was being burned to the extent that some of the wilder of these stories suggested.

Other tales seem more curious, such as the description of the entrance process by one resident: "Our relationship with the base is not as good as it was during the past [that is, the Soviet period]. It is now almost impossible for us to enter the base. Those who enter are scanned at six different gates. The X-rays they use for scanning are very harmful for your health. Some of the workers on the base are now infected by skin diseases and cancer by those X-ray machines." For the Westerners on the base, such claims seemed ridiculous, though I certainly remembered the odd sensation the first time I walked through the entrance checkpoint. As I was funneled down the narrow razor wire–lined walkway into a small empty room, the heavy metal door closed with a definitive thud. It was eerie how the remotely controlled scanner whirled around me before the door on the far side of the room clicked open automatically. For local laborers the sensation of entering a science fiction movie must have been even more extreme, giving a certain sensibility to their stories.

We can see the impact of the strange relationship and disconnection between the base and the surrounding communities in the stories and rumors that circulated around it, in part by tracing the dramatic events in February 2012 following an initial report of Koran burnings on the base. Although a full-scale investigation later suggested that only four Korans had been unintentionally burned in an incinerator (although a later report stated that an additional fifty-three were on the verge of being burned), in the days that followed the first reports it was difficult to get a clear picture of what had happened from either the international press or in the nearby bazaar.[15] Instead, the stories built on each other and eventually took on a life of their own.

Stories about the incident, which occurred on February 20, spread quickly among those living around the airbase. Coalition soldiers had brought a large amount of written material out from the detention facility to be burned. There were reports that the detainees had been using these materials to pass secret messages among each other. Several Afghan laborers had been working near the incinerators when materials to be burned arrived. A watching Afghan soldier had tried to intervene, warning the Americans not to burn the material, but they continued with the process. It was not until another Afghan laborer stepped in and pulled out a scorched Koran that the burning was stopped.[16]

Laborers left work that day, and the tale quickly spread. The first protest of the incident occurred the next morning, drawing a crowd of over 3,000, many of whom worked on the base. The normally bustling bazaar outside the base was instead filled with young men hurling stones. Business stopped, and garbage was set on fire. Later, when some soldiers from inside the base began firing rubber bullets, protestors hid behind the cement pillions designed to prevent suicide bombers from ramming the front gate. As the protest continued, it became violent. Even the laborers who wanted to return to work were not allowed to by the protesters out of fear of reprisals. One told a reporter, "Whoever goes back to work will be killed. They think of us as traitors."[17]

After the incident, General Allen, the commander of NATO forces in Afghanistan, and President Obama quickly issued apologies, and Karzai lamented the incident while calling for calm. The military responded further by allowing a group of local elders onto the base to see the evidence firsthand. Instead of reducing tension, this actually further fueled rumors in the bazaar, with some of the men returning claiming that they had seen ten to fifteen Korans desecrated.[18]

Despite these attempts to calm the population, the Bagram protests gained momentum and spread across the country. The following week saw thousands of protesters in a number of different provinces. Many of these protests turned violent, with dozens of Afghan protesters killed both by coalition troops and by Afghan police in various locations, as well as several coalition troops members killed in a series of attacks that followed. In most of the incidents, it was Afghan police who were injured while protecting coalition bases. In some instances, however, the Afghan police actually turned and joined protesters.[19]

The following week also saw an increase in the number of security incidents aimed at the international presence across the country. This included the shooting of two international advisors working at the Ministry of the Interior, a large car bomb at the airbase in Jalalabad, and the tainting of food with bleach at another Forward Operating Base, which the Taliban claimed was an attempt to poison coalition soldiers. It was difficult to determine whether these events were genuinely linked to the Bagram protests, but they all contributed to a general sense of strain in the relations between Afghans and the international community. NGO workers like Will were put on lockdown by their organizations. In the span of a few brief days, the entire country was on high alert.

In the wave of criticism and public statements by Afghan officials about the burning of the Korans on the base, other political issues and concerns about the American presence were quickly raised and seemed to intertwine with each other. Condemnation from the Taliban was predictably extreme, but even members of the Afghan government began making more incendiary statements than they had in the past. One conservative parliamentarian from an area just to the west of the base called the Americans "invaders" and told local mullahs to urge their followers "to wage jihad against Americans." Those closer to the Karzai government were more circumspect but still ambivalent. After getting pelted by stones at one of the protests, the chief of police in Kabul told *The New York Times*, "I do not blame people for throwing rocks at us, because this is their right to protest their anger about dishonoring our Holy Koran."[20]

The frustration among protesters across the country built on some previous protests where the international community was perceived as not respecting Afghan traditions or religion. Cases such as the Roman Catholic convert (mentioned in Chapter 1) who was released due to international pressure had contributed to a growing sense among the Afghan population that the international community respected neither their religion nor their sovereignty. The Taliban encouraged this by highlighting these links in a statement about the incident, claiming, "Since the invasion of Afghanistan by the animal Americans, this is almost the 10th time they have degraded the holiest values of Muslims."[21] The Taliban had previously used incidents involving Korans and public outrage to encourage insurgency against the Afghan government. Most notably, in January 2010, after a Special Forces raid in Garmser, a contested district in Helmand, a Koran was found stabbed with a knife. The next day, 500 protestors threw rocks at Marines and Afghan police outside of the Garmser FOB. During the protest, a handful of Taliban fighters attempted to work the crowd into a violent frenzy, knowing the Marines would hesitate to fire on a group primarily of civilians. In the days that followed, insurgents mixed with thousands of protestors across the district, seriously setting back the American effort in the troubled district.[22] A few months later when I visited the district and spoke to both military officials and local elders, both sides were relieved the incident had not caused more deaths but were clearly concerned by the underlying tensions that were far from resolved.

In the eyes of many Afghans, these incidents were not separate accidents, but these examples of cultural insensitivity and a lack of respect for local opinions were linked. In interviews and discussions I had around the base after the Bagram riots, the story of the Koran burning on the base intermingled with other cases such as photos of U.S. soldiers urinating on Afghan corpses and the case of Army Staff Sergeant Robert Bales, who walked off his base in southern Afghanistan and killed seventeen civilians.[23] Most of these cases had very little to do with the actual insurgency, but they gave the Taliban and other government opponents the opportunity to link the growing resentment of the international community with the cause of the insurgents.

Gauging the general mood of Afghans around such incidents was difficult. For the most part Owen suggested that the ANA troops he worked with did not treat him differently after such incidents: "If one American does something shitty, they don't condemn the whole group." Similarly, Will's partners were understanding on the days he could not go to work due to security threats like the protests. The response of individual communities could be more extreme. Fighting against a handful of insurgents harassing a base was one thing, but once an angry group of civilians joined them, there was no real military solution. Owen, who had been stationed not far from where the Bales incident occurred, said the incident set the international troops and the ANA troops they were partnered with "back years."

In instances like these, the walls of Bagram and other bases, which prevented communities from looking in, also allowed those outside to imagine a variety of insulting behaviors by the international community occurring there. The higher the walls, the more difficult it became to determine what was really happening inside the base and the easier it became to imagine all sorts of depravity. The incident provided an opportunity for the Taliban and other groups opposing the intervention to "prove" the true colonial intentions of the Americans, and it is perhaps unsurprising that there were reports of protesters singing Taliban songs outside the base.[24] Incidents like these made the narrative around the conflict increasingly two sided, with the international invaders on the one side and all Afghans, including insurgents, on the other.

When I spoke with several American officials about the Koran burning incidents, they often expressed incredulity and exasperation over the Afghan responses. The burnings were accidental and did not reflect the true sentiments of those on base, they argued. Why such an extreme response? Could they really hold the entire international community accountable for the actions of a few shell-shocked soldiers? What the officials often did not seem to grasp was the way in which the communities near the base did not at all see these as isolated incidents. Instead they understood them from the perspectives of those who had been living in a skewed political-economic world. For almost a decade, they had watched the walls grow, corrupt businessmen get rich, and young men snatched away in the night for interrogation by NATO forces. At the same time they had seen the immense wealth of the foreigners in their intimidating vehicles that threatened to run taxis off the road and in the flow of goods that continued to fall off trucks on their way into the base. Was it possible for such powerful neighbors to make such simple mistakes? By 2012, those in the communities around the base no longer gave them the benefit of the doubt; when I visited later that summer, new barriers had been installed around the base, and there were still burn marks on the ground, remnants of the protests earlier that spring, all making the base seem even more distant and impenetrable. It had been over two years since Obama had announced the initial troop surge and a year since American forces had passed the 100,000 mark, but clearly the surge had not brought the intended stability, and Afghans and internationals alike began to doubt both the intentions and the usefulness of the international presence in the country.

Prisons and Walls

The Koran burning incident did much to shape conversations both around the base and in diplomatic circles about the agreement on the long-term presence of American troops in the country. With an insurgency that seemed to be growing worse instead of better, the international presence was under more scrutiny by Afghan officials than it ever had been before. Following widespread allegations of fraud on Karzai's part during 2009, relations between the U.S. government and the Karzai administration deteriorated significantly. Obama's relationship with Karzai was chilly, and none of the American ambassadors who followed Neumann seemed to be as close to Karzai as Neumann had been.[25] Karzai began using press appearances as an opportunity to criticize the international presence and the Americans in particular. Three of the concerns that had been pressed most firmly by the Afghan government in the media were the issues of American forces conducting night raids in Afghan homes, Afghan civilian casualties, and the detention of insurgents at an American facility on Bagram Airbase.

Bagram Airbase had been a center for the detention for insurgents caught by American and ISAF forces since members of the coalition first arrived at the base. However, as the intervention went on, the detention process grew more centralized, and an increasing number of the detainees from across the country were sent to Bagram. As Anand Gopal, who tracked detainees, many of whom were arrested by accident, based on bad intel or on intel that had been directly manipulated by a rival commander to settle a grudge, described the process:

From the Field Detention Site, you would be shipped to one of the main prisons at either Bagram or Kandahar Airfield. You would then be questioned by a new set of interrogators, who made little attempt to reconcile existing intelligence with any fresh information that they obtained. Your journey would likely end here, locked away for months or even years—unless you were one among the two hundred Afghans destined for Guantanamo. There you would be assessed by officials even farther removed from the battlefield, with even foggier knowledge of the country's politics.[26]

To deal with these increased numbers, the detention facility at Bagram was rehabbed in 2009, and by 2011 there were 3,000 known prisoners there. This was a fivefold increase since Obama had taken office and meant that Bagram had approximately eighteen times the number of detainees that the detention facility at Guantanamo Bay did.[27] Most of the detainees were Afghan, but a good number came from a range of other places: Pakistan, Uzbekistan, Saudi Arabia, Chechnya. They were treated as "enemy combatants," and, despite campaign promises to shut prisons like Guantanamo, the Obama administration upheld an approach to these detainees initiated by the Bush administration that essentially stripped those housed in the facility of all legal rights.[28] Stories of mistreatment leaked out with prisoners who had been freed from the compound, but, at the same time, one civilian who visited the facility told me that prisoners in the neighboring Afghan jail thought that conditions at the international facility were so much better they actually tried to get themselves labeled as terrorists so that they would be transferred.[29]

Part of the issue surrounding the transfer of prisoners was the fact that the Afghan legal system could not legally detain prisoners without trial the way that coalition forces could (because they would no longer be enemy combatants).[30] This had been greatly complicated by ISAF's provision, pushed for by the Dutch and the British, that prisoners detained by international forces had to be turned over to Afghan authorities within ninety-six hours. This created a rather chaotic system that was prone to what Neumann called "revolving door releases back onto the battlefield." Speaking to other American officials at the time, however, it was clear that American officials were less concerned with the legal rights of the detainees than they were with what would happen once the detainees entered the Afghan legal system. Among international diplomats and military officials there was a widespread distrust of the Afghan legal system and fear that many of the combatants would simply be freed.

These concerns grew as Karzai continued his practice of routinely pardoning large number of prisoners on holidays, including the narcotics traffickers discussed in the previous chapter. There was particular concern about "IED makers" who had been caught with incriminating materials but no solid evidence that they were in the process of planting explosives. It was felt that transferring such prisoners would mean they would be quickly released and back out making explosives.

Eventually, in 2012, a memorandum was signed transferring the bulk of the facilities gradually over to Afghan control. In the hopes of retaining some control or influence over the prisoners to be transferred, the United States paid for the construction of a large Afghan prison facility adjacent to the international airbase.[31] Despite the transfer to Afghan control, reports continued to surface of another classified American detention facility on the base where prisoners were held outside of the Afghan legal system or where they were brought from the Afghan Parwan detention facility to be interrogated. The U.S. government also put up significant resistance when the Afghan judicial system decided to release eighty-eight prisoners the Americans still deemed "dangerous" in 2014, resulting in much diplomatic debate and a delay in the release of the prisoners.[32] More important than these diplomatic issues for those living in the area, this transfer highlighted the weakness of the Afghan state and fueled the growing resentment that many felt toward the troops on the base.

Although human rights organizations regularly attacked American policy throughout the intervention for this lack of any due process, it was interesting how rarely the issue of the prisoners' rights came up in my conversations with people outside the base. The fact that there was no due process was not particularly shocking to most Afghans; their judicial system was notoriously corrupt, and this was not new. When they referred to the foreign detainees in particular, there was also little sympathy. These were fighters who had come from other countries to destabilize their country; they saw little reason not to lock them up and throw away the key.

What was more concerning for many around the base was the way in which the presence of a detention facility, which Afghans had no access to, undermined the sovereignty of the Afghan state. As if to emphasize the issues with sovereignty, official documents referred to the detention center as "the Parwan Detention Center," named after the province where it was located, attempting to disassociate it from the base itself. The name, however, did not lessen the symbolic link between the new Afghan prison and the base, and, perhaps as evidence of this, the head of the prison narrowly escaped an assassination attempt in 2014 near his home, twenty minutes south of the base. Publicly, President Karzai, on several occasions, presented emotional ultimatums about the transfer of the facility, which suggested to many Afghans listening that he saw the facility as a threat to his own position. He also linked the transfer of the facility to the issue of civilian casualties and wider concerns about the American presence in the country. At one point during the Koran burning riots outside Bagram, Karzai's spokesman directly linked the two concerns together, stating, "The sooner you turn over the Bagram prison to Afghan authorities the sooner we will avoid such incidents," referring to the protests that were happening at that time.[33]

For residents around the base, stories and rumors about the detention facility were less an individual insult than they were evidence of the strange ambiguity of political space around the base. They were living in Afghanistan, yet the Afghan government did not seem to possess ultimate sovereignty over the land in the area or the Afghans who lived there. There was an international military presence that was said to be protecting them, and, yet, as daily attacks showed, these military forces could not even secure the entire area around the base, particularly at night. If anything, the base seemed to attract attacks, making it more dangerous to live in the area, a complaint that local residents raised to me regularly.

Afghans elsewhere in the country, focused on the day-to-day politics of life and earning a living, could essentially ignore the intervention. In more stable areas, Afghans primarily interacted with the Afghan government, not the international community; even in more insurgent-controlled areas, Taliban commanders were calling the shots. Around centers like Bagram, however, the ambiguity of the intervention was fully exposed. Nowhere else was it so clear that military presence, stability, and development had little to do with each other.

On one level it may seem like a coincidence that Bagram was the site of both the detention facility and the riots over the Korans, but in another sense it made sense that the gates of Bagram Airbase had become a symbolic point where worlds collided. The walls suggested that on one side the Afghan state was sovereign and on the other side coalition forces were sovereign, but the

Afghans in the bazaar and even the troops on the base knew that this was not true. The broken concrete barriers and burnt dumpsters suggested that the intervention was messier than that, with countless actors competing for resources and complicating the political landscape for ordinary Afghans. As the surge continued, the resentment and frustration grew.

People commented in particular how on the bazaar side of the wall it was almost impossible to see anything happening within the base. But it turns out that neither was it much easier to look out from the inside.

10 How to Host Your Own Shura

You will never understand this country as clearly as on the day you arrive.

— Ambassador Neumann

THE KORAN BURNING INCIDENT was one of several wake-up calls to the international military that their strategies for winning local communities to their side were falling short. These incidents frustrated the international community generally and the military in particular. Resources were not the issue. There was plenty of money available, but what did these communities want? How could they figure this out? The COIN approach of trying to win the hearts and minds of local communities had multiple strategies that required analysis of local political conditions using a series of defined steps. These approaches required an assessment of local needs, an analysis of the threats facing the community, and then the implementation of projects. All of these stages could be tricky.

As one of the State Department's most experienced officials in southern Afghanistan, after spending two years embedded in a district in Helmand, concluded, "The most powerful tribal leaders in Garmser were a mystery to us."[1] One of the central strategies in trying to solve this mystery was the engagement of key local elders or, for the military, KLEs (for Key Leader Engagements). These meetings were used to gather intelligence but also to establish stronger ties with the community and get a better sense of how best to proceed with stabilizing the area. But how do you train a young American soldier to engage with a tribal elder?

The Shura Strategy

The military was, of course, not the only group trying to understand the needs of local communities. NGOs and aid groups had been doing this in

Afghanistan for much longer, and the issue of community consultation had long been addressed in a variety of ways. Because Afghan communities and social groups had a history of council or shura meetings that ranged in size from neighborhood groups to large-scale tribal councils, holding similar meetings seemed like a way to create community consensus and give internationally sponsored projects legitimacy. This approach was used by humanitarian organizations working with refugee communities years before the invasion; however, the idea of community consultation increasingly became a key element of many projects, particularly as the criticism of early development and military projects grew.

The best-known national-level attempt at community consultation was probably the World Bank–funded National Solidarity Program (NSP), which set up councils to determine what types of small development projects a community needed, in thousands of villages across the country. Started in 2003 and designed by now-president Ashraf Ghani, this program was widely viewed by the international community as fairly effective, even by the normally critical Office of the Special Inspector General.[2] Although there were instances of corruption and misspent funds, most felt that the emphasis on involving local communities in decision-making processes was more effective than top-down approaches. Additionally, the sums being handed out were small enough so that if a few of these councils were not actually representative of their communities, it would not greatly undermine the overall perception of the program. In the years that followed, other projects tried to replicate this process with varying degrees of success.

In the case of the NSP and other effective instances, development councils actually determined how international donor funds would be spent in the community and which types of projects to prioritize, a rare move toward local democratization in Afghanistan's highly centralized system. In other cases, international groups were less interested in actual input from the communities they were working in but still craved the aura of legitimacy that these meetings seemed to create. In these instances, such community consultation was little more than a rubber stamp, meant to justify a program that had been designed in some distant Western capital. Of course, even if they were just rubber stamps, local elders increasingly saw these bodies as a means of attracting international funds. Some of the local elders in Istalif were quick to pull together a small group of elders when visiting NGOs stopped by to give the meetings an increased air of legitimacy. NGOs were then quick to take photos of such meetings and put them on the covers of their donor reports. Eventually such meetings became, in some ways, self-generating, as communities increasingly set them up to try to attract more international development work and NGOs used them to justify work they were doing.[3]

Initially using the light footprint approach, the international military was more than happy to leave these local elders and their complicated political worlds alone. As things grew steadily worse, however, the military found itself rushing to try to figure out everything that they had not been paying attention to during the first six years of the intervention. Regardless of how effective these development shuras were, by 2009 the international military had clearly decided that these were an important concept in their counterinsurgency approach in Afghanistan. The increased prominence of shuras also obviously had something to do with the gradual realization in the international community that the government in Kabul was not meeting local expectations. Instead, the military clearly felt that there was something to be gained both by reaching out to local elders directly and by taking local Afghan government officials with them to these meetings. Soon, the military tried to meet with elders to discuss everything from where small development projects might

Figure 10.1. Internationally sponsored shura meeting. Photo by Casey Garret Johnson.

be set up to whether certain prisoners should be released, and Anne Marlow in the *New Republic* dubbed this shift the "shura strategy."[4] Soon the military was scrambling to train their soldiers in how "to engage with local communities" and, essentially, host shuras.

In our conversations, Owen was quick to point out that most of his training had done nothing to prepare him and his colleagues to do things like hold a meeting with local Afghan elders. Indeed, SEALs were particularly poorly equipped to do this. For example, Owen explained that when he was originally assigned to missions to meet with elders he treated these meetings as primarily intelligence-gathering exercises. When he needed information to complete a mission, he would go in to ask about the local insurgent threats and then would promptly leave. Unfortunately, this was essentially the opposite of what really made a shura useful. For the elders, these council meetings were much more about reaffirming social bonds and paying respect. It was the gathering together that gave the shura's decisions legitimacy, much more than the details of their discussions. In many instances, while researching Afghan approaches to dispute resolution, I found that the dispute would actually be resolved *before* the shura meeting, privately, among the key parties of the dispute. They would still need to hold the shura, however, to ratify the agreed solution and make it valid in the eyes of the community. Having international military officials come to a meeting, only to leave after a few minutes when they had the information that they needed, as Owen did at first, was disrespectful and short-circuited the entire process.

Often, from the Afghan elders' perspective, meeting with the military had nothing to do with intelligence; it was about establishing relationships, and the military was unlikely to get anything of real substance from them at such meetings. The gathering would establish a connection between the elders and the military forces, put forth a public display of loyalty, and demonstrate the potential for an open dialogue.[5] For elders around Bagram, meeting with the international military like this could, first of all, make them seem more powerfully connected than they actually were but could also suggest to their communities that the elders were voicing many of their concerns about the cultural insensitivities of the international military to officials. Even though Owen clearly realized there was more going on at these meetings than the intelligence gathering, he still felt limited in what he was really trying to accomplish in these venues. His training had not prepared him for this type of task, and adapting to these cultural practices was a challenge.

When I asked Owen how the military could have been better prepared for these types of missions, he quickly turned it back to me: "We rely on people [like anthropologists] to come in and say 'Actually while you think you're doing a good thing building this well, you're really pissing off his neighbor, and it's going to cause thirty more years of fighting between these tribes.' The military, we just think that we're doing a good thing. It's not really any fault of ours. It's not our expertise." This also applied to the shift toward local development, and Owen continued: "To be honest, I think it's terrible that we've asked soldiers to be social workers. It's confusing when you hand a rifle to a nineteen-year-old and say, 'Hey, defend yourself, don't just go over and die needlessly. Defend yourself.' At the same time, your instincts should not be to pull the trigger but to ask a different question altogether. And that's not a smart military strategy." At the same time, however, Owen acknowledged that, the way the situation had evolved in Afghanistan, increasingly the burden fell on soldiers to do much of this type of work. "But the military, I feel, are the only ones willing to go. Who in the State Department is willing to go into a village in western Kandahar?"

In fact, I knew many people in the State Department in Kabul who were very willing to go but were prohibited by increasingly strict embassy regulations. Even when State Department or USAID officials were stationed at PRTs or FOBs, their movements were highly restricted. As one official pointed out to me, for most military officers with civilians at their post, the potential repercussions of having a civilian die under their command greatly outweighed any benefits that having that official go out in the field may have brought, even for the most COIN oriented. This led many military officers to severely restrict the movement of any civilians on their bases.

As a result, as security deteriorated in places like Bagram, it became increasingly incumbent on the military to do much of this work themselves, including the gathering of information about communities on topics ranging from tribal structures to development needs.

Knowing the Terrain

The military's attempt to remedy this lack of training in relationship building that Owen focused on led, in part, to the creation of a controversial program, the Human Terrain System (HTS), to better understand local communities. The HTS was run by the American Army and embedded social scientists into the military units in Iraq and Afghanistan. These social scientists were expected to provide cultural information that would allow troops to be sensitive to cultural norms and provide them with political and social knowledge about their region.

The program immediately caused an uproar in the anthropological community, which was concerned about the role of social scientists in providing the military with intelligence.[6] Concern over the ethics of how social science was being used by the military, what the information was being used for, and anthropology's long, troubled relationship with colonial powers fueled much of the initial apprehension. The debate revolved particularly around the difference between cultural "knowledge" (soldiers should take their boots off before entering a mosque) and cultural "intelligence" (this compound should be targeted because the Taliban were active there).[7] The concern was that HTS was essentially weaponizing anthropological knowledge, and the American Anthropological Association issued a strong condemnation of the program.

Perhaps unsurprisingly, the protests by the academic community did little to slow the growth of the actual program, and soon, following an initial phase in Iraq, there were HTS teams made up of social scientists operating at Bagram and across southern and eastern Afghanistan. Depending on their locations, teams were expected to meet with local elders and brief officers on the local political landscape. As I watched some of the teams operate from a distance and later spoke with former team members, I was struck by their frustration with their inability to do any of their assigned tasks. Understanding a community meant speaking with community members, but, like other civilians on FOBs, officers were reluctant to allow them to leave the base. Once they were allowed out, they were generally accompanied by a large number of soldiers in their protection detail, who viewed the journey more as a military maneuver than as an attempt to build any type of relations. Those soldiers on security detail were primary concerned with protecting the HTS team members, which meant, in many instances, actually restricting their access to local Afghans. The conclusion of many as the program developed was that anthropological research and the military simply did not mix. For my part, from a purely logistical standpoint, I could not imagine doing some of the research I did while wearing Kevlar and being guarded by Marines. Surely those running the program knew that the kind of information these anthropologists were gathering with soldiers with guns standing right next to them was not likely to be very helpful. What Afghan elder in his right mind would give sensitive information to American soldiers in front of community members who might then report back to insurgents? Doing so would certainly put them in danger. Furthermore, in many more dangerous areas where the American military had thus far failed to provide any stability, why should they give such information?

Another key issue that soon became apparent was that soldiers and anthropologists have distinct languages, both filled with jargon, difficult to translate, and, at times, mutually unintelligible; commanders were often at a loss for what to do with the information they were receiving, and the social scientists were unsure about what type of information these commanders wanted.[8] Even if the anthropologists could provide information about the local tribal composition of an area and its connection with the insurgency, what was the commander to do with this information? After several years of frustration and several highly publicized and tragic deaths, the program was eventually greatly scaled back.

Ultimately, the HTS teams had little impact that I could discern in the communities around Bagram (there were plenty of patrols coming out and meeting with locals; the HTS teams were just one of many), and the program failed to gain much traction for numerous reasons, including the deaths of several of the social scientists who worked on HTT.[9] However, the real reason HTS teams failed to create the change within the military many had hoped for actually had little to do with the academic or moral issues around the project. It was more a victim of the contracting model that plagued so many other projects around Bagram.

Although the academic community was not successful at stopping the program, they were effective at scaring away many of those who were most qualified. As a graduate student at the time, I was told by more senior scholars that young academics risked putting their entire career in jeopardy if they joined. As a result, I tended to give the HTS teams a wide berth, even when I was in a district where I knew they were operating and even though one of my friends from graduate school did join the program. At the same time, as the counterinsurgency approach gained momentum and the surge put more soldiers into the field, there was a sudden demand for anthropologists, sociologists, and any other social scientist who knew anything about the country. However, due to the years of conflict along with concerns like my own about the repercussions of even speaking to these groups, the military had difficulty finding people who were both qualified and had any sort of background in the region—anthropologists had flocked to the country in the 1960s and

1970s, but few had on-the-ground research experience since the Soviet invasion. Furthermore, most of those anthropologists from the earlier generation were of an age where they had comfortable jobs, homes, and families and thus little interest in embedding with Marine units and living in tents. Because the program was placing civilians with military units, it used a contractor to find and employ these social scientists. Having the Department of Defense hire the social scientists would have forced those selected for the HTS teams to comply with many more regulations, something that some felt might not be a bad thing, but it would have massively slowed the program down. So a contract was awarded to BAE Systems, a multinational British-based defense contractor, to find and employ the social scientists.

Of course, BAE got paid only if they actually hired social scientists, so it was in their best interest to fill rosters completely, even if they could not find candidates with the appropriate experience. Qualified candidates were difficult to find; for many, the idea of working in a war zone was simply not worth the six-digit salaries that were being offered; for others, hoping to work in the academic world later, the career risk was too great. Unable to identify well-qualified candidates, the contractor started cutting corners in the hiring process to recruit less-qualified candidates. To their embarrassment, many of these hires were then unflatteringly publicized in the media (most famously this included one individual who had written a thesis on dumpster diving and several other team members who went on months of paid leave, which allowed the contractor to continue billing their salaries).[10] The international military on the ground might have wanted HTS anthropologists who knew Afghanistan well and could provide cultural advice, but, once again, the contracting model meant that the contractors had no real incentive for the HTS teams to actually be any good at their jobs; their greatest incentive was getting the teams out in the field as soon as possible. Initial reports from commanders about HTS teams were good, in part because they were filled with the few qualified candidates that BAE Systems could find and in part because it was in almost everyone's best interest that the teams at least appear successful. For the contractors, this would ensure more contracts in the future; for military officers, it was evidence to their superiors that they were truly embracing COIN strategy. As the teams expanded, however, the applicant pool became more diluted, initial expectations were not met, and the reputations of these teams worsened among military officers.

Producing reports of limited use, commanding officers who were already concerned about the safety of civilians serving under them were less likely to authorize movement outside the bases where the teams were stationed. This, of course, became a vicious cycle because the less they were permitted off these bases, the worse their information was, and the less useful their reports were, making commanders even less likely to let them outside the wire.

With the training of anthropologists to accompany the military in hostile areas increasingly seeming like a fool's errand, the military turned to training soldiers themselves in how to operate in these culturally sensitive areas. For soldiers to fulfill this function, however, they needed a crash course in Afghan politics and culture.

Shura School

On the edge of Kabul, near the ruins of the former parliamentary palace, was a relatively small ISAF camp called Camp Julien. It shared the area with an ANA base where many of the young ANA recruits were trained; when approaching, one could often watch Afghan recruits practicing moving in formation under the watchful eye of international trainers contracted by DynCorp, one of the larger military contractors in the country. The cluster of temporary structures at this small base served mostly as housing as well as a small presentation hall, a dining facility, and a couple of offices, all connected by the ubiquitous gravel paths of international bases. In these buildings an odd international conglomeration of primarily midlevel officers from the various NATO countries represented in ISAF, along with Afghan officials from a range of bodies, including the army, the police, and NDS (the National Directorate of Security), came for three or four days at a time for a series of workshops focused on issues connected to counterinsurgency theory and practice.

A series of lectures was developed, where, typically, military officers presented on an array of topics, such as strategies for Afghan–coalition partnering and evidence gathering in the field to ensure that insurgents could be more effectively tried in Afghan courts. Students with cups of coffee and notepads sat on wooden benches with Afghan officers in chairs closer to the front, where they could use the translation service. This created a rather incongruous image of Afghan policemen, sitting around with simultaneous translation headphones on, listening to international military officers lecture them in English on Afghanistan's government and military structures.

As what must have been primarily a public relations move, the COIN Academy, as it was called, also allowed some international civilians, NGO workers, and the occasional anthropologist to attend some of these talks. This gave me the opportunity to observe several of these sessions and talk with participants about the instruction. Chatting with one of the Australians charged with designing the modules provided a window on how the international military thought about "teaching" Afghan politics and culture. Given my own previous background in informal dispute resolution and local shuras, one of the most interesting modules for me was entitled "Effective Traditional Consultation with the Population." As the instructor who designed the course told me, the basic goal was to teach the soldiers "how to run a shura."

With Afghan policemen and a mixture of other coalition soldiers surrounding a slightly raised platform, I watched the module from the back of the room. The soldiers were quiet as the narrator began to read from a script, the first slide appearing on the screen behind him. At the center of the slide was an idyllic picture of about thirty Afghan elders, sitting on a series of blankets with three international soldiers. All were cross-legged, listening to an elder across from the international soldiers speak, and below the picture was a quote from a passage of the Koran stating that those that conduct their affairs "by mutual consultation" are praised. As the speaker began to introduce the topic, the next slide came up with a list of "Terminal Learning Objectives." These include the ability to "understand the cultural significance of traditional meetings" and to "demonstrate an understanding of the debriefing and documentation requirements" for those attending such meetings.

The narrator standing at the podium gave a brief introduction explaining the learning goals, and then about a dozen international officers and Afghan translators walked onto the small stage to begin an extended role-playing session, where one of the "village meetings" was acted out in front of the audience. The session described a mission from "Forward Operating Base Tuna" that was required to go into an area that had not previously had contact with either the Afghan army or police. The mission of the ISAF soldiers was to help facilitate a "meet and greet" between the commander of the Afghan army and the police, with several of the key local elders. They were also hoping to assess the needs of the community and gather information on Taliban activity in the area.

Behind the actors, a detailed satellite image of the area was displayed on the screen. I was struck by the contradiction of having so much detailed

Figure 10.2. Shura school. Photo by the author.

information about some aspects of the village while remaining totally clueless about others. I would have loved to have imagery like this when I conducted my research; instead I only had what the Afghans had: vaguely sourced stories and rumors about who lived where and what leaders were most important. These stories mapped out the politics of the area and the social relations between various groups. The map in the presentation attempted to do some of this by overlaying mug shots where certain commanders held sway, but it provided few such additional details. Instead it emphasized where the different roads were, where the local mosques were located, and where the most recent Taliban attacks had occurred. In particular, several points were noted as hostile terrain, and there were suggestions for meeting points for a potential gathering but also extraction routes if the group needed to flee. The emphasis of these slides remained tactical even while trying to integrate elements of what politics in the district might have actually looked like; there was little political strategic depth.

As the scene unfolded, the actors, most of whom were instructors at the counterinsurgency academy, stepped forward to join the narrator. Because the audience was familiar with many of these "actors" from lectures on previous days, there was some chuckling as different instructors came on the stage and some smiles at some of the more wooden performances, but for the most part the audience was attentive. Although it was easy on an international military base to find people to play the coalition soldiers in the skit, one of the issues that became apparent immediately was the fact that the only Afghans who actually worked in Camp Julien were translators.[11] These translators were usually in their twenties. This meant that, during the role-playing exercises, these young translators were required to play the parts of all the Afghans in the scenario, including the "village mullah," "elder 1," "elder 2," and so on. I watched, smiling, as one of the young men tried to straighten the turban atop his colleague's head, a garment that clearly neither of these young urban elites had ever worn before or were likely to wear anytime soon outside this international base. Despite these disjunctures, both the Afghans and international performers approached the scene seriously, and the audience members took notes as the skit unfolded.

After each brief scene, the narrator would pause and ask the audience to take note of certain things. He asked: "Who entered the meeting first, and what did this show?" Answer: "ANSF [Afghan National Security Forces]—shows that they are in the lead." The module suggested several tactical considerations, such as "choosing the meeting location is the responsibility of your ANSF counterpart and the Village Elder" and that "you may go further into a village than initially planned or desired." The narrator suggested that members of the meeting should "talk family" and share tea, also giving recommendations on how to sit during the meeting and to make sure weapons were not pointed at any of the participants. The narrator also instructed them not to ask about women and not to come across as an "Arrogant Westerner."

A series of questions about the political and economic situation were raised before the simulated council meeting with the local elders. ("What basic civil needs does the community require? Who are the key leaders in the village?") Most of these questions were then answered over the course of the mock shura. (The village needed a well and "agricultural guidance." The Village Elder was Haji Matin, the Village Mullah was Mullah Rahimi, and the Village Teacher was Mualam Burhan—I found the fact that these positions were all capitalized throughout the script interesting, suggesting that the role of "Village Elder" was somehow a formalized position worthy of the capitalization of a proper noun as military rankings are.) The audience then watched as the coalition forces' commanding officer debriefed with his note taker, who suggested questions for the next time they had a meeting with the elders. ("What is the current network diagram in the village? And why was the local farmer included in the meeting?")

When the session was over, there was brief, polite applause, and then the soldiers filed out to the mess hall next door for lunch. As we sat at long tables, I asked a few of the international soldiers across from me how they thought the presentation went. For the most part they thought that it had been interesting, but most of the soldiers I spoke with pointed out that they had few opportunities to engage in such meetings with local Afghans. Instead, most of them, as midlevel officers, had administrative or logistical duties on large bases like Bagram. It was the Special Forces guys, like Owen, who actually did this type of interaction, they said, and they never attended the COIN academy. The conversation over lunch quickly shifted, and the soldiers started discussing the accommodations they had next door, comparing the housing with the barracks at their more permanent posts.

I left the presentation with perhaps more questions than I had when I arrived. The entire experience was odd. This was especially true because, during my previous field research, I had sat on numerous occasions with exactly this type of gathering of actual Afghan elders. It almost felt like a parody of these experiences that I had had previously, rather than an actual representation, and it left me scratching my head. Why did they use a quote from the Koran to justify the use of shuras? Were they trying to justify them to the coalition soldiers watching the skit? To the Afghan villagers? (And how odd was it for Christian soldiers to be quoting Muslim scripture to Afghan villagers to justify a meeting?) Or was this justification for the Afghan police and security forces in the audience? This seemed unlikely, considering the fact that most of the training seemed aimed directly at the international soldiers, with the presence of Afghans almost an afterthought to demonstrate cooperation between the ANA and NATO.

It was also interesting to watch how the module integrated elements of what the military really wanted to see into the scenario. For example, the fact that the villagers wanted "agricultural guidance" seemed convenient because many FOBs had recently been given agricultural advisors (and, really, few villagers wanted "guidance"; mostly they wanted seeds and fertilizers and simply put up with training programs to get them). Similarly, the fact that on the next mission they were planning on asking about the "current network diagram in the village" was clearly a projection of how the military wanted Afghan villages to work. I wondered if, even on the best day, these soldiers would bump into such usefully packaged information.

The other issue the presentation raised was that in many of my conversations both in Kabul and around Bagram: It was often the Afghan police and other Afghan government officials who were most opposed to the type of COIN approach that hosting shuras seemed to represent. If the international community was working to set up meetings with village elders and relying on informal councils to gather information, this seemed to directly circumvent the state. In the skit, the coalition soldiers (and, ironically, the Afghan security forces in the room) were essentially being taught to work around government officials, communicating directly with local elders. It was in moments like these that the friction was most apparent between those like the State Department, who wanted to state build by expanding the Afghan government, and those, particularly in the military, who were using counterinsurgency tactics that often reached around the state. I asked some of these Afghan officers about it in the mess hall after the performance, but it was clear that being selected to participate was an honor for them and a means of advancement, and so they seemed not particularly bothered by the fact that they were being lectured on their own culture by Australian soldiers for much of the day. Similar to many of the international soldiers, they were more interested in chatting about the quality of the food being served.

The presentation itself went out of its way to try to bridge some of the tensions between the state-building approaches that favor building the institutions of the government and the counterinsurgency tactics that ignored weak state officials and focused on the informal elders who had the real power in local communities. One of the central bullet points on the third introductory slide stated that "Village Meetings are a legitimate means for GIRoA [Government of the Islamic Republic of Afghanistan] to consult and connect with people" and suggested that this was supported by the Afghan National Development Strategy. Although shuras I had attended might have been a method that both the government and elders used in rural areas, including Bagram, to build some additional political legitimacy for themselves locally by demonstrating their ability to bring people together, this legitimacy was local and did not connect to a wider sense of national development.

Such training, however, was not happening just in Afghanistan, and Owen laughed as he recounted some of the similar training he had been sent to observe back in the United States:

They do shuras with Afghan role players and bring in Afghans. No shit. I went with one of the Green Berets that we were going to work with. I went, and I witnessed some of this training. We went to Fort Knox to see this training that they were doing and were like, what the fuck? It was eye opening that this is how they approached this thing. When we got put on the VSO thing [Village Stabilization Operations—an attempt to insert teams at a local level to provide support for local villages, requiring an amount of cultural and social understanding that was not typical for the SEALs], we, I mean the SEAL community, we were like . . . what the fuck? I'm going to have to go in there and have tea with a village elder?

Everything we do in our training is about kinetic in nature. Everything we do. If it's not about killing someone, it's about getting to where you are going to kill somebody. Riding in a helicopter, driving a boat, jumping out of a plane, we're just getting to the X and then on the X we're shooting someone in the face. That's why people go to BUDS because of that, people make it through BUDS because of that, and people join teams because of that. Every piece of training we do is to that end. And now we're being told we need to sit around and drink tea? What? People's minds were doing backflips.

The soldiers in the room were perhaps not doing backflips, but it was clear that they were having trouble connecting what they were watching with what they had experienced on the bases and PRTs where they normally resided. For them, the training was little more than a welcomed three-day break from their normal duties. Owen, himself, was all for any type of training that was going to actually help his mission. Sitting at Camp Julien, however, it was not clear to me that any of the officers in the room were likely to use this type of training in the field. However, as the surge continued, the coalition forces were faced with new problems as their numbers swelled, problems such as the increasing number of Afghans who had been detained by international forces and were being held at places like Bagram. Here, high-ranking officers decided, was a place where they could use the shura strategy.

The Prisoner Release Shura

With the surge also came an immense increase in the number of Afghan and foreign fighters who were detained by the international military. As prisons in Bagram and elsewhere filled, there were increasing logistical questions about what to do with the numerous detainees whose status was murky. For soldiers like Owen, who were busy fighting a war, there was little emphasis on legal processes, such as evidence collection, on the battlefield or while conducting raids. As a result, it was often difficult to charge these detainees in Afghan courts. Other detainees had been picked up simply because they were in the wrong place at the wrong time. With facilities filled to capacity, there were many whom the international military wished had not been detained in the first place. Simply releasing these men, however, seemed problematic. How could officials be sure they would not return directly to the battlefield? Would the military transfer them back to their home provinces? Would they just walk out of the front gate at Bagram? So, working with the State Department and ISAF, the U.S. military began seeking alternative methods of dealing with these detainees. One of the more popular ideas was to release these prisoners into the care of community elders in a public ceremony. Tying this situation into the wider strategy of community consultation, these ceremonies became known as Prisoner Release Shuras.

As they began piloting these shuras, I was working on an access to justice project for the United States Institute of Peace and was invited to observe one of these gatherings. At the time, detainees held at the facility at the Bagram Airfield were having their cases reviewed, a long and slow process according to those involved. Those prisoners who had a sufficient amount of evidence against them were handed over to the Ministry of Justice. Those on whom they had no evidence or who were accused of lesser crimes were being released in these new ceremonies to local elders. In addition to moving many of these detainees who seemed to be not much of a threat out of the prisons, it was the hope of COIN practitioners that such programs could also help win hearts and minds. This was in part a response to one of the major criticisms of the international military presence by Afghan communities, that the detention of young men was arbitrary and lacked transparency, but State Department offi-cials also felt that it could help build bridges between the Afghan state and the local leaders involved by holding council meetings. I knew what these shuras might look like in the provinces, and I was interested in seeing how they were recreated by the military, who were putting so much hope in them.

Many of these detention cases demonstrated the difficulties both sides seemed to have in communicating with and understanding the other: Was a group of men with shovels walking down the road off to their fields to work planting crops, or were they being paid by the Taliban to lay a roadside bomb? The Marine who had recently had a comrade killed in an attack was likely to have a tendency to reach a conclusion very different from that of someone else. Similarly, once a young man was detained, where did he go? Was he at the local international base, or had he been flown someplace like Bagram? How could his family find out more about the case? Considering some of the problems I had just with finding the doors of certain bases, it was certainly not surprising that Afghan families would have even more problems getting information or even finding someone to speak to inside the base.

The complex relationships of the international military with a corrupt Afghan judicial system that was not running at full capacity further complicated the situation. Once detained, many things could happen to the young man. He could be handed over to the NDS. He could enter the Afghan court system. He could remain in American custody. Oftentimes this happened without any information being released to the young man's family. Prisoner Release Shuras were meant not simply to deal with the great number of detainees but were also meant as a move toward transparency. Theoretically they were also designed to suggest to Afghan communities that they were involved in the justice process and that they had a say in whether these young men were a danger to the community.

In theory, these meetings would be held in designated places, such as mosques, guestrooms of influential men, or outside on carpets in the centers of local communities. By the time I received my invitation, it was clear that, although the design of these meetings was simple, the logistics of setting up such meetings were more complicated. Military officials were at times unsure where the best place to hold such gatherings would be, and because they were partnering with the ANA it was decided that initially holding some of these meetings at ANA facilities would be easiest. Simultaneously, it would help the image of the ANA in the wider community. This decision was somewhat strange at the time because it was not clear to me that communities in unstable areas would really have had a much more positive relationship with ANA bases than they did with international bases. In the eyes of the American military who were sponsoring the program, however, such an approach felt much more "Afghanized."

So, on a sunny morning, I was invited as part of my research to observe one of these meetings held at a facility on the outskirts of Kabul, not far from the Counterinsurgency Academy, to see if this was indeed helping Afghans gain access to justice. Despite being technically on the grounds of an ANA base, the meeting still had the feeling that it was being hosted by the international military—the large meeting hall was surrounded by temporary structures, thrown up hastily by the military, paid for with international funds, and all attendees had to pass through a series of checkpoints staffed by both American and Afghan soldiers and were carefully searched each time.

This particular shura brought together a handful of ISAF officers, the Minister of Justice, four members of parliament, a State Department representative, a few other Afghan government dignitaries, 140 elders, and perhaps forty former detainees. The group of dignitaries sat on a stage. A few ISAF reporters and other Westerners sat at the back of the room. Between us, around long tables, with their heads at the levels of the feet of the speaker, sat the local elders and recently released detainees.

The folding chairs that the elders and detainees sat in were in sharp contrast with the deep plush sofas that the dignitaries had sunk into. Such sofas and similar overstuffed armchairs were often associated with government officials and other members of the ruling elite. They were found in the offices of many ministers, and the Dari term for such a sofa, *diwan*, could actually either mean *palace* or refer to a piece of furniture.[12] This historic symbolic image of the state, with the ruler relaxing on a sofa while petitioners brought their cases to be judged by him, contradicted the collective nature of the local shura, where attendees generally sat on cushions on the floor in a circle. The entire structure of the affair contributed to the feeling that the release of prisoners was purely at the mercy and grace of the ruler, the same way that Karzai's sporadic releasing of prisoners from Afghan jails on certain holidays reinforced this sense.

The meeting was opened by the Minister of Justice, who called on those who had been released to join the side of the Afghan government and accept the Constitution. His speech emphasized religious themes, and he began with the reminder that Afghanistan is a Muslim country, assuring those in the room that those prosecuted under Afghan law were really being prosecuted under *shariah*, or Islamic law. The seemingly unnecessary reminder that Afghanistan was a Muslim country helped give his speech an almost ritualized feel, as he reassured everyone of their national identity and thus their unity. He then explained that prayer and respect for religion were the only real purposes of life. He highlighted the importance of prayer as a ritual that made them all Muslims and suggested that all the current fighting made prayer impossible for both those who were fighting and those in disrupted communities (threatening their status as true Muslims). At the same time, however, he also referred in his speech to the internationals in the room and called on ISAF to provide evidence for those detained or to release them. This seemed, however, to be aimed less at the internationals in attendance (few of whom were paying much attention to his speech) and seemed intended more to demonstrate to the elders in the room that he was not simply doing the bidding of the internationals. As was typical of many upper-level Afghan officials at such meetings, he concluded his speech by apologizing for how busy he was, and, as soon as his speech was over, he rapidly shook some hands of the key elders and officials and then left the room—another act that would not have been acceptable in any true shura meeting.

The ANA general who spoke after him was gruff, as was typical of Afghan officers. His speech was briefer and less theatrical. He focused on the security of the prisoners more than religion. He told the prisoners that "Afghanistan will always protect you," a particularly meaningful, but also questionable, statement, because many were returning to insurgent-filled areas where suspicions would run high that those who had been detained had also become spies for the Americans. If anyone could help ensure their protection, it was probably actually the elders in the room, and for most, it was not clear at all that the government would actually do much to protect them as they returned home.

The general's brevity contrasted with the series of Afghan parliamentarians who followed. They gave longer, vigorous speeches, calling on ISAF and the Ministry of Justice to immediately release all those who were innocent (suggesting at the same time, of course, that all those in the room actually may have been innocent). The way the criticism was phrased also suggested that it was the Ministry's fault when international forces kept innocent Afghans detained. One suggested that the minister, in particular, could do more to pressure international forces to release detainees. Another parliamentarian who said that he himself was a former Taliban member described his own detention and said that reconciliation should have started in 2001, not nine years later. This statement was, perhaps, not strictly true, because there had been a process for disarmament, demobilization, and reintegration (referred to as DDR) in the years just after the initial American invasion, but the program had been limited in its success, and therefore the recent attempt to reach out to former Taliban fighters was likely to feel to many in the room like a brand-new process. With new parliamentary elections scheduled for a few months after the meeting, these members of parliament appeared to be using the gathering as an opportunity to campaign for votes, and it was easy to see how their tough stances against the international military and an increasingly unpopular Afghan government might play well with the Afghan elders there, who could potentially be useful in later mobilizing votes.

It was then time for the international representatives to speak. The speeches made by ISAF officers were more formulaic (I wondered if there was a PowerPoint for giving introductory remarks at Prisoner Release Shuras as there was a PowerPoint on how to host a shura). They focused on statistics, such as the number of detainees who had already been released, and laid out the process of gathering testimony and evidence, such as fingerprints and residue from explosives. This seemed meant to impress on the attendees the seriousness of the process and the supposed logic of ISAF's detainee policy. An ISAF general, the highest-ranking member of the international military present, talked about their desire to hand over the system to the Afghan government as soon as possible, so that ISAF could become primarily advisors in the detention process. This statement was not disingenuous; in more private conversations, many of these international officials appeared anguished over their inability to move detainees out of the international system. Within the system they created, however, this was incredibly difficult; in the meantime, the number of detainees only increased.

There was a certain irony in the ISAF general's emphasis on the ongoing handing over of detention facilities and responsibilities for prosecuting prisoners to the Afghan government as quickly as possible, despite the fact several in the room described how they felt that they were treated much better in ISAF custody rather than being held by the Afghan government in the notorious Pul-i Charki prison. As one detainee told me, "It is better to be in Bagram for eight months than Pul-i Charki for one day." The ISAF officers and Afghan officials throughout the day also subtly snipped back and forth at each other over who was responsible for the woeful process. The ISAF general, for example, addressed the fact that a list of an additional eighty-four detainees from the ANSF centers had been given to the Ministry of Justice for immediate release but that they had not yet been released. Several other speakers criticized the Minister of Justice for this ("this government is not a government, and the minister should be ashamed of himself"). As the meeting went on, the tensions between the various representatives seemed to grow, and the lack of coordination among the various groups was clear to everyone in attendance.

The elders and detainees spoke last, toward the end of the day. They were briefer, and most of them were subdued, perhaps simply looking forward to heading home. Many of the detainees spoke of their innocence and described how they had been arrested after local rivals had given the international military false information about them. Some were more animated. One elder repeatedly emphasized the fact that we were in the *Islamic* Republic of Afghanistan and then led the room in three chants of "Allahu akbar," during which the international attendees shuffled their feet uncomfortably. However, the blame for long detentions was spread fairly evenly. Several speakers pointed out that the international military should not be detaining people, and some emphasized that the Afghan government did not have the capacity to deal with such cases and that perhaps the international troops should be involved because they were less biased against different tribes and ethnic groups than Afghan officials were likely to be.[13] A number of prisoners also pointed out how well they had been treated while detained, one showing off his new pair of eyeglasses.

The meeting was not always smooth. As the speeches were being delivered, participants came in and out of the building and attention wandered. Translation was also slow and sloppy, as well as difficult to hear through static-filled simultaneous translation headsets. I switched back and forth between using the headsets and listening to the speeches in Dari, to get a sense of whether the internationals in the room were hearing the same thing the Afghans were. In many instances, it seemed as if they were not. During one more animated presentation from a member of parliament, the translator abandoned trying to keep up with the torrid pace of the speech, explaining to the English-speaking listeners that the man "is simply repeating himself, and he seems drunk."

It was also hard to determine, particularly from the military side, whether the meeting was judged to be a success. Attendance was not taken, so it was impossible to tell whether the elders were actually from the communities that represented the prisoners. The initial idea of the shura was to release detainees from just one area, but that had not seemed feasible, so eventually detainees from several provinces were included in the ceremony. A couple of the elders in attendance suggested to me that they were not even from the same areas. If the elders were from different communities, the entire point of the meeting would have been undermined because they would not have the influence to convince the younger men not to rejoin the insurgency, but it was difficult to track this with all the comings and goings. The fact that even the officials in charge of the event did not seem to have a clear list of the attendees participating in the release suggested that those running the meeting did not have much more information than I was able to gather during the day. There is also some irony in the fact that security constraints meant this shura was held on an ANA base to keep a handful of internationals safe while forcing elders to travel from distant provinces on dangerous roads. For Afghan elders, who often use ritualized visiting to pay respect with the host almost always having more status than the guest, being hosted by the ANA also inherently made them subservient to the Afghan officials and internationals on the base there. This was certain to make the meeting feel less cooperative than I am sure the international officials involved had hoped it would be.

Those among the international military, however, still clearly thought that the stakes for the meeting were high. An official had come in from the U.S. embassy to observe the proceeding, and many of the international military officers were high ranking with busy schedules. One explained to me that one of those being released was known to be the head of an IED (improvised explosive device) manufacturing team, but the evidence against him was not conclusive enough. The governor from his province had "begged" them not to release him, but apparently he had influential friends in the presidential palace who had advocated for his release. With the governor lobbying the international military at the PRT in his province, and the president lobbying the U.S. embassy in Kabul, even this small meeting was being watched carefully.

At a lull in the meeting, a series of elders gathered around some of the ISAF officials toward the front of the room. They swamped the overly taxed translators with questions about other neighbors and relatives who had been detained during military operations and not heard from again. The midlevel ISAF officials who were running the event had no real information with them about other detainees but dutifully took down names and phone numbers, although they were clearly overwhelmed and did not seem optimistic that they would be able to assist. They tried to convince the elders that, even though this meeting was only for those who had already been released, there would be more like it. One elder, looking discouraged, told the official that any information he could give him about those who were still detained would be helpful for the families from his village. The ISAF officials could do little more than encourage him to stay for lunch.

At the end of the meeting, all of those released received a certificate in a picture frame. I was left struggling to imagine those who were still living in insurgent-filled areas returning home to hang the certificate from NATO declaring their innocence proudly on their walls for the Taliban and others to see.

Building Relationships, Not Dams

Although it was difficult to judge the usefulness of that meeting, the fact that the military soon moved away from such approaches suggests that few saw real benefits from the political and economic capital spent setting them up. Part of this was the fact that, as the number of troops began to decline in the country, there were fewer detainees filling facilities. There was also an increasing emphasis on having the ANA immediately take custody of detainees, so on Owen's first deployment there were a lot of detainees in what he referred to as the "gray area" between Afghan and American custody, but by his redeployment in 2014 he estimated that only 1 percent of detainees were ever in American control. Beyond this, however, the oddly ineffective shura fit into a wider pattern of the international community's failure to understand the motives of those Afghans with whom they were interacting, while also failing to make meaningful changes when they did have a sense of what these motives were.

One of the problems with both the Prison Release Shura and the shura training session at the Counterinsurgency Academy was, in part, the fact that they seem to have inverted the ways in which these meetings work. In Afghan towns and villages, shuras met because there was trust and cooperation between the key individuals. A shura meeting was then a public demonstration of that trust and respect, with everyone sitting together as equals. In this case of the Prisoner Release Shura, as well as other such meetings sponsored by the international military, the military was attempting to use these gatherings to establish relationships before there was any real trust between the parties. They were also relying on Afghan officials who were often from Kabul or had lived abroad as refugees. Such Kabuli officials often had deep biases and spoke condescendingly to those from rural areas, a practice that predated the years of war. The international officials organizing the shura meetings really did want to build relationships with these Afghan elders, but they prioritized the structures of the meetings over the relationships themselves, ignoring the details of who was actually attending and how the meeting was set up. All this essentially put the cart before the horse.

Around Bagram, we can see how a similar lack of trust doomed many of the outreach and consultation programs that the international community attempted to organize. These programs were almost always initiated by the ruling elite who had already made so much money off contracting with the base that the community had little trust in them. A businessman like Omar knew it was far more lucrative to maintain private contacts both within the Afghan government and, even better, with those on the base than to waste time with these performances. Furthermore, those in the communities around Bagram had already watched millions being spent without previous consultation and had little reason to believe that international attempts to reach out, during what was then the eighth year of the war, were anything other than decorative. Even when meetings were held, there was no trust in the room to begin with and little reason to think that it would grow out of such ceremonies that served primarily to demonstrate the power of the international community and the ruling elite.

This was part of a wider failure of understanding how to operate in the Afghan political world. The technical, bureaucratic approaches of those in the intervention were not suited to learning about culture, building on lessons learned or establishing the relationships that were at the heart of how Afghan politics work, even when figures like Owen and Ronald Neumann really did want these things to work. As Neumann reflected back, "Our assumption is that technical experience is plug in/plug out and that you can simply take it into another culture. Now it's true that the technical aspects of an electric line are the same from one country to another, but you need to find out how the local people, officials, whatever the level is, define the problem before you tell them a solution that they will buy into, and we don't do that."

The problem was not an Afghanistan problem as much as it was a problem with how internationals were thinking about intervention. Neumann continued: "This is something I've seen us do in Iraq and Afghanistan with technical people, who will see a problem, and they will see the technical solution, and their solution might be technically valid, but if you don't understand the problems and priorities of the locals you're not addressing the problem." The blueprints for refurbishing the Kajaki dam may have been technically sound, but they did not address the instability in the area or many of the political issues that communities near the dam had with the project. Neumann added:

"Without buy-in, you're either getting nothing or you're getting something that's simply going to collapse once we walk away, but that comes back to how much time you need to spend developing a relationship and how much time you need to spend talking about issues."

This related more broadly to how both diplomats and international military officials thought of their Afghan counterparts. As Neumann reflected, "Afghans tend to relate to people more as individuals, whereas we relate to them as the functional holders of a position. Look at our bio collection in Afghanistan; this is something I've been complaining about for years—you ask for a bio of a local commander or official and what you get is a list of the jobs that they have held mostly since 2001." I found myself agreeing with the ambassador. While working on my dissertation, I had also drawn up the political histories of various key figures in town. The long biographies written by the embassy, however, were extremely different from the types of notes that I drew up, and I had always been surprised by how much work went into the embassy versions, just to record the formal positions and offices that the leaders had held. These documents, however, said little about the leader's position in Afghan politics vis-à-vis other tribes, commanders, or government officials. In Istalif, simple political résumés would not have explained the complex dynamics on the ground that evolved after decades of shifting alliances and relationships. Referring to these official biographies, Neumann continued, "They don't tell you where they fought, who they fought with, who betrayed them, who killed their father. They're as useless as an ashtray on a motorcycle. Yet twelve years in, we still don't collect useful biographical information. A lot of people might end up knowing this stuff, but we can't capture it." Many of the higher-up political advisors at the embassy who had been in Afghanistan for a while might come to know these things through conversations, but, as vital as this information was, it rarely made the more formulaic sheets that were supposed to describe the individual's political history. It also meant that, as soon as a new official rotated in, all they had to start with were these bland fact sheets, and the insider knowledge all left with the outgoing political officer.

After spending a couple of hours on Owen's boat on Chesapeake Bay talking about the various challenges he and his guys faced, and the ways in which things went wrong, I tried to turn the conversation around toward what had worked during his time in the country. He paused and said "the colonel," referring to the ANA colonel whom he was partnered with for much of his time:

Honestly, he was pretty easy, because I was giving money to his guys. I was providing training. There were some things he would get mad about. We'd talk about training, and then he'd start talking about his garden, this garden that he wanted. He needed a well for his garden [he'd tell me], and I was like, "Hey man, my job is not for the beautification of your base, my job is to make sure that your soldiers can go out to these places and not get themselves killed." And he didn't like hearing that, but after a while I was able to show him how much more important military training was than making his base look good. After a period of time, if I had some money that I could throw toward it, I would.

The colonel had originally seen the internationals whom he worked with primarily as a source of income, Owen continued: "The Green Berets had this job before I did. I turned over with the ODA [Operational Detachment-Alpha, the Army Special Forces Team that he replaced]. They gave them all sorts of stuff, here, here, here, here," Owen said making grabbing gestures, "and then when we got there, we were like, the floodgates stopped, and they were pissed at first. We changed it from a sense of entitlement . . . 'No, no, no, you're Americans, you're here to give us this,' to 'Yes, I'm an American, but I'm here to train you.' And that worked because we were relying on each other." From this tense beginning, a stronger working relationship gradually emerged; in the end, Owen and the colonel created an effective coalition partnership.

But Owen's time there was short, just as the surge was short. Although this relationship might have lasted the length of his deployment, there was no guarantee that those replacing him would continue it. In fact, more often than not, this was not the case in Afghanistan where relationships are built on personalities, not the positions that the individual inhabits.

Unfortunately, the surge was over before the international community was able to build meaningful understanding or connections. People who had the most experience, like Ambassador Neumann, were often not there long enough to maintain many of the meaningful relationships in a way that might have changed the outcome of the intervention. For others, like Will Locke, who took the time to build such relations, the world of the surge moved too fast to make a place for his thoughtful approaches to sustainable energy. The development money was, in too many instances, gone before young Afghan entrepreneurs like Omar had a chance to build the businesses and organizations that could bring real economic change to Afghanistan. Although he remained hopeful, he also faced a long struggle against an entrenched ruling elite of former commanders and corrupt government officials and was likely going to need to adapt further to extreme economic swings as the market veered wildly in response to a decrease in international attention.

By announcing that the drawdown of troops would start just years after, Obama's surge created a fast-paced world, where money was spent, contradictions arose, and tensions mounted, but where relationships were too rarely built. Those who took part in the intervention were left to ask what this burst of effort actually achieved.

11 The Pieces Left Behind

The military was like: We're going to put boots on the ground and kick AQ [al Qaeda] where it counts, and we're probably not going to kill them all, but we're going to kill a lot of them . . . I just think it got out of hand. After ten years, we're no longer there kicking AQ's ass, we're handing out money and we're stepping on IEDs.

—Owen

Was It Worth It?

By the spring of 2015, the drawdown of international troops was nearly complete; outside of Bagram, everything, it seemed, was for sale. Despite the fact it had been announced that the United States would maintain a presence of some 10,000 troops and most bases would be transferred over to the ANA, most of Bagram was being disassembled, and raw materials were pouring off the bases.

Young men were busy at shops outside the center of the bazaar, pulling nails out of piles of wooden boards to be reused. Others were breaking apart shipping containers with blowtorches and crowbars, so the pieces could be shipped more easily to Pakistan. Closer to the base, more valuable materials were for sale, and as I approached the gate I passed a shopping compound with stacks of portable toilets and another with office chairs straight from the base. Chatting with people in the bazaar, it was clear that businessmen like Omar thought this might be their last chance to take advantage of the international presence, and, although people complained of the decrease in funds, it was clear that in this moment most shops seemed to be doing well. At the same time, however, there was a sense that everything from the intervention was slipping away, making the base just another archeological site among all the others in the Shomali Plain.

Speaking to audiences in the United States, I am often pressed to give an assessment of the intervention. Was the intervention *worth it*? Was it *successful*?

These are never easy questions to answer. How can we measure the impact of the intervention? In the small town where I did my original research, which the Taliban had effectively leveled, Istalifis overwhelmingly saw the intervention as a good thing. NATO forces had pushed the Taliban from the area, businesses were growing, and the district was relatively stable. Schools and mosques had been built; people were marrying and thinking about the future. There was resentment toward the Afghan government due to its corruption and frustration with the unevenness of international aid, but these issues were relatively minor. For Istalifis, life during the intervention was a great improvement over life before it.

On a national level, however, the question is far more difficult to answer. In one sense, the advances in Afghanistan since 2001 in public health and education have been staggering. In 2001, one in every four children in Afghanistan died before reaching the age of five. By 2010 that number was one in ten.[1] School enrollment increased from 1 million to 8 million, with 2.5 million of those girls (under the Taliban there had been virtually no girls in government schools). Although there is some debate over the precise numbers, life expectancy in Afghanistan had also increased by at least ten years since 2001 (some reports have it as high as twenty years).[2] In a population of 30 million, that is potentially 60 million years of human life. Such incredible changes were the result of hardworking Afghans and internationals who revolutionized public health and education in the country in a very short time.

Of course, the costs were as astounding as the gains, and it is easy to find similarly impressive statistics that suggest the intervention has been a fool's errand. With over 2,000 U.S. soldiers killed, 20,000 civilian causalities, and at least 4 million people displaced, the numbers are both notoriously difficult to calculate and difficult to contemplate.[3] Programs such as iCasualities and the "Costs of War" program at Brown University have attempted to maintain statistics on the human, economic, and social costs of the interventions in Afghanistan and Iraq, but even these attempts face serious challenges. For example, military deaths often do not include contractors, who in 2014, as American troop numbers declined, outnumbered actual soldiers working for the U.S. military by 40,000.[4] Other numbers are impossible to manage because of the long-term repercussions of the intervention we are just beginning to understand, such as the $63 billion that has already been spent on medical care and disability benefits to American veterans of the wars in Afghanistan and Iraq since 2001, a figure that has been predicted to rise to $3 trillion as veterans age.[5]

The anthropologist in me almost always tries to return to the human level to ask such questions about how individuals evaluate their lived experience of the intervention. Asking those individuals who were a part of the intervention to assess their time there provides more context than these politically motivated statistics but also demonstrates some of the challenges in thinking more broadly about the experience. When I asked Owen, he reflected for a moment: "Did I make that place any better? Did I make America any safer? I don't know . . . maybe. Sometimes when people thank me for my service, I think, thank a local cop for keeping you safe."

But what about fighting terrorism? What about the patriotism that Owen had felt in the wake of the September 11 attacks? Owen answered:

> On the national-level counterterrorist initiative, I see a much more direct line to keeping Americans safe, but what I was doing in Afghanistan? This was the most dangerous thing I've ever done or probably will do . . . Maybe in some isolated cases it did some good for Afghanistan, but I don't think Afghanistan will change, and I don't think our presence there was helping things to that end. My presence there might have been keeping a village safer for a limited amount of time, but since then maybe that village has been completely routed by the Taliban, because they came in and said, "We're going to kill everyone because you let the Americans into your village." That could have very easily happened. I don't know that it hasn't. We took great personal risk, and if that happened, we actually made it worse.

Will was more direct and perhaps more optimistic. Will, like Owen, focused on the personal relationships that the intervention created. The real benefit of AWP for Will, he said with a pause, was that "we trained some people." Although the company itself did not take off and his dream of seeing hydropowered wind pumps in the area surrounding Bagram was never realized, all of the men who worked for the company had been exposed to a variety of techniques for working with wind energy that were actually applicable to a rather wide array of other energy projects. The people whom Will has stayed in touch with went off to work for very different companies, but for the most part they were using at least some of the skills they had built working with Will. It was the relationship, the knowledge that was passed on, that ultimately made much more of a difference than the funds that were spent.

Like Will, Owen continued to talk about the impact he had on those whom he was closest to, the men under his command: "I had the opportunity to write some good awards for my guys . . . [while I was doing this] I read cita- tions from World War II . . . this guy went ashore at Normandy or Iwo Jima and stopped Japanese Imperialism. I read the citations that my guys got, and it's like 'these guys stood up for each other when shit went sideways. A lot of guys went over there, some guys didn't make it back, a lot of guys came back horribly changed, a lot of guys got promoted out of it.'"

Owen continued, telling the story of a soldier who was blinded by a mine, "He gave up his eyesight. Did that make America safer? Did it make anyone in Afghanistan safer? But you can't really think about it that way . . . every single death. Without those 70,000 Americans that died on D-Day, think about that, the net result was that we defeated Nazism."

What Was the Intervention?

Of course all of these debates over whether the intervention was a success or failure beg the question, failed or succeeded *to do what*? What was the in- ternational community hoping to achieve in Afghanistan? This is a difficult question to answer because there were so many different answers to the ques- tion and because many of those in the international community answered the question in contradictory ways: If the United States was fighting a war against terrorism, why did it not stop when Osama bin Laden was killed? If the in- ternational community was promoting international values like democracy and human rights, why did they continue to coddle warlords, who had well- documented histories of past and current crimes? If, as some argue, this was really just a neocolonial affair, why did the international community spend so much money, while extracting no natural resources from Afghanistan? (In fact, Chinese firms thus far have benefited the most from Afghanistan's po- tential mineral wealth, which is ironic because they are one of the least visible international presences in the country.)

Even the way American leaders discussed the intervention changed dras- tically over time. Bush's War on Terrorism eventually morphed into a state- building operation that was then replaced by counterinsurgency doctrine. Not every aspect of these shifts was a complete change in policy and implementa- tion, but the shifts did change the tone of politicians when discussing the in- tervention and the ways in which programs were prioritized. Debates within the Bush and Obama administrations over how to think about and address the problems in Afghanistan had far-reaching implications. For example, was the problem in Afghanistan terrorists or insurgents? The question might seem like semantics, but in the Obama administration's review of America's strategy in the country, the answer would have direct impact on how many troops were sent to the country, how their mission was defined, where funds were spent, and how the government treated various groups both inside and outside the country. With Vice President Joseph Biden pushing for a counter-terrorist approach that would favor a smaller number of troops, particularly Special Forces, and General Petraeus and others in the military pushing for a more thorough counterinsurgency approach that would demand a massive influx of troops and funds, Obama's decision to favor the military's counter-insurgency approach reshaped the entire conflict.[6] The decision had direct impact on how Owen's mission of supporting ANA troops, instead of acting on his own, shaped the ways in which Will sought out funds, reorganized the strategies of Omar's business, and restructured the role of the State Department in the conflict.

Each member of the intervention experienced the ways that these un-resolved approaches, competing theories, and the methods derived from them had the potential to contradict and undermine each other, particularly when the approaches were employed simultaneously. A counterinsurgency approach, for example, suggested that the international community concen-trate its efforts in the areas where the insurgency was the most intense, using development projects to win hearts and minds and to decrease the likelihood that young men would join the insurgency. An approach that prioritized de-velopment, however, argued that resources should be more evenly distrib-uted around the country; if anything, they should go to areas that were more secure where projects were likely to have a higher chance of success rather than to unstable areas where insecurity might endanger staff. At the same time, a state-building approach might favor the promotion of technocratic officials who could run the government's administration in the provinces, whereas a stabilization model would favor any local commander who might be able to control local violence regardless off his ability to govern effectively or legally.

Different countries and even institutions within countries oftentimes seemed to have different goals in Afghanistan. American troops were clearly the greatest promoters of the counterinsurgency approach, particularly when General McCrystal and General Petraeus were leading ISAF, but they were greatly supported by the Australians, who also favored such an approach. At the same time, the German military tended to favor stabilization and pushed the Afghan state to take the lead. Within the U.S. government, approaches clashed, with the State Department almost always inclined to emphasize state building over either counterinsurgency or counterterrorism. These conflicting strategies created a revolving door of policy decisions that seemed at times to spin Afghans around and leave them right back where they started.

For example, in the initial years of the intervention, few internationals paid much attention to the rapidly reviving opium industry in the south of the country, which the Taliban had actually been very successful in suppressing. A few years later, however, the British government, with encouragement from the Americans, began an aggressive campaign of opium eradication, based primarily on the logic that the Taliban were using the proceeds from the opium trade to fund the insurgency. Destroying one of the few viable crops for farmers in this part of the country, however, earned the international community few allies among local Afghans. Furious farmers with wrecked crops were not helpful in winning hearts and minds, and analysts became increasingly concerned that this was leading young underemployed farmers to join the insurgency. Soon the international military was back to turning a blind eye to the opium issue and in some cases even paying compensation to farmers whose opium crops were damaged by helicopters landing in their fields.[7]

These varying goals that occasionally contradicted each other all undermined the coherence of international efforts. In particular, they also made evaluating different projects and priorities challenging. When one program was working but no longer fit the general strategy of the donor country, it was too often abandoned. NGOs, even when they were successful at one type of project, were often forced to submit proposals to do very different things, simply to keep funds coming in and fickle short-term donors happy. This contributed to the inability of many of the institutions that comprised the intervention to effectively assess either their failures or their successes.

Learning Lessons

If there is any lesson to be learned from the intervention in Afghanistan, it is perhaps the difficulty of learning lessons. Will, Owen, Omar, and Ron all spoke of the various ways in which the different organizations that were a part of the intervention failed to learn and adapt as the intervention went on and their goals, programs, and missions changed. So, on one level, suggesting that there is a better way to "do" an intervention would hobble those involved in

206 The Pieces Left Behind

the next one, just as those in Afghanistan were hampered by lessons learned in places like Iraq and East Timor.

One of the challenges of learning lessons was that institutions had poor memories and that the people who were a part of the intervention were changing all the time. In the military this often meant tours of around a year, though some countries such as Great Britain had even shorter tours. NGO workers and contractors might have stayed somewhat longer than this on average, but they were still on fixed timeframe contracts that gave them less incentive to look toward the future of projects. Funding was often on an annual cycle, so even NGO workers who were remaining in Afghanistan were often working on something new or radically changed each year as programming shifted. Perhaps most problematic were Western diplomats who required deep cultural and political understandings of the place but were oftentimes rotated through on one-year stints. The American State Department made this even worse by tending to rotate everyone at the same time each summer. Ambassador Neumann lamented: "With one-year duty tours, almost the whole embassy staff was turning over during the summer, a kind of institutional frontal lobotomy of lost experience. We recommended to Washington various ways of improving the situation: tours linked with Washington jobs so that two officers would rotate back and forth and the staggering of some jobs so that rotation would occur in the winter and spread out the loss of critical knowledge. Nothing happened."[8] As a result, almost none of the State Department's diplomats were likely to gain the intimate familiarity with a country and its leaders that Neumann was able to build over the years.

There was an upside to this, in that people who were new to Afghanistan oftentimes had an optimism and an energy that the old-timers lacked, but even this could be problematic. Neumann suggested: "The fact that we change people all the time means that you are always getting some new enthusiasm that tends to divert resources. The enthusiasm or enthusiasms tend to come faster than your resources. So when you have command pressures to move resources to whatever is a higher priority they need to come out of something that is now deemed a lower priority. But that often means that we lose focus, and we lose attention." In the process, older projects were forgotten or at least deprioritized, Neumann indicated: "We don't keep our gaze on things. Did you ever read *The Wind in the Willows* when you were a child? Do you remember Mr. Toad sitting in the road with a canary yellow car in a ditch, looking at the ditch and the car, saying 'oh my, oh my'? We do that a lot."

Another issue was that, despite talk of civilian–military projects, the military and civilian groups, including both independent NGOs and government bodies like the Department of State, still rarely cooperated in a meaningful manner. This meant not only were those in the intervention not well placed to create relationships with Afghans, but also that they struggled to create relationships even with each other. Change here seemed easier to facilitate. Neumann discussed this: "Another brainstorm of mine, which is also not happening, is to put some embassy officers with Special Forces. Put them with the military, so that they are under military ROE [Rules of Engagement] because, frankly, if someone gets killed then it is not a political issue [as much as a military issue], though frankly I'd prefer to have them out with Special Forces because I think intellectually they have a better understanding of the need to build relationships as opposed to just having a Key Leader Engagement, which is a term that I absolutely despise," referring back to much of the type of work that Owen had felt the least prepared for: "You're a diplomat, we deal with relationships and in building them, and that has nothing to do with me having a meeting and then running away and saying I had an engagement. Put an embassy officer out there with them in Kandahar or Helmand, with a Special Forces group, not as a classic PolAd role [political advisor], but as a reporter . . . They [the Special Forces members] know that they don't know this stuff. They are always working on, and they've got some very good people out there, [but the coordination is lacking]."

Yet, as we saw in Owen's case, although the military might have similarly craved such interactions, no institutions on either side of the civilian–military line were really set up to cooperate in such a manner. Instead, both individuals and organizations themselves were more concerned that what they were doing made sense within their own institutional framework, continually looking back to Washington for guidance. With too few people thinking about the overarching goals of the intervention, individuals were left to make decisions that best suited their own interests.

Although both Bush and Obama advocated for better civilian–military coordination and Obama mentioned the strategy frequently when referring to Afghanistan on the campaign trail, these attempts at better coordination were not a question of politics, Neumann concluded: "This failure to comprehend implementation is neither partisan nor ideological; rather, I believe, it stems from a lack of the information and experience that would lead intelligent people to understand a complicated phenomenon they have never actually witnessed. And since very little is written about how the complex civilian part of counterinsurgency and armed nation building works, it is difficult to gain that understanding."[9] Military–civilian and donor coordination meetings may have been set up to satisfy governments in Washington, London, and Brussels, but groups were cagey about sharing information, and genuine cooperation was all but impossible.

All this meant that independent donors continued to fund ineffective contracts; smart, innovative projects like Will's were ignored; and the various groups and individuals that made up the intervention simply muddled along instead of learning from their experiences and adjusting their strategies accordingly. Institutional structures have not changed, and even attempts to simply gather information, like HTS, fell flat. When considering the experiences of those in this book, there is little here to suggest that the next time America intervenes in a country that it will have learned anything from the intervention in Afghanistan at all.

The Pieces Left Behind

So what did this stilted intervention, confounded by its own bureaucracy and lack of innovation, ultimately do for Afghanistan? When I asked the four individuals who are at the heart of this book, their answers had some surprising thematic unity.

Retired, but still consulting and lecturing on Afghanistan, Ambassador Neumann was pessimistic about much that was going on in Afghanistan, though he still saw "shreds of hope." With the U.S. government less and less committed to a sustained presence, it was difficult for him to believe that the Taliban would not make something of a comeback in at least a few key areas across the country—a scenario that began playing out in 2015. Additionally, although the economy had experienced significant growth, this growth had still created an inflated war economy, and Afghanistan seemed destined, in Neumann's mind, for some sort of economic shock. He felt that much of this, however, was still avoidable. With a continued American commitment, in the form of a limited troop presence and dependable funds to support Afghan government initiatives, there would be opportunities for Afghanistan to avoid serious economic or military instability. Afghan leaders, however, would then need to take advantage of the opportunities that the continued troop presence and funding would create.

Omar was still looking for the next business opportunity and thought the economic instability could also create some opportunities he could leverage to his advantage. He, however, had little hope that the current leaders or political parties would do much to lead the country toward a more democratic and equitable order that would include youth. Like many, Omar primarily had disdain for the so-called political parties that had fought during the Civil War. These parties tended to be ethnically based and dominated by a specific commander, and they resembled militias more than anything else, he argued. The leaders of these parties and their allies were the ones making money off the stripping down of Bagram, a process that was not producing any of the types of sustainable business growth that Omar genuinely favored. The emerging generation of youths tended to be distrustful of the older commanders and their parties. Many of the parties, however, were successfully co-opting local youth branches by providing them with funds in exchange for political affiliation. Omar referred to these as little more than "franchises."

As one of Omar's friends reflected:

> There is a generational shift going on in the area around Bagram. A lot of youth are taking advantage of educational opportunities in Kabul and beyond. The youth are developing a new perspective on the Shomali area, on Afghanistan, and on the world beyond. They will eventually replace, in the medium term, the generation that was so shaped by the war [a generation who is loyal to the older commanders]. A youth from the area no longer dreams of becoming a bodyguard for a commander as it used to be until recent years. Now, he sees different opportunities. Some have enlisted in the army or the police, institutions that may be weak but are thought of as national [instead of regional]. I know a dozen or so other youth from the area who are looking further and are receiving their schooling in America, Europe, and beyond.

The intervention has left a political landscape that is fragmented, a mixture of old and new figures who will have to find new ways to compromise or face serious conflict. Thinking about the next generation of leaders, Neumann reflected:

> You've got political mobilization, in a sense [among young people] . . . if this group tried to take power prematurely, they will get quashed, but right now they have a measure of power. Short term [the older generation] can buy power [by co-opting young people and getting their votes]. Longer term, they

Figure 11.1. U.S.-constructed Afghan police station. Photo by the author.

may have to pay attention. When you look at these people, are you seeing something essentially traditional, or are you seeing something new, like civil society? It would be a mistake to put [this new group of young people] analytically into a box, which is our civil society box . . . instead what you have is something different.

Will and Owen were both more reflective about their own personal roles in the intervention. Perhaps this is in part because they are more removed now than Omar and Ron are. Will still has friends in the country and continues to think about sustainable energy, but he has no real plans to return to Afghanistan or work further in other parts of the developing world. In my follow-up conversation with Owen, it was clear that Afghanistan was still on his geopolitical radar, but he was more anxious to talk about the rise of terrorist groups in West Africa and what that might do to American strategic interests.

One of the concerns that this raises is how we think more widely about intervention and the role of America in global politics. For the most part, the internationals I worked with, lived with, and interviewed in Afghanistan were people who were genuinely altruistic. Although this was often framed in different ways, with the military using the language of security and patriotism and relief workers talking about basic needs and human rights, these were people who were concerned with making the world better. Despite this, in many instances, the fractured political and economic landscape around Bagram was actually made worse by the international presence. Rarely was this intentional, but the international community, trapped in its own bureaucratic structures, struggled to learn from its mistakes or adapt to changing local conditions.

This frustrated figures like Omar who thought the international presence in the area had the opportunity to create real change. Instead, Omar and the rest of his generation are now left to watch most of Bagram get stripped down, sold primarily as scrap, and to deal with the repercussions of a hectic, disruptive, and uneven presence in the country. Navigating these unstable economic and political waters will be challenging even for the most optimistic youth.

More generally, however, the concern is that the lessons of Afghanistan are ignored and that the stories of Will and Owen are forgotten. This is a place where I believe that anthropology has the opportunity to make a real impact, to bring together disciplinary approaches holistically to ask on deeper levels, what is international intervention and when is it useful, particularly if intervention is going to continue to be a central piece of American foreign policy. If, however, we do not take the time to ask these more complex questions and reflect on the consequences of our actions on multiple levels, history will repeat itself again and again, despite our best intentions.

Reference Matter

Acknowledgments

THIS WORK GREW OUT OF over five years spent in Afghanistan between 2005 and 2015 and the increasing sense that standard approaches to writing and thinking about the intervention there, whether these lenses were policy based or academic, were missing much of what was actually going on during the crucial years of this conflict on the ground level. As a result, I am grateful to many people for the time and thoughtful conversations that helped me develop the account presented here. First and foremost I am indebted to the four characters who are at the center of this story, as well as those living in communities around Bagram, who all took their time to speak with me and, for the most part, good-naturedly debated many of the issues at the center of this book. In many ways multisited ethnographies that are not conducted in one single research stint present serious challenges, but the fact that I was looking at the intervention at the same time that both the communities around the base and the internationals in Afghanistan were asking existential questions about the intervention made this process easier, and the material in this book came from formal interviews but also from discussions over dinner, chats in the tea shop, and complaints from shopkeepers when a convoy drove by kicking up dust. I am grateful to everyone who took the time to allow me into these conversations and debates.

In addition, I was assisted in conducting the research for this book by grants from the United States Institute of Peace and Skidmore College. During the writing process Bennington College generously provided funds and time to bring many of the pieces here together. During various phases of the research, I was assisted by Sediq Seddiqi, Sanaullah Tasal, and Assad Sahil and was accompanied on several trips by Gregory Thielker, whose artist's eye added much to my understanding of the place. His work in our joint exhibition, titled "(Un)governed Spaces," gives life to much of what this text is reflecting on. I also appreciate the assistance of the Usdan Gallery at Bennington College, the Schmucker Art Gallery at Gettysburg College, and Rick Chrisman at Skidmore College for their support in making the exhibition possible in its various forms.

Some of the material in Chapter 10 appeared in a different form in a chapter entitled "The International Community and the 'Shura Strategy' in Afghanistan" in the volume *Perspectives on Involving Non-State and Customary Actors in Justice and Security Reform*, edited by Peter Albrecht, Helen Maria Kyed, Deborah Isser, and Erica Harper.

This manuscript itself was further assisted by formal and informal conversations with and feedback from Shahmahmood Miakhel, Zubair Ahmad, Whitney Azoy, David Edwards, Farid Ahmad Bayat, Muneer Salamzai, Mohammad Hassan Wafaey, Zuhal Nesari, Charles Lindholm, Kimberly Arkin, Michael Keating, Matt Waldman, Rohullah Amin, Nazif Shahrani, Andrew Wilder, Scott Smith, Tim Luccaro, John Dempsey, Jawan Shir, Sonia Ahsan, and Omar Sharifi. My former advisor, Thomas Barfield, continues to be a steadfast mentor, encouraging me to think about how these issues have grown out of Afghanistan's past, while working with Anna Larson has always challenged me to consider what they mean for the future.

In the publication process, Michelle Lipinski's constant and enthusiastic support at Stanford University Press was vital to bringing this work together, and I am appreciative of the valuable recommendations made by the anonymous reviewers. I am deeply indebted to Elizabeth Ruane, Anna Larson, and David Bond, who provided invaluable feedback and encouragement at important moments in the development of the book, while my students at Bennington College, particularly those in "Cultural Localities" and "Displaying Culture," with their cheerful—and at times relentless—questioning, pushed me to sharpen my points. I hope that this book encourages them and others to question what they think they know about the world and the ways that we think about these politically turbulent times.

—March 2015, North Bennington, VT

Notes

Chapter 1

1. Barfield and Szabo (1991) present a series of case studies of typical Afghan domestic architecture, including a *qala*, or fort, style compound from the area. These structures remain the dominant form of residence type in the plain.

2. Dobrydney 2012.

3. See Rubin September 16, 2012.

4. Throughout this book names, and in some cases identifying details, have been changed, except in cases of public officials and those who asked that their names not be changed.

5. Belasco March 29, 2011. The costs of the intervention in Afghanistan and elsewhere are notoriously and worryingly difficult to calculate due to their political nature. For an innovative attempt to explain some of these costs, see the Watson Institute's Cost of War project at www.costofwar.org.

6. International Assistance Mission n.d.

7. See Tarzi March 22, 2006, and Afshar 2006 for some of the legal issues with this setup.

8. Suspicion about cultural imperialism, particularly couched in religious terms, meant that some organizations were accused of proselytizing even when they were not at all faith based.

9. International Assistance Mission n.d.

10. In the years that followed, the price of solar panels and the batteries that they charge fell drastically, leading to something of a boom in solar energy in Afghanistan. Issues with repairs, however, remained, and most of these solar panels were used for only small-scale electrification, making hydropower still more appealing to communities with the potential for waterpower.

Chapter 2

1. For more, see Coburn 2011a, particularly chapter 7.

2. For more, see Coburn 2013.

3. International Security Assistance Force December 2008.

4. Chandrasekaran 2012, 64.

5. Sinders July 8, 2008.

6. See, for example, *Air Force Print News Today* September 25, 2012.

7. The term *commander* or *commandon* was used by Afghans to describe former and current militia leaders. Particularly in the press, it has often been translated as *warlord*. In previous work (Coburn 2011a), I have used *commander* to stress the ambiguity that many Afghans feel toward these figures whom they admired for fighting the Soviets and hated for destroying much of the country during the Civil War. In some instances, however, *commander* does not have enough of the negative connotations of *warlord*, particularly around Bagram, so I use both terms here, depending on the emphasis of the speaker. For more on some of these nuances and how this category has evolved in recent years, see Mukhopadhyay 2014.

8. I first spent time in the area in the summer of 2005 and have returned every year since. I conducted more systematic research in the communities outside the base, which is the basis for much of this account, in the winter of 2012, the summer of 2013, the summer of 2014, and the spring of 2015 as well as conducting interviews between 2010 and 2015 in Bagram; Kabul; Washington, DC; New York; Norfolk, VA; London; and the Adirondacks, as well as by phone, Skype, and email.

9. The vast majority of these rockets and mortars did little damage, though on occasion they do cause casualties. See, for example, the attack that killed four American troops in the spring of 2013 (Voice of America June 19, 2013). For the most part, however, rocket attacks were a symbolic part of the insurgents' public relations campaign, demonstrating loudly to those in the community that the international military had failed to fully secure the area.

10. Although Pashtuns around the base organized themselves by tribes, not all groups in Afghanistan do. Tajiks in the area tend to organize themselves by geographic locations (thus a Tajik from the Panjshir Valley is Panjshiri) and refer to these groups as *qaums*. Qaums, however, still operate politically in what is a fairly similar way to tribes, creating similar patterns of conflict and cooperation. For more, see Coburn 2011a, chapter 2.

11. Refugees, particularly those returning from Iran and Pakistan, also put pressure on land prices in the area, though oftentimes they did not have the funds to compete for the high-value land around the base and were more of a factor in other parts of the Shomali Plain.

12. Much of this critique was triggered by a volume edited by James Clifford and George Marcus (1986). For a review of the ensuing debate that influenced my conception of this ethnography, see Westbrook 2008.

13. James Ferguson and Akhil Gupta's work on transnationalism (2002) has done much to crystalize some of the shifts that have occurred in the field.

14. There are, of course, some exceptions to this, such as Anand Gopal's nuanced story of how the war shaped the lives of three Afghans, *No Good Men among the Living* (2014). Such nuances, however, rarely made it into the stories that were printed in newspapers and posted on popular websites.

Chapter 3

1. See Scott 1998, in particular chapter 2.

2. There is much overlap here with Noam Chomsky's analysis of terms like *failed state* (2006).

3. In some insurgent areas, ISAF forces went so far as to distribute "*shona ba shona*" medals to those elders who supported their operations. For an example, see Sandell September 24, 2011.

4. After becoming commander of ISAF, Stanley McCrystal, whose already prickly personality made many of his NATO allies bristle, earned few friends by shutting down the beer garden in the ISAF headquarters in Kabul at the beginning of his command. The beer garden was also a good example of the confusion created by assembling a multinational military force because drinks in the garden had to be purchased in euros, which, as an American anthropologist living in Afghanistan, I rarely carried. Adding to the confusion, DFACs on bases and in the U.S. embassy often gave change in paper tokens instead of coins. These, of course were usable only in facilities on bases run by similar contractors. In one of the houses where I lived with a series of journalists and aid workers, we had a jar of these from various visits to the bases by the door, but we never could remember to stock up on our way out, so the contents of the jar seemed simply to grow.

5. Freston January 9, 2013.

6. Synovitz September 16, 2003.

7. There is also certain irony to the fact that Sherpur was the site of the ill-fated British cantonment during the first Anglo-Afghan war, whose design and placement in a low area surrounded by hills Dupree refers to as a "masterpiece of military stupidity" (1980, 384).

8. For an account of some cases of land grabs in Sherpur, see Filkins January 1, 2009, and for an assessment of the impact of these moves, see Luccaro March 23, 2012.

9. For example, counterterrorism expert Peter Bergen (March 31, 2005) viciously attacked *Afghanistan: The Mirage of Peace* by veteran aid workers and diplomats Chris Johnson and Jolyon Leslie (2005), calling it "tone deaf or simply wrong." Despite this, most of their predictions about the mismanagement of the intervention and the failings of the Afghan state ultimately proved correct, whereas much of the early COIN (counterinsurgency) optimism eventually proved misplaced. For those promoting

the surge, however, dissent or criticism, particularly from junior officials, was not tolerated.

10. I watched interactions between elders and international military officers near both Bagram and Istalif and was struck by how much more tense the interactions were near the base than they were in the small-town bazaar, where most of both the shopkeepers and soldiers appeared more curious than anything else.

11. Ironically, at times this made this group even more biased against Afghans living in villages, whom they dismissed as poor and uneducated, than their international counterparts.

12. The Insightful Approaches group website, now defunct.

13. Afghan Online Business Directory (n.d.).

Chapter 4

1. Thanks to Thomas Barfield, who pointed out to me that this is probably a reinterpretation of Alexander's marriage to Roxana, who was not from the area but instead was from the north of the Hindu Kush. Such details had clearly been reworked locally to emphasize the importance of the area in ancient history.

2. For a full account of the disaster at Charikar, see the account by Colonel Haughton, one of the two survivors (1879). For other such cases, see Coburn 2011a, chapter 5.

3. Abdur Rahman Khan was particularly active in moving thousands of members of antagonistic tribes to new lands; see Dupree 1980, 419.

4. This was an interesting contrast with my experience in Istalif, where, for Istalifis, the experience of living as refugees in Kabul and in Pakistan among various other ethnic groups seemed to increase the practice of interethnic marriage and business. In contrast, it seems that tensions among these groups in the Bagram area cut down on the practice. Although there is not quantitative evidence to support it, even if the trend is not true, the fact that Bagramis have the perception that there is less interethnic marriage seems to reveal something about their suspicions about other ethnic groups in the area.

5. This also explains the fact that there were relatively fewer Afghan-American or Afghan-European immigrants who were able to return to the area to make money, compared to a place like Kabul. To succeed in business in the Shomali, one needed to at least be aware of the complex tribal tensions that shaped politics and economics in the area.

6. A contract in 1956 with the Soviet Union for arms from various Soviet bloc countries for $25 million in military equipment drastically increased military spending in the country (Dupree 1980, 522).

7. Neumann 2009, xvi.

8. For a history and sharp analysis of the development of "Little America" and its impact on the post-2001 conflict, see Chandrasekaran 2012.

9. See Canfield 1973 and Azoy 2012, respectively.

10. For the Wakhan Corridor, see Shahrani 2002 [1979]; for Nuristan, see Jones 1974; and for various nomad groups, see Barfield 1981, Pedersen 1994, and Olesen 1994.

11. Dupree 1977, 98.

12. Ibid., 105 and 120.

13. See Barfield 2010, Tanner 2009, Rubin 2002, Ewans 2001, and Roy 1990 for some of the best of these various accounts.

14. For a romantic account of these days written by Jouvenal's friend and fellow Frontline reporter, see Loyn 2005.

15. Gandamack Lodge (n.d.).

16. For more on the rise of the Taliban more generally, see Rashid 2000; on the role of the United States during this period, see Coll 2005.

17. Loyn 2005, 378.

18. Similar things are said of the various neighborhoods in Kabul built by the Soviets called Microrayon, which were also coveted despite their distinctly un-Afghan architecture.

Chapter 5

1. Loyn 2005, 352.

2. For a deeper analysis of some of some of these lost opportunities, see Johnson and Leslie 2005; Rashid 2008, part 3; and Wissing 2012, chapter 4.

3. Neumann 2009, 8–9.

4. The White House, Office of the Press Secretary, December 1, 2009.

5. The gate had actually been there all along, but Neumann pointed out that "the problem in getting it open was bureaucratic; different procedures and badges for entry into each compound. To this day there are separate guards for the two sides of the gate and different passes are necessary to cross over."

6. These numbers are difficult to track, but for a fairly reliable reporting of coalition causalities, see iCausalities.org.

7. Neumann 2009, 110, 113.

8. Chandrasekaran April 23, 2010.

9. Trofimov August 9, 2012.

10. Several years later the billing system has just begun to function in Kabul, and cities like Kandahar lag far behind.

11. Jones 2009, 186–189.

12. For an in-depth report on the struggles to refurbish the dam during this period, see Vogt January 6, 2013.

13. Wissing 2012, 70–71.

14. Office of the Special Inspector General for Afghanistan Reconstruction September 25, 2013.

Chapter 6

1. Aikins February 2013, 52–53.

2. In some other instances, international groups running training exercises would give participants a test at the beginning and at the end of the day on their knowledge of the Afghan legal system, which might have been slightly more useful in terms of monitoring progress, but it still did nothing to try to evaluate whether the participants actually did anything with this knowledge once they returned home.

3. For a more extensive review of these issues, see Coburn 2013.

4. As it became clear that the counterinsurgency strategy was facing challenges in rural parts of Afghanistan, it became popular to debate slight modifications of this doctrine, such as "Shape, Clear, Hold, Build," and "Clear, Hold, Build, Transfer."

5. There were some notable areas, such as the notoriously dangerous eastern mountains in Kunar and Nuristan. For an account of some of these challenges, see Junger 2012. For analyses that touch on these various approaches and the connections between security and development, see Suhrke 2011 and Gopal 2014.

6. Department of Defense 2007, 2–41.

7. Of course, many of the more for-profit contractors had far fewer qualms about chasing contracts and were much more willing to work in provinces where they were not at their most effective.

8. Johnson, Ramachandran, and Walz September 2011, 2.

9. Compare this with the fact that only 10 percent of those deployed during World War II were contractors (McFate 2014, 19).

10. Center for Army Lessons Learned April 2009.

11. Hedgpeth and Cohen August 11, 2008. An additional matter was whether CERP funds ever got spent the way in which they were intended, and the Department of Defense increasingly fell short on the obligation of CERP funds as opposed to the amounts actually appropriated by Congress. In 2012, for example, only $43.5 million was obligated of the $200 million that Congress had appropriated (Spoko January 16, 2014).

12. Chivvis et al. 2014.

13. Johnson et al. September 2011, 3.

14. Johnson, Ramachandran, and Walz 2013, 84.

15. Johnson et al. September 2011, 2.

16. Shuras can take many forms, but the military generally understood them as local council meetings. They will be discussed further in Chapter 10.

17. Unsurprisingly, it was groups such as the Department of State who clearly were more comfortable with state-building approaches and human rights groups who were concerned about the extrajudicial powers of these groups that were most critical of them. American military officers were most likely to embrace the use of militias, though this was not true in all cases.

18. The bidding for these contracts could become nasty and political. In addition to lobbying members of Congress to get contractors, in some instances contractors leaked reports to the media to undermine bids from competitors. Part of the oddness of all this, however, was that it was very common for contracting staff to move from one firm to another, so often they were competing with those whom they had previously worked with. For some examples, see Coburn 2013.

19. Neumann 2009, xii.

20. It is difficult in many instances to compare expenditure on contractors to that on soldiers because overhead is rarely taken into account in military figures; however, the figures are still striking, with one 2007 study of contractors in Iraq putting the average salary of a DynCorp contractor at $445,000, whereas a U.S. Army sergeant earned between $51,00 and $69,000 (McFate 2014, 29).

Chapter 7

1. For more, see Coburn 2011a, chapter 3.
2. World Bank 2014.
3. Fry 1974, 16.
4. Stevens July 28, 2009.
5. Mossotti November 4, 2011, 1253.
6. Timmons June 29, 2012.
7. Fry 1974, 221–222.
8. In less economically important parts of Afghanistan, the skewing effect of the international military presence was even more significant; in one district in Helmand, the only industry was gravel crushing, which one State Department official concluded "would be unsustainable past the boom resulting from the construction of hundreds of gravel-hungry US bases throughout Helmand" (Malkasian 2013, 234–235).
9. At the time there were approximately fifty Afghanis to the dollar.
10. For a memoir that provides an intimate look at the running of a job creation program in the south of the country, see Joel Hafvenstein's *Opium Season* (2007).

Chapter 8

1. By this time insurgents had used nearby buildings or construction sites to help facilitate a number of spectacular attacks around the country, making internationals weary of any nearby structures. In one of these cases insurgents actually used a nearby house to tunnel under the prison in Kandahar, freeing almost 500 prisoners in one night (see Shah and Rubin April 25, 2011); in another, they used a twelve-story shopping complex construction site to stage an attack on the U.S. embassy in Kabul (see Aikens March 2012).

2. Cullison and Wonacott (August 12, 2008), as well as the Associated Press (December 16, 2008).

3. For a thorough account of how funds were being redirected to insurgents, see Wissing 2012, particularly chapter 5.

4. Office of the Special Inspector General for Afghanistan Reconstruction October 30, 2013, 11.

5. Department of Justice, Office of Public Affairs February 12, 2013.

6. Associated Press February 12, 2013.

7. When fueling my own car I never actually found it cheaper closer to Bagram, but presumably this fuel was being bought by locals on the black market, not at the main pump stations.

8. Department of Justice, Office of Public Affairs June 18, 2009.

9. CBS News November 1, 2007.

10. Department of Justice, Office of Public Affairs February 11, 2015.

11. Department of Justice, Office of Public Affairs October 24, 2012.

12. Office of the Special Inspector General for Afghanistan Reconstruction January 30, 2014, 52–53.

13. Petrishen February 18, 2015, and DiMauro May 26, 2014. Remarkably, as of early 2015, both these men still had their employment in Afghanistan, as well as their experience overseeing government contracts, listed as experience on their online resumes.

14. DiMauro May 26, 2014.

15. Salahuddin July 9, 2009. In response to the release of one group of traffickers, the State Department stated that they found Karzai's decision "disappointing," particularly given the $6 million that had been given to develop the Criminal Justice Task force (Department of State July 15, 2009). Other embassy officials were much more candid in privately expressing their anger to me about the decision, which was announced in the lead-up to the 2009 presidential elections.

16. This was a much larger issue with insurgents detained by coalition forces, and significant effort went into designing evidence bags for soldiers that would be acceptable in insurgency cases that were transferred to Afghan courts.

17. Johnson October 10, 2009.

18. Johnson and Lydersen October 22, 2009.

19. See Barfield 2010, chapter 2.

20. See Azoy 2012.

21. In particular, see Azoy 2012, chapter 6.

22. Leadership forms in Afghanistan have long been dynamic despite the assumed "timeless" nature of tribes. Nazif Shahrani has written extensively about some of these shifts; for an earlier example of changing forms of leadership, see his study of the Kyrgyz (1986).

23. The term *malik* was often used to describe the role of the elders charged with representing the community, particularly to the Afghan government or even inter-

national groups like NGOs. There are other terms such as *arbab* and *khan* that were also occasionally used in the Bagram area, though *malik* was far more common, so I predominately use that term. In other parts of the country, *arbab* and *khan* were used much more frequently; there were occasionally slight nuances in the definition, but they were conceptually similar. For more, see Coburn 2011a, chapter 5.

24. Coburn 2011a chapter 6. For other examples of studies of leadership, see, for example, Azoy 2012 and Jones 1974. Much of this work was inspired and framed by Fredrik Barth's ethnographic work in Pakistan (1959) and the debate that arose from Talal Asad's critique of it (1972).

25. See Coburn and Larson 2014a, chapter 5.

26. For more, see Coburn May 2010.

27. These leaders, who were both nonstate actors and state officials simultaneously, were something of a break from the 1960s and 1970s model of state officials, who came from a technocratic elite that ruled Kabul but was largely looked down on in the provinces. For more on political structures in the era, see Barfield 2010 (compared with Barfield 1981) and Azoy 2012.

28. For more on Razziq, see Aikins September 21, 2011.

29. Coburn and Larson January 2014b.

Chapter 9

1. For more on the local politics of the area and how these figures related to each other, see Coburn and Larson 2014a, chapter 5.

2. Further complicating the matter, parliamentarians, ministers, and other government officials were sometimes assigned police details for their protection. At the same time, however, they might have their own guards as well, creating essentially a militia of mixed origins.

3. Partlow August 17, 2010.

4. The imprecise nature of militias around Bagram reflects some of the challenges that policy makers and academics have when discussing non-Western political systems. Although there have been increasingly sophisticated analyses of militias and other "nonstate actors," there still seems to be an assumption that these are clearly defined units, with precise membership. Particularly around Bagram this was often not true, and it was often difficult to tell the exact difference between a militia and a group of men who were friendly with each other and would be willing to arm themselves if called on. For some of the better analyses that raise some similar points in the Afghan case, see Giustozzi 2009, Mukhopadhyay 2014, and Keen 2012.

5. For a local in-depth account of the U.S. government's attempt to use a variety of types of militias to provide security in one district, see Malkasian 2013.

6. For insights into the Uruzgan area and the rise of Matiullah Khan, see Gopal 2014.

7. For a sophisticated review of these figures in particular, see Mukhopadhyay 2014.

8. This all contrasted with Istalif, the town where I had originally conducted my research, where there were fewer resources to fight over and fewer actors to do the fighting, which meant less instability despite the fact that there was much less of an international military presence. For more, see Coburn 2011a, chapter 7.

9. This fits Charles Lindholm's observations about how the contrasting values of egalitarianism and individualism simultaneously shape political structures historically across the Islamic Middle East (2002, chapter 4).

10. For more on these local political mechanisms, see Coburn 2011a, chapter 5.

11. They are sometimes contrasted with *jirgas*, a Pashtun term for a gathering of elders who generally meet on an ad hoc basis to solve a specific dispute. There are exceptions in the usage of this term as well, of course, such as the *Wolesi Jirga*, or parliament.

12. For more, see Coburn 2013.

13. For more on the proliferation of shuras and particularly the ways in which this was driven by the international presence, see Coburn and Miakhel September 2010.

14. For more, see Coburn and Larson 2014a.

15. British Broadcasting Corporation August 28, 2012. Most of the Afghan opinions I quote here about what happened during these events come from interviews that I conducted several months later in the summer of 2012.

16. This information came from a final report on the incident, not released until several months later. Accounts at the time were far more contradictory. British Broadcasting Corporation August 28, 2012.

17. Sieff February 21, 2012.

18. Rubin February 22, 2012.

19. Harooni and Shalizi February 24, 2013, and Sieff February 24, 2012.

20. Rubin February 22, 2012.

21. Zwak February 21, 2012.

22. For a complete account of the riots in Garmser, see Malkasian 2013, 166–172, who states that intelligence later showed that the Taliban had planted the damaged Koran.

23. Dreazen April 29, 2012.

24. The Taliban, however, were clearly not as directly involved in the Bagram riots as they had been earlier in Garmser (Rahimi and Rubin February 21, 2012).

25. Indeed, in 2015, after leaving the office of president, Karzai went on to jointly author a policy piece with Neumann.

26. Gopal 2014, 144.

27. Numbers of detainees at Bagram, Guantanamo, and other American military facilities are contested because the United States rarely releases official numbers, and,

in some instances, so-called secret facilities alongside official facilities contain detainees who do not appear on official lists. When possible, the figures here have been correlated with the numbers from groups like the International Committee of the Red Cross who attempt to monitor prisoner populations; see Doane and Hirschkorn November 15, 2011, and Andersson May 11, 2010.

28. For a discussion of this decision, see Savage February 21, 2009.

29. For an account of the conditions in the facility, see van Bijlert March 9, 2011.

30. Kate Clark has tracked this issue for a number of years. For more on some of the legal issues surrounding the transfer of the detention center, see her pieces from March 21, 2012; May 23, 2012; July 25, 2013; and February 13, 2014. This account draws heavily on her work as well as the Afghan Ministry of Public Affairs's "Memorandum of Understanding between the Islamic Republic of Afghanistan and the United States on Transfer of US Detention Facilities in Afghan Territory to Afghanistan."

31. Diplomats and military officials also actively advocated for certain Afghan officials to be assigned to work at the facility, feeling they were less corrupt and more likely to cooperate with international officials.

32. Clark July 25, 2013, and AAN Team and Guests January 8, 2014.

33. Rubin February 22, 2012.

Chapter 10

1. Malkasian 2013, 162.

2. Office of the Special Inspector General for Afghanistan Reconstruction March 22, 2011.

3. For more on this phenomenon, see Johnson and Leslie 2005a prescient analysis of the ways in which the international community attempted to deliver aid and stabilize the country in the early years of the intervention.

4. Marlowe May 13, 2010.

5. This also helps explain why, when coalition forces hosted "mandatory" shura meetings that required men from the community to attend, they were often highly ineffective.

6. See, for example, the Executive Board's Statement from the American Anthropological Association (October 31, 2007).

7. This debate is covered in Gezari 2013, chapter 2.

8. For the most nuanced assessment of HTS, see Edwards December 27, 2010, where he concludes most notably that "there is a fundamental discrepancy between how anthropology conceives of and carries out its work and how the military conceives of and carries out its work."

9. Although assessment of the ongoing HTT project is still not complete, it has been roundly criticized in the mainstream media (Gezari 2013), and a congressional report on it also saw far more problems than benefits arising from the program (Clinton, Foran-Cain, McQuaid, Norman, and Sims November 2010).

10. This has been covered extensively in a variety of mainstream media sources, but for a good overview see Gezari 2013, especially chapters 8–9.

11. Most of the laborers and those working in the dining hall were "third-country nationals," often from India or some other South or Southeast Asian country.

12. I thank Thomas Barfield for pointing this parallel out to me.

13. This complaint about the inherent ethnic bias among Afghan officials was also the reason that many Afghans gave me for wanting international officials involved in election oversight and other processes where they were perceived as more impartial.

Chapter 11

1. Afghan Public Health Institute, Ministry of Public Health, Central Statistics Organization, ICF Macro, Indian Institute of Health Management Research, and the World Health Organization Regional Office for the Eastern Mediterranean 2011.

2. See Sandefuroct October 10, 2013, and Diehl September 11, 2011.

3. See UN Assistance Mission in Afghanistan and the UN Office of the High Commissioner for Human Rights July 2014 and Watson Institute March 2013.

4. Department of Defense April 2014.

5. Watson Institute March 2013, 11, and Stiglitz 2008. For a more nuanced discussion of the concept of the "costs" of war, see chapter 5 of MacLeish 2013.

6. The nuances and personalities involved in this debate are thoroughly recounted in Woodward 2010.

7. *Opium Season* is an engaging memoir of one contractor attempting to navigate these shifting polices (Hafvenstein 2007).

8. Neumann 2009, 16.

9. Ibid., xii.

Bibliography

AAN Team and Guests. (January 8, 2014). "Innocent, Guilty—Useful? What's Behind the US–Afghan Clash over 88 Prisoners from Bagram," War and Peace. Kabul: Afghan Analysts Network.

Afghan Ministry of Public Affairs. (March 9, 2012). "Memorandum of Understanding between the Islamic Republic of Afghanistan and the United States on Transfer of US Detention Facilities in Afghan Territory to Afghanistan." Kabul: Author.

Afghan Online Business Directory. (n.d.). "Insightful Approaches Construction Co. Ltd." http://kabullist.com.

Afghan Public Health Institute, Ministry of Public Health, Central Statistics Organization, ICF Macro, Indian Institute of Health Management Research, and the World Health Organization Regional Office for the Eastern Mediterranean. (2011). "Afghanistan Mortality Survey 2010." Calverton, MD: Author.

Afshar, Mandana Knust Rassekh. (2006). "The Case of an Afghan Apostate: The Right to a Fair Trial between Islamic Law and Human Rights in the Afghan Constitution," in Armin von Bogdandy and Rudiger Wolfrum, eds., *Max Planck Yearbook of United Nations Law*, 591–605. Leiden: Martinus Nijhoff Publishers.

Aikins, Matthieu. (September 21, 2011). "Our Man in Kandahar." *The Atlantic.*

———. (March 2012). "The Siege of September 2012." Newsmakers, *GQ.*

———. (February 2013). "Kabubble: Counting Down to Economic Collapse in the Afghan Capital." *Harper's Magazine*, 44–54.

Air Force Print News Today. (September 25, 2012). "455 ESFS Visits Bagram ANP, Delivers Supplies."

Alexander, Chris. (2011). *The Long Way Back: Afghanistan's Quest for Peace.* New York: Harper Collins.

American Anthropological Association. (October 31, 2007). "American Anthropological Association's Executive Board Statement on the Human Terrain System Project." Arlington, VA: Author.

Andersson, Hilary. (May 11, 2010). "Red Cross Confirms 'Second Jail' at Bagram Airbase." *BBC News*.

Asad, Talal. (1972). "Market Model, Class Structure, and Consent: A Reconsideration of Swat Political Organization." *Man* 7(1): 74–89.

Associated Press. (December 16, 2008). "US Downplays Attacks on Afghan Supply Line."

———. (February 12, 2013). "Contractor Faces Sentencing for Smuggling Cash."

Azoy, Whitney. (2012 [2003]). *Buzkashi: Game and Power in Afghanistan*, 3rd ed. Long Grove, IL: Waveland Press.

Barfield, Thomas. (1981). *The Central Asian Arabs of Afghanistan: Pastoral Nomadism in Transition*. Austin: The University of Texas Press.

———. (2010). *Afghanistan: A Cultural and Political History*. Princeton, NJ: Princeton University Press.

Barfield, Thomas, and Albert Szabo. (1991). *Afghanistan: An Atlas of Indigenous Domestic Architecture*. Austin: The University of Texas Press.

Barth, Fredrik. (1959). *Political Leadership among Swat Pathans*. London: Athlone Press.

Belasco, Amy. (March 29, 2011). *The Costs of Iraq, Afghanistan and Other Global War on Terror Operations since 9/11*. Washington, DC: The Congressional Research Service.

Bergen, Peter. (March 31, 2005). "After the Taliban." *The Washington Post*.

British Broadcasting Corporation. (August 28, 2012). "US Troops Punished for Koran Burning and Urination Video."

Canfield, Robert Leroy. (1973). *Faction and Conversion in a Plural Society: Religious Alignments in the Hindu Kush*, Anthropological Papers No. 50. Ann Arbor: Museum of Anthropology, University of Michigan.

CBS News. (November 1, 2007). "Fuel Fraud Latest in Army Contracting Woes."

Center for Army Lessons Learned. (April 2009). *Commander's Guide to Money as a Weapons System: Tactics, Techniques and Procedures*, No. 9-27. Fort Leavenworth, KS: Author.

Chandrasekaran, Rajiv. (April 23, 2010). "US Military, Diplomats at Odds over How to Resolve Kandahar's Electricity Woes." *The Washington Post*.

———. (2012). *Little America: The War within the War for Afghanistan*. New York: Knopf.

Chayes, Sarah. (2007). *The Punishment of Virtue: Inside Afghanistan after the Taliban*. New York: Penguin.

Chivvis, Christopher, Olga Oliker, Andrew Liepman, Ben Connable, George Will-coxon, and William Young. (2014). "Initial Thoughts on the Impact of the Iraq War on US National Security Structures." Washington, DC: Rand.

Chomsky, Noam. (2006). *Failed States: The Abuse of Power and the Assault on Democracy.* New York: Henry Holt.

Clark, Kate. (March 21, 2012). "The Bagram Memorandum: Handing over 'the Other Guantanamo,'" Rights and Freedom, Kabul: Afghan Analysts Network.

———. (May 23, 2012). "The 'Other Guantanamo 2: The Afghan State Begins Internment,'" Int. Engagement. Kabul: Afghan Analysts Network.

———. (July 25, 2013). "The 'Other Guantanamo' 6: Afghans Still Struggling for Sovereignty at Bagram," Intl. Relations. Kabul: Afghan Analysts Network.

———. (February 13, 2014). "65 'Innocent'/ 'Dangerous' Detainees Released from Bagram: What Secret Documents Say about Afghan and US Claims," Rights and Freedoms. Kabul: Afghan Analysts Network.

Clifford, James, and George Marcus, eds. (1986). *Writing Culture: The Poetics and Politics of Ethnography.* Berkeley: University of California Press.

Clinton, Yvette, Virginia Foran-Cain, Julia Voelker McQuaid, Catherine E. Norman, and William H. Sims. (November 2010). "Congressionally Directed Assessment of the Human Terrain System." CRMD0024031.A1/Final. Washington, DC: CNA.

Coburn, Noah. (November 2009). "Losing Legitimacy: Some Afghan Views on the Government, the International Community, and the 2009 Election." Post-Election Brief 2. Kabul: AREU.

———. (May 2010). "Connecting with Kabul: The Importance of the Wolesi Jirga Elections and Local Political Networks in Afghanistan." Parliamentary Election Brief. Kabul: AREU.

———. (2011a). *Bazaar Politics: Power and Pottery in an Afghan Market Town.* Palo Alto, CA: Stanford University Press.

———. (2011b), "The International Community and the '*Shura* Strategy' in Afghanistan," in Peter Albrecht, Helen Maria Kyed, Deborah Isser, and Erica Harper, eds., *Perspectives on Involving Non-State and Customary Actors in Justice and Security Reform.* Rome: International Development Law Organization.

———. (2013). "Informal Justice and the International Community in Afghanistan." Peaceworks. Washington: USIP.

Coburn, Noah, and Anna Larson. (2014a). *Derailing Democracy in Afghanistan: Elections in an Unstable Political Landscape.* New York: Columbia University Press.

———. (January 2014b). "Youth Mobilization and Political Constraints in Afghanistan: The Y Factor." Special Report. Washington, DC: USIP.

Coburn, Noah, and Shahmahmood Miakhel. (September 2010). "Many *Shuras* Do Not a Government Make: International Community Engagement with Local Councils in Afghanistan." Washington, DC: USIP.

Coll, Steve. (2005). *Ghost Wars: The Secret History of the CIA, Afghanistan and Bin Laden from the Soviet Invasion to September 10, 2001*. London: Penguin Books.

Cullison, Alan, and Peter Wonacott. (August 12, 2008). "Taliban Is Seizing, Destroying More NATO Supplies." *The Wall Street Journal*.

Department of the Air Force. (October 31, 2013). "Bagram Airfield, Afghanistan, Deployment Guide." Bagram Afghanistan: 455th Air Expeditionary Wing.

Department of Defense. (2007). *US Army Counterinsurgency Manual*. Foreword by Lt. Gen. David Petraeus and Lt. Gen. James Amos. New York: Skyhorse Publishing.

———. (April 2014). "Contractor Support of US Operations in the USCENTCOM Area of Responsibility." DoD website.

Department of Justice, Office of Public Affairs. (June 18, 2009). "Former Military Contractor Convicted of Participating in Scheme to Steal Large Quantities of Fuel from US Army in Afghanistan." Press Release.

———. (October 24, 2012). "Former Employee of Army Contractor Pleads Guilty to Bribery for Facilitating Theft by Trucking Contractor in Afghanistan." Press Release.

———. (February 12, 2013). "Former Department of Defense Contractor Sentenced to 30 Months in Prison for Smuggling Kickback Proceeds from Afghanistan to the United States." Press Release.

———. (February 11, 2015). "Two U.S. Army Sergeants Plead Guilty to Taking Bribes while Deployed in Afghanistan." Press Release.

Department of State. (July 15, 2009). "Afghanistan: President Karzai Pardons Convicted Drug Traffickers." PRN:2009/730.

Diehl, Jackson. (September 11, 2011). "Ryan Crocker's 'Strategic Patience' in Afghanistan." *The Washington Post*.

DiMauro, Julie. (May 26, 2014). "Ex-State Department Contractor in Afghanistan Pleads Guilty to Fraud." The FPCA Blog.

Doane, Seth, and Phil Hirschkorn. (November 15, 2011). "Bagram: The Other Guantanamo?" CBS News.

Dobrydney, David. (December 28, 2012). "Just Passing Through: Bagram Terminal Busiest in DoD." 455th Air Expeditionary Wing Public Affairs, Air Force Print News Today.

Dreazen, Yochi. (April 29, 2012). "The US Military Is Struggling to Police Itself in Afghanistan." *The Atlantic*.

Dupree, Louis. (1980 [1973]). *Afghanistan*. Princeton, NJ: Princeton University Press.

Dupree, Nancy Hatch. (1977). *An Historical Guide to Afghanistan*, 2nd ed. Kabul: Afghan Tourist Organization.

Edwards, David B. (1996). *Heroes of the Age: Moral Fault Lines on the Afghan Frontier*. Berkeley: University of California Press.

———. (2002). *Before the Taliban: Genealogies of the Afghan Jihad*. Berkeley: University of California Press.

———. (December 27, 2010). "Counterinsurgency as a Cultural System." *Small Wars Journal*.

Ewans, Martin. (2001). *Afghanistan: A Short History of Its People and Politics*. London: Curzon Press.

Ferguson, James. (1994). *The Anti-Politics Machine: Development, Depoliticization, and Bureacratic Power in Lesotho*. Minneapolis: University of Minnesota Press.

Ferguson, James, and Akhil Gupta. (2002). "Spatializing States: Toward an Ethnography of Neoliberal Governmentality," *American Ethnologist*, 29(4): 981–1002.

Filkins, Dexter. (January 1, 2009). "Bribes Corrode Afghans' Trust in Government." *The New York Times*.

Fishstein, Paul, and Andrew Wilder. (January 2012). "Winning Hearts and Minds?: Examining the Relationship between Aid and Security in Afghanistan." Medford, MA: Feinstein International Center.

Freston, Tom. (January 9, 2013). "The Poppy Palaces." *Vanity Fair*.

Fry, Maxwell J. (1974). *The Afghan Economy: Money, Finance, and the Critical Constraints to Economic Development*. London: E. J. Brill.

Gandamack Lodge. (n.d.). "Peter Jouvenal." Retrieved on October 1, 2014, from http://gandamacklodge.co.uk/peter.htm.

Gezari, Vanessa M. (2013). *The Tender Soldier: A True Story of War and Sacrifice*. New York: Simon and Schuster.

Giustozzi, Antonio. (2009). *Empires of Mud: Wars and Warlords in Afghanistan*. New York: Columbia University Press.

———, ed. (2012). *Decoding the New Taliban: Insights from the Afghan Field*. New York: Columbia University Press.

Gopal, Anand. (2014). *No Good Men among the Living: America, the Taliban, and the War through Afghan Eyes*. New York: Metropolitan Books.

Hafvenstein, Joel. (2007). *Opium Season: A Year on the Afghan Frontier*. Guilford, CT: The Lyons Press.

Harooni, Mirwais, and Hamid Shalizi. (February 24, 2013). "Twelve Killed in Protests across Afghanistan." Reuters.

Haughton, J. (1879, second edition). *Char-ee-kar and Service There with the 4th Goorkha Regiment (Shah Shuja's Force) in 1841: An Episode of the First Afghan War*. Uckfield, UK: The Navy & Military Press.

Hedgpeth, Dana, and Sarah Cohen. (August 11, 2008). "Money as a Weapon," Special Report. *The Washington Post*.

International Assistance Mission. (n.d.). "Who We Are" and "Renewable Energy." Retrieved on October 1, 2014, from http:// iam-afghanistan.org.

International Security Assistance Force. (December 2008). "ISAF Regional Commands and PRT Locations." Kabul: Author.

Johnson, Carrie. (October 10, 2009). "Afghan Men Tricked into US Trip, Detained." *The Washington Post.*

Johnson, Carrie, and Kari Lydersen. (October 22, 2009). "Afghan Witness, Detained 14 Months, Finally Testifies in Bribery Case." *The Washington Post.*

Johnson, Chris, and Jolyon Leslie. (2005). *Afghanistan: The Mirage of Peace.* London: Zed Books.

Johnson, Gregory, Vijaya Ramachandran, and Julie Walz. (September 2011). "The Commander's Emergency Response Program in Afghanistan: Five Practical Recommendations." Brief. Washington, DC: Center for Global Development.

———. (2013). "CERP in Afghanistan: Refining Military Capabilities in Development Activities," *PRISM* 3(2).

Jones, Schuyler. (1974). *Men of Influence in Nuristan: A Study of Social Control and Dispute Settlement in Waigal Valley, Afghanistan.* London: Seminar Press.

Jones, Seth. (2009). *In the Graveyard of Empires: America's War in Afghanistan.* New York: W. W. Norton.

Junger, Sebastian. (2012). *War.* New York: Twelve.

Keen, David. (2012). *Useful Enemies: When Waging Wars Is More Important than Winning Them.* New Haven, CT: Yale University Press.

Larson, Anna. (2009). "Toward an Afghan Democracy: Exploring Perceptions of Democratisation in Afghanistan." Kabul: AREU.

———. (2011). "Deconstructing 'Democracy' in Afghanistan." Kabul: AREU.

Lindholm, Charles. (2002 [1996]). *The Islamic Middle East: Tradition and Change.* Malden, MA: Blackwell Publishing.

Loyn, David. (2005). *Frontline: The True Story of the British Mavericks Who Changed the Face of War Reporting.* London: Michael Joseph.

Luccaro, Tim. (March 23, 2012). "What Kabul's Chic Homes Say about Corruption and Governance." Washington, DC: USIP.

Luttrell, Marcus. (2007). *Lone Survivor: The Eyewitness Account of Operation Redwing and the Lost Heroes of SEAL Team 10.* New York: Little, Brown and Company.

MacLeish, Kenneth. (2013). *Making War at Fort Hood: Life and Uncertainty in a Military Community.* Princeton, NJ: Princeton University Press.

Malkasian, Carter. (2013). *War Comes to Garmser: Thirty Years of Conflict on the Afghan Frontier.* London: Oxford University Press.

Marlowe, Ann. (May 13, 2010). "*Shura* to Fail?" *The New Republic.*

McCrystal, Stanley. (2013). *My Share of the Task: A Memoir.* New York: Portfolio.

McFate, Sean. (2014). *The Modern Mercenary: Private Armies and What They Mean for World Order.* New York: Oxford University Press.

Monsutti, Alessandro. (2005). *War and Migration: Social Networks and Economic Strategies of the Hazaras of Afghanistan.* New York: Routledge.

Mossotti, Victor. (November 4, 2011). "Cement in Afghanistan," in Stephen Peters, Trude Kin, Thomas Mack, and Michael Chornack, eds., *Summaries of Important Areas for Mineral Investment and Production Opportunities of Nonfuel Minerals in Afghanistan.* USGS Open-File Report 2011-1204. Washington: USGS.

Mukhopadhyay, Dipali. (2014). *Warlords, Strongman Governors, and the State in Afghanistan.* New York: Cambridge University Press.

Neumann, Ronald E. (2009). *The Other War: Winning and Losing in Afghanistan.* Washington, DC: Potomac Books.

Office of the Special Inspector General for Afghanistan Reconstruction. (March 22, 2011). "Afghanistan's National Solidarity Program Has Reached Thousands of Communities but Faces Challenges That Could Limit Outcomes." SIGAR Audit 11-8, Social and Economic Development/NSP. Washington: Author.

———. (September 25, 2013). "Audit of USAID/Afghanistan's Kandahar-Helmand Power Project." Audit Report No. F-306-13-001-P. Washington: Author.

———. (October 30, 2013). "Quarterly Report to the United States Congress." Washington: Author.

———. (January 30, 2014). "Quarterly Report to the United States Congress." Washington: Author.

Olesen, Asta. (1994). *Afghan Craftsmen: The Cultures of Three Itinerant Communities.* New York: Thames and Hudson.

Partlow, Joshua. (August 17, 2010). "Karzai Wants Private Security Firms out of Afghanistan." *The Washington Post.*

Pedersen, Gorm. (1994). *Nomads in Transition: A Century of Change among the Zala Khan Khel.* London: Thames and Hudson.

Petrishen, Brad. (February 18, 2015). "Worcester Man Admits to Bilking Feds of $120K while Working in Afghanistan." *Worcester Telegram & Gazette.*

Piggot, Hugh, Smail Khennas, and Simon Dunnett. (2003). *Small Wind Systems for Rural Energy Services.* Rugby, UK: Practical Action.

Rahimi, Sangar, and Alissa Rubin. (February 21, 2012). "Koran Burning in NATO Error Incites Afghans." *The New York Times.*

Rashid, Ahmed. (2000). *Taliban: Militant Islam, Oil and Fundamentalism in Central Asia.* New Haven, CT: Yale University Press.

———. (2008). *Descent into Chaos: The United States and the Failure of Nation Building in Pakistan, Afghanistan and Central Asia.* New York: Viking.

Roy, Olivier. (1990). *Islam and Resistance in Afghanistan,* 2nd ed. Cambridge, UK: Cambridge University Press.

Rubin, Alissa. (February 22, 2012). "Afghan Protests over the Burning of Korans at a US Base Escalate." *The New York Times.*

———. (September 16, 2012). "Audacious Raid on NATO Base Shows Taliban's Reach." *The New York Times.*

Rubin, Barnett. (2000). "The Political Economy of War and Peace in Afghanistan." *World Development* 28(10):1798–1803.

———. (2002). *The Fragmentation of Afghanistan*, 2nd ed. New Haven, CT: Yale University Press.

Salahuddin, Sayed. (July 9, 2009). "Karzai Pardons Five Afghan Heroin Traffickers." Reuters.

Sandefuroct, Justin. (October 10, 2013). "Here's the Best Thing the US Has Done in Afghanistan." *The Atlantic.*

Sandell, Kevin. (September 24, 2011). "Combined Task Force Spartan Hosts District-Wide Reintegration Shura, Unites Influentials around Insurgents' Peaceful Return to Communities." Defense Video and Imagery Distribution System.

Savage, Charlie. (February 21, 2009). "Obama Upholds Detainee Policy in Afghanistan." *The New York Times.*

Scott, James C. (1998). *Seeing Like a State: How Certain Schemes to Improve the Human Condition Have Failed.* New Haven, CT: Yale University Press.

———. (2009). *The Art of Not Being Governed.* New Haven, CT: Yale University Press.

Shah, Taimoor, and Alissa Rubin. (April 25, 2011). "Taliban Breach Afghan Prison; Hundred Free." *The New York Times.*

Shahrani, M. Nazif. (1986). "The Kirghiz Khans: Styles and Substance of Traditional Local Leadership in Central Asia." *Central Asian Survey* 5(3/4): 255–271.

———. (2002 [1979]). *The Kirghiz and Wakhi of Afghanistan: Adaptation to Closed Frontiers and War.* Seattle: University of Washington Press.

Sieff, Kevin. (February 21, 2012). "Afghans Protest Burning of Korans at US Base." *The Washington Post.*

———. (February 24, 2012). "In Kabul, Afghan Police Sympathize with Protesters Angry over Koran Burning." *The Washington Post.*

Sinders, Christina. (July 8, 2008). "Coast Guard Augments Army at Bagram Air Base." American Forces Press Service.

Smith, Scott Seward. (2010). *Afghanistan's Troubled Transition: Politics, Peacekeeping and the 2004 Presidential Election.* Boulder, CO: Lynne Rienner Publishers.

Spoko, John. (January 16, 2014). Letter to John Dunford, Robert Hale, and John McHugh, SIGAR 14-22-SP/CERP Funding Inquiry, Office of the Special Investigator General for Afghan Reconstruction.

Stanton, Doug. (2009). *Horse Soldiers: The Extraordinary Story of a Band of US Soldiers Who Rode to Victory in Afghanistan.* New York: Scribner.

Stevens, Lory. (July 28, 2009). "US Development Team Assesses Afghan Cement Plant." American Forces Press Service.

Stiglitz, Joseph E. (2008). *The Three Trillion Dollar War: The True Cost of the Iraq Conflict.* New York: W. W. Norton.

Suhrke, Astri. (2011). *When More Is Less: The International Project in Afghanistan.* New York: Columbia University Press.

Synovitz, Ron. (September 16, 2003). "Afghanistan: Land-Grab Scandal in Kabul Rocks the Government." Radio Free Europe/Radio Free Liberty.

Tanner, Stephen. (2009). *Afghanistan: A Military History from Alexander the Great to the War against the Taliban,* rev. ed. Cambridge, MA: Da Capo Press

Tarzi, Amin. (March 22, 2006). "Afghanistan: Apostasy Case Reveals Constitutional Contradictions." Radio Free Europe/Radio Free Liberty.

Timmons, Heather. (June 29, 2012). "Afghanistan Woes Foreign Investors in New Delhi." *The New York Times.*

Trofimov, Yaroslav. (August 9, 2012). "Afghans Fear US Pullout Will Unplug Key Projects." *The Wall Street Journal.*

UN Assistance Mission in Afghanistan and the UN Office of the High Commissioner for Human Rights. (July 2014). "Afghanistan, Midyear Report 2014: Protection of Civilians in Armed Conflict." Kabul: Author.

van Bijlert, Martine. (March 9, 20011). "Stories People Tell (2): Bagram Prison; Not a Single Good Day." Rights and Freedoms. Kabul: Afghanistan Analysts Network.

Vogt, Heidi. (January 6, 2013). "US Pushes to Finish Afghan Dam as Challenges Mount." *The Associated Press.*

Voice of America. (June 19, 2013). "Taliban Claim Killing of 4 US Troops."

Watson Institute. (March 2013). "The Costs of War since 2001: Iraq, Afghanistan, and Pakistan." Providence, RI: Brown University.

Westbrook, David. (2008). *Navigators of the Contemporary: Why Ethnography Matters.* Chicago, IL: Chicago University Press.

The White House, Office of the Press Secretary. (December 1, 2009). "Remarks by the President in Address to the Nation on the Way Forward in Afghanistan and Pakistan."

Wissing, Douglas. (2012). *Funding the Enemy: How US Taxpayers Bankrolled the Taliban.* Amherst, NY: Prometheus Books.

Woodward, Bob. (2010). *Obama's Wars.* New York: Simon and Schuster.

World Bank. (2014). "4.2 World Development Indicators: Structure of Output." Data Catalog, Tables. Washington, DC: World Bank.

Zwak, Samar. (February 21, 2012). "Afghans Vent Frustration over Koran Burning, US Apologizes." Reuters.

Index

Abdur Rahman Khan, 64, 220n3
access to justice projects, 15, 16–17, 103–4, 188
acronyms, 18, 40–41
Afghanistan: Civil War of 1929, 62, 66; Civil War of 1990s, 6, 8, 30, 73, 77, 78, 127, 156, 157, 159, 209, 218n7; Constitution, 9; economic conditions, 29–32, 33, 57–58, 59, 123–24, 125–36, 154, 161–62, 198–99, 203, 205, 208–9, 218n11, 223n8; elections in, 15, 16, 85, 103, 150–51, 153, 191–92, 224n15, 228n13; government officials, 7, 12, 15, 18, 26, 37, 87, 131, 132–33, 149–50, 165–66, 175, 181, 186, 190–92, 193, 194, 195, 199, 201, 208, 225nn27,2, 227n31, 228n13; vs. Iraq, 79, 80, 89, 109, 113, 119, 178, 206; leadership forms in, 148–49, 224n22; legal system, 15, 16–17, 144–45, 169–70, 188, 189, 222n2, 224n16; Ministry of Justice, 16, 17, 188, 190–91, 192; Ministry of Public Affairs, 227n30; Ministry of the Interior, 165; political parties, 72, 157, 158, 159, 209; sovereignty of, 170–72. See also Afghan Local Police (ALP); Afghan National Army (ANA); Afghan National Police (ANP); Karzai, Hamid
Afghan Local Police (ALP), 68, 103, 114, 156, 222n17
Afghan National Army (ANA), 114, 194, 195, 200; insider attacks, 43; relations with U.S. military, 19, 22–24, 35, 43, 112–13,

167, 185, 189, 191, 197–98, 204; training of recruits, 181
Afghan National Development Strategy, 186
Afghan National Police (ANP), 23, 114, 115, 132, 151, 186
Afghan translators, 57, 220n11
Afghan women, 36–37
Aga Khan Foundation, 24–25, 84
agriculture, 1, 10–11, 109
Akhunzada, Sher Mohammad, 157
Alexander, Chris: *The Long Way Back*, 32
Alexander the Great, 4, 70; marriage to Roxana, 61, 220n1
Allen, John R., 165
Alliance Wind Power (AWP), 4–7; and Locke, 5, 6, 10–11, 12, 26, 43, 58, 87–88, 90, 92–98, 99, 100, 118, 121–23, 162, 167, 202, 208
Almas, Haji, 150, 155, 156
ALP. *See* Afghan Local Police
al Qaeda, 40, 79, 87
American Academy of Diplomacy, 68
American Anthropological Association, 178
Amu Darya, 67
ANA. *See* Afghan National Army
Anglo–Afghan war, first, 3, 61–62, 219n7
ANSO (Afghanistan NGO Safety Office), 85
anthropologists, 182, 211; ethnography, 32–38, 39, 218n12, 225n24; fieldwork, 13–14, 16, 33–34; and HTS, 69, 177–80, 227n8
Anwar Khan, 150, 156